P 61   Elinor Glyn

The Best of the Raconteurs

The Best of the Raconteurs

SELECTED BY
Sheridan Morley and Tim Heald
WITH A PREFACE BY
Sheridan Morley
AND ILLUSTRATIONS BY
John Lawrence

LONDON
The Folio Society
2000

Fourth printing 2003

Typeset at The Folio Society in Bembo.
Printed on Caxton Wove paper at Butler & Tanner Ltd,
Frome, and bound by them in full cloth
printed with a design by the artist.

Contents

6

7

8

Preface

According to the *Shorter Oxford English Dictionary*, this book has no right to exist at all. A raconteur, we are told simply enough, is a 'teller of anecdotes', and one of the features of an anecdote is that it is more often transmitted verbally than on paper, while its teller is by definition not at that moment a writer. But from the moment that The Folio Society suggested the magical idea of this anthology of raconteurs, I could hardly wait to contribute to it, let alone write its Preface.

I come from a family of raconteurs: from my father Robert Morley through to my godfather Peter Bull, most of the men in my family for a generation or two have made at least part of their living from the business invented by Coleridge's ancient mariner—that of buttonholing passing strangers and trying to fix them, if not with a glittering eye, then at least with a glittering anecdote.

My own introduction to the guest-speaker racket came from a great and infinitely elegant humorist called Basil Boothroyd, with whom I had the amazing good fortune to share an office at the old *Punch* premises just off Fleet Street back in the late 1970s. Boothroyd was the comic writer, now shamefully underrated, who bridged the gap from A. P. Herbert to Alan Coren, but he was also an accomplished post-prandial speaker who had more or less invented, on this side of the Atlantic, what has always been known in America as the 'rubber-chicken circuit', that loose-limbed collection of clubs, societies, charities, bookshops and other organizations and groups who nationwide are, or were, forever in need of a speaker to round off their gatherings.

Boothroyd, Bull, my father and I and a few hundred others indeed once belonged to an agency which thrived between the early sixties and the late eighties by sending us out, for a three-digit fee minus their commission but plus train fare (often first class), across the country to address serried ranks of quite large ladies, often still sporting equally large hats, who required a bit of a laugh and sometimes even enlightenment after a monthly luncheon. Sadly, the business rather fell apart during the recession, when my father was the first to notice a drop in his annual engagements; phoning the agency to enquire whether it was only his star that was on the wane, he was told by their secretary that in the light of the economic situation, several ladies' luncheon clubs had been forced to choose between a sweet and a speaker, and had plumped for the former. My father was curiously delighted; to be replaced by a jam sponge, possibly even a trifle, seemed to him not so much a career setback as the fulfilment of his lifetime's work as a pudding evangelist.

For me, however, it was Basil who signalled the end of that particular era; he came into the office one morning ashen, announcing that he was never again going to make a speech or public appearance of any kind, at home or abroad, for fee or charity, not even to sell a book. What had happened, I discovered, was that on the previous day he had attended some kind of ladies' luncheon in Cornwall, run by the vicar of the local parish. After the ritual chicken and apple pie plus custard, he had risen to his feet to deliver his usual fifty-minute comic monologue. During this, out of the corner of his eye, he had noticed the vicar removing one of the ladies from the audience, taking her into a kind of antechamber, returning her after ten minutes or so, and taking out another. This the man of God continued to do all through the speech, and driving back to the station Basil felt bound to enquire what precisely had been going on out there.

'Ah, so you noticed, Mr Boothroyd,' replied the vicar; 'I was hoping you wouldn't, but perhaps I ought to explain. I only get my ladies together once a month for these lunches, and when I do I like them to have their feet done, so I get the chiropodist round and he sits just outside the hall and does their bunions.' One of the greatest of all twentieth-century English public speakers had ended his career as the straight man to a chiropodist.

There have been other, similar, mishaps on the circuit, albeit none quite so final; the writer Christopher Matthew once recalled being at a Yorkshire speaker's dinner with my father thus: 'Robert was much as his customers had always imagined him—flamboyant, theatrical, larger than life. Few could ever guess how nervous he was, but he soon got into his stride, telling them about his childhood and early days in the profession, about Marie Tempest and Louis B. Mayer and John Barrymore and Bernard Shaw, and his beloved mother-in-law, Gladys Cooper. For over an hour the stories tumbled out, sometimes sad, often touching, always funny. "Is this the sort of thing you want, dears?" he asked his audience at the end of a story about Greta Garbo; "or would you perhaps like to ask a few questions?"

' "I have a question," said a man in the front row; "why are your fly-buttons undone?" "I had rather hoped", Robert replied, calmly adjusting his dress, "that it would add to the general air of informality." '

Most of the great raconteurs seem to have left us now in search of celestial audiences elsewhere, though John Mortimer and Peter Ustinov are still triumphantly in their anecdotage. When my grandchildren ask what Robert, their great-grandfather, was really like I always think first of Mortimer and Ustinov, but realize with a kind of shock that when they go, there will really be nobody else to point them towards. We are dealing here with a dying art form, largely perhaps because fast-food outlets and frozen television dinners are somehow inimical to storytelling; a world that has chosen to graze, rather than eat, doesn't have the twenty-first-century time to sit down at table, let alone remain there after coffee listening to someone talking to them in person rather than via television or the internet. One of the last refuges of the rent-a-speaker is, oddly enough, the ocean liner; once on board, audiences have little else to do but eat and listen until the casino opens, and not the faintest chance of escape unless they happen to be unusually good swimmers. It might even now be worth trying to pioneer the aeroplane speaker, one who for hard cash would roam the aisles of jetplanes entertaining bored travellers at several thousand feet. They too would find it hard to escape the anecdotes.

All of which, of course, makes it all the more important that we should celebrate the great talkers in the pages that follow. Inevitably you will find the selection reflects the taste of its editors: the triumph of the theatre over sport is entirely my fault, though you could argue that every anecdotalist is really an actor in personal disguise, and that all great stories have in common a kind of theatricality, either in the event itself or else just in the retelling.

Remember also that what you are reading here is what the great raconteurs wrote, or what was written about them: where you can recall the tones of their voices, or the looks on their faces, it may well help to do so. Liberties have been taken, of course, with the great talkers of history: we can't possibly know whether or not John Aubrey was as scintillating a gossip in the flesh as he was in the pages of *Brief Lives*, or whether the duc de Saint-Simon let himself go among the courtiers at Versailles with quite the relish he employed when writing his memoirs; but their style is the style of the raconteur. We hear authentic voices, authentic accents, behind the printed words. Inasmuch as there is a criterion for selection in this book, this is it.

As for what we have left out—and the names are legion—there is always a chance of a second volume. For a number of reasons, I made my contribution to this book in its early stages, so as I write this Preface I have, in effect, been granted a sneak preview. I hope I will not be misunderstood if I say it is a hugely enjoyable book with which to start the new century: an unexpectedly early present for 2000 for me—and, I trust, for you too.

SHERIDAN MORLEY
London, 2000

Mensa, A Table

'You have never done any Latin before, have you?' he said.

'No, sir.'

'This is a Latin grammar.' He opened it at a well-thumbed page. 'You must learn this,' he said, pointing to a number of words in a frame of lines. 'I will come back in half an hour and see what you know.'

Behold me then on a gloomy evening, with an aching heart, seated in front of the First Declension.

Mensa	a table
Mensa	O table
Mensam	a table
Mensae	of a table
Mensae	to or for a table
Mensa	by, with or from a table

What on earth did it mean? Where was the sense in it? It seemed absolute rigmarole to me. However, there was one thing I could always do: I could learn by heart. And I thereupon proceeded, as far as my private sorrows would allow, to memorize the acrostic-looking task which had been set me.

In due course the master returned.

'Have you learnt it?' he asked.

'I think I can *say* it, sir,' I replied; and I gabbled it off.

He seemed so satisfied with this that I was emboldened to ask a question.

'What does it mean, sir?'

'It means what it says. *Mensa*, a table. *Mensa* is a noun of the First Declension. There are five declensions. You have learnt the singular of the First Declension.'

'But', I repeated, 'what does it mean?'

'*Mensa* means a table,' he answered.

'Then why does *mensa* also mean O table,' I enquired, 'and what does O table mean?'

'*Mensa*, O table, is the vocative case,' he replied.

'But why O table?' I persisted in genuine curiosity.

'O table—you would use that in addressing a table, in invoking a table.' And then seeing he was not carrying me with him, 'You would use it in speaking to a table.'

'But I never do,' I blurted out in honest amazement.

'If you are impertinent, you will be punished, and punished, let me tell you, very severely,' was his conclusive rejoinder.

Such was my first introduction to the classics from which, I have been told, many of our cleverest men have derived so much solace and profit.

WINSTON CHURCHILL

Billycart Racing

None of this meant that I was a good practical hand. For example, I could not build billycarts very well. Other children, most of them admittedly older than I, but some of them infuriatingly not, constructed billycarts of advanced design, with skeletal hard-wood frames and steel-jacketed ball-race wheels that screamed on the concrete footpaths like a diving Stuka. The best I could manage was a sawn-off fruit box mounted on a fence-paling spine frame, with drearily silent rubber wheels taken off an old pram. In such a creation I could go at a reasonable clip down our street and twice as fast down Sunbeam Avenue, which was much steeper at the top. But even going down Sunbeam my billycart was no great thrill compared with the ball-race models, which having a ground-clearance of about half an inch and being almost frictionless were able to attain tremendous velocities at low profile, so that to the onlooker their riders seemed to be travelling downhill sitting magically just above the ground, while to the riders themselves the sense of speed was breathtaking.

After school and at weekends boys came from all over the district to race on the Sunbeam Avenue footpaths. There would be twenty or thirty carts, two-thirds of them with ball-races. The noise was indescribable. It sounded like the Battle of Britain going on in somebody's bathroom. There would be about half an hour's racing before the police came. Residents often took the law into their own hands, hosing the grim-faced riders as they went shrieking by. Sunbeam Avenue ran parallel to Margaret Street but it started higher and lasted longer. Carts racing down the footpath on the far side had a straight run of about a quarter of a mile all the way to the park. Emitting shockwaves of sound, the ball-race carts would attain such speeds that it was impossible for the rider to get off. All he could do was to crash reasonably gently when he got to the end. Carts racing down the footpath on the near side could go only half as far, although very nearly as fast, before being faced with a right-angle turn into Irene Street. Here a pram-wheeled cart like mine could demonstrate its sole advantage. The traction of the rubber tyres made it possible to negotiate the corner in some style. I developed a histrionic lean-over of the body and slide of the back wheels which got me around the corner unscathed, leaving black smoking trails of burnt rubber. Mastery of this trick saved me from being relegated to the ranks of the little kids, than which there was no worse fate. I had come to depend on being thought of as a big kid. Luckily only the outstanding ball-race drivers could match my fancy turn into Irene Street. Others slid straight on with a yelp of metal and a shower of sparks, braining themselves on the asphalt road. One driver scalped himself under a bread van.

The Irene Street corner was made doubly perilous by Mrs Branthwaite's poppies. Mrs Branthwaite inhabited the house on the corner. She was a known witch whom we often persecuted after dark by throwing gravel on her roof. It was widely believed that she poisoned cats. Certainly she was a great ringer-up of the police. In retrospect I can see that she could hardly be

blamed for this, but her behaviour seemed at the time like irrational hatred of children. She was a renowned gardener. Her front yard was like the cover of a seed catalogue. Extending her empire, she had flower beds even in her two front strips, one on the Sunbeam Avenue side and the other on the Irene Street side—i.e., on both outside edges of the famous corner. The flower beds held the area's best collection of poppies. She had been known to phone the police if even one of these was illicitly picked.

At the time I am talking about, Mrs Branthwaite's poppies were all in bloom. It was essential to make the turn without hurting a single hair of a poppy's head, otherwise the old lady would probably drop the telephone and come out shooting. Usually, when the poppies were in bloom, nobody dared make the turn. I did—not out of courage, but because in my ponderous cart there was no real danger of going wrong. The daredevil leanings-over and the dramatic skids were just icing on the cake.

I should have left it at that, but got ambitious. One Saturday afternoon when there was a particularly large turnout, I got sick of watching the ball-race carts howling to glory down the far side. I organized the slower carts like my own into a train. Every cart except mine was deprived of its front axle and loosely bolted to the cart in front. The whole assembly was about a dozen carts long, with a big box cart at the back. This back cart I dubbed the chuck-wagon, using terminology I had picked up from the Hopalong Cassidy serial at the pictures. I was the only one alone on his cart. Behind me there were two or even three to every cart until you got to the chuck-wagon, which was crammed full of little kids, some of them so small that they were holding toy koalas and sucking dummies.

From its very first run down the far side, my super-cart was a triumph. Even the adults who had been hosing us called their families out to marvel as we went steaming by. On the super-cart's next run there was still more to admire, since even the top-flight ball-race riders had demanded to have their vehicles built into it, thereby heightening its tone, swelling its passenger list, and multiplying its already impressive output of decibels. Once again I should have left well alone. The thing was already famous. It had everything but a dining car. Why did I ever suggest that we should transfer it to the near side and try the Irene Street turn?

With so much inertia the super-cart started slowly, but it

accelerated like a piano falling out of a window. Long before we reached the turn I realized that there had been a serious miscalculation. The miscalculation was all mine, of course. Sir Isaac Newton would have got it right. It was too late to do anything except pray. Leaning into the turn, I skidded my own cart safely around in the usual way. The next few segments followed me, but with each segment describing an arc of slightly larger radius than the one in front. First gradually, then with stunning finality, the monster lashed its enormous tail.

The air was full of flying ball-bearings, bits of wood, big kids, little kids, koalas and dummies. Most disastrously of all, it was also full of poppy petals. Not a bloom escaped the scythe. Those of us who could still run scattered to the winds, dragging our wounded with us. The police spent hours visiting all the parents in the district, warning them that the billycart era was definitely over. It was a police car that took Mrs Branthwaite away. There was no point waiting for the ambulance. She could walk all right. It was just that she couldn't talk. She stared straight ahead, her mouth slightly open.

CLIVE JAMES

Educating the Mitford Girls

Boud [Unity] was the bane of governesses, few of whom could stand up for long to her relentless misbehaviour, and as a result we never had the same one for any length of time. They came and left in bewildering succession, and each replacement brought with her a new slant on the sum total of human knowledge.

Miss Whitey taught us to repeat, 'A-squared-minus-B-squared-equals-A-squared-minus-2-AB-plus-B-squared', but she did not stay long enough to explain why that should be. Boud found out that she had a deadly fear of snakes, and left Enid, her pet grass snake, neatly wrapped around the WC chain one

17

morning. We breathlessly awaited the result, which was not long in coming. Miss Whitey locked herself in, there was shortly an ear-splitting shriek followed by a thud. The unconscious woman was ultimately released with the aid of crowbars, and Boud was duly scolded and told to keep Enid in her box thereafter. Miss Whitey was succeeded by Miss Broadmoor, who taught us to say *Mensa, Mensa, Mensam* all the way through. Nancy, even in those early days preoccupied with U and Non-U usage, made up a poem illustrative of the main 'refainments' of Miss Broadmoor's speech: 'Ay huff a löft, and öft, as ay lay on may ayderdown so söft (tossing from sade to sade with may nasty cöff) ay ayther think of the löft, or of the w-h-h-h-h-eat in the tröff of the löft.' We couldn't resist reciting it each morning as lesson time drew near.

Latin lessons came to an end after Miss Broadmoor left. Miss McMurray grew beans on bits of wet flannel and taught the names of different parts of these growing beans—Plumule, Radical, Embryo.

She was soon followed by Miss Bunting, whose main contribution to our education was to teach a little mild shoplifting. Miss Bunting was a dear little round giggly woman, shaped like a Toby jug, with a carefree and unorthodox approach to life that we found most attractive. Boud towered over her, and sometimes scooped her up and put her, squealing, on the schoolroom piano.

We made occasional trips to Oxford. 'Like to try a little jiggery-pokery, children?' Miss Bunting suggested. There were two main methods: the shopping-bag method, in which an accomplice was needed, was used for the larger items. The accomplice undertook to distract the shop-lady while the lifter, or jiggery-poker in Miss Bunting's idiom, stuffed her bag with books, underclothes or boxes of chocolates, depending on the wares of the particular store. The dropped-hanky method was

suitable for lipsticks or small pieces of jewellery. Miss Bunting in her governessy beige coat and gloves, Boud and I in matching panama straw hats, would strut haughtily past the deferential salespeople to seek the safety of Fuller's Tea Room, where we would gleefully take stock of the day's haul over cups of steaming hot chocolate.

JESSICA MITFORD

Protestant

Our family was dirt poor, which I figured out as a child from the fact we had such a bad vacuum. When you vacuumed the living-room, it would groan and stop and you had to sit and wait for it to groan and start up, then vacuum like mad before it quit again, but it didn't have good suction either. You had to stuff the hair-balls into it. I also knew it because Donald Hoglund told me. He asked me how much my dad earned, and I said a thousand dollars, the most money I could imagine, and he shrieked, 'You're poor! You're poor!' So we were. And, in a town where everyone was either Lutheran or Catholic, we were neither one. We were Sanctified Brethren, a sect so tiny that nobody but us and God knew about it, so when kids asked what I was, I just said Protestant. It was too much to explain, like having six toes. You would rather keep your shoes on.

Grandpa Cotten was once tempted toward Lutheranism by a preacher who gave a rousing sermon on grace that Grandpa heard as a young man while taking Aunt Esther's dog home who had chased a Model T across town. He sat down on the church steps and listened to the voice boom out the open windows until he made up his mind to go in and unite with the truth, but he took one look from the vestibule and left. 'He was dressed up like the pope of Rome,' said Grandpa, 'and the altar and the paintings and the gold candlesticks—my gosh, it was just a big show. And he was reading the whole darn thing off a page, like an actor.'

19

Jesus said, 'Where two or three are gathered together in my name, there am I in the midst of them,' and the Brethren believed that was enough. We met in Uncle Al's and Aunt Flo's bare living-room with plain folding chairs arranged facing in toward the middle. No clergyman in a black smock. No organ or piano, for that would make one person too prominent. No upholstery, it would lead to complacency. No picture of Jesus, He was in our hearts. The faithful sat down at the appointed hour and waited for the Spirit to move one of them to speak or to pray or to give out a hymn from our Little Flock hymnal. No musical notation, for music must come from the heart and not off a page. We sang the texts to a tune that fit the meter, of the many tunes we all knew. The idea of reading a prayer was sacrilege to us—'if a man can't remember what he wants to say to God, let him sit down and think a little harder,' Grandpa said.

'There's the Lord's Prayer,' said Aunt Esther meekly. We were sitting on the porch after Sunday dinner. Esther and Harvey were visiting from Minneapolis and had attended Lake Wobegon Lutheran, she having turned Lutheran when she married him, a subject that was never brought up in our family.

'You call that prayer? Sitting and reciting like a bunch of schoolchildren?'

Harvey cleared his throat and turned to me with a weak smile. 'Speaking of school, how are you doing?' he asked.

There was a lovely silence in the Brethren assembled on Sunday morning as we waited for the Spirit. Either the Spirit was moving someone to speak who was taking his sweet time or else the Spirit was playing a wonderful joke on us and letting us sit, or perhaps silence was the point of it. We sat listening to rain on the roof, distant traffic, a radio playing from across the street, kids whizzing by on bikes, dogs barking, as we waited for the Spirit to inspire us. It was like sitting on the porch with your family, when nobody feels that they have to make talk. So quiet in church. Minutes drifted by in silence that was sweet to us. The old Regulator clock ticked, the rain stopped and the room changed light as the sun broke through—shafts of brilliant sun through the windows and motes of dust falling through it—the smell of clean clothes and floor wax and wine and the fresh bread of Aunt Flo which was Christ's body given for us. Jesus in our midst, who loved us. So peaceful, and we loved each other too. I thought perhaps the Spirit was leading me to say that, but I was just a boy, and children were supposed to keep still. And my affections were not pure. They were tainted with a sneaking admiration of Catholics—Catholic Christmas, Easter, the Living Rosary, and the Blessing of the Animals, all magnificent. Everything we did was plain, but they were regal and gorgeous—especially the Feast Day of St Francis, which they did right out in the open, a feast for the eyes. Cows, horses, some pigs, right on the church lawn. The turmoil, animals bellowing and barking and clucking and cats scheming how to escape and suddenly leaping out of the girl's arms who was holding on tight, the cat dashing through the crowd, dogs straining at the leash, and the ocarina band of third-graders playing Catholic dirges, and the great calm of the sisters, and the flags, and the Knights of Columbus decked out in their handsome black suits—I stared at it until my eyes almost fell out, and then I wished it would go on much longer.

'Christians', my uncle Al used to say, 'do not go in for show', referring to the Catholics. We were sanctified by the blood of the Lord, therefore we were saints, like St Francis, but we didn't go in for feasts or ceremonies, involving animals or not. We went in for sitting, all nineteen of us, in Uncle Al's and Aunt Flo's living-room on Sunday morning and having a plain meeting and singing hymns in our poor thin voices while not far away the Catholics were whooping it up. I wasn't allowed inside Our Lady, of course, but if the Blessing of the Animals on the Feast Day of St Francis was any indication, Lord, I didn't know but what they had elephants in there and acrobats. I sat in our little group and envied them for the splendor and gorgeousness, as we tried to sing without even a harmonica to give us the pitch. Hymns, Uncle Al said, didn't have to be sung perfect, because God looks on the heart, and if you are In The Spirit, then all praise is good.

GARRISON KEILLOR

No Good at Sports

I think this is the proper moment to state that Emily and I are not of the breed of amazons. We're no good at sports and we weren't then. At Bryn Mawr I played hockey only because it was compulsory. My team was the seventh, which seldom met, owing to the fact that there was no other team inadequate enough to meet us. I tried basketball (also compulsory) but if anyone had the lack of judgement to toss a ball at me I ducked it and ran. The only outstanding feat I ever accomplished in that repulsively degrading activity known familiarly as 'gym' was to knock myself senseless with an Indian club. Emily wasn't one whit better, if truth were told. But in her case truth wasn't told and the thought riles me to this day. She was small and moved gracefully (I was tall and moved like a McCormick reaper). Moreover, she had sidestepped all regulation college athletics by having talked somebody into allowing her to be an instructor in an activity she chose to call 'rhythmic dancing'. I don't believe she had the remotest notion of what she was doing, let alone

teaching, but she had picked up an Isadora Duncan outfit and a few Attic postures and when she told the head of the athletic department she had a special contribution to give the students, the head of the athletic department, whose only contribution wasn't much more than a hockey-stick and an old pair of sneakers, let her get away with it. I am not one to write with authority about Emily's class in Greek whatever-it-was. I attended it only once. Emily on this occasion wore a lovely little purple tunic, very bacchanalian, very Ballets Russes. The only reason she wasn't carrying a bunch of grapes in her teeth was because the grape season was over. The rest of us bacchantes had perforce to wear our regulation athletic attire, middy-blouse, serge bloomers, woollen stockings and some tasty black footgear known as 'gym shoes', which looked as if they'd been cut down out of arctics. Emily, who by comparison had no trouble at all looking like Pavlova, had us all prancing, expressing joy, sorrow, frolic and greeting, while a grim individual at an upright accompanied us with 'Narcissus' and 'Nights of Gladness'. Despite my middy-blouse and serge bloomers I tried my most passionately to act like something hot off Keats' Grecian urn, but Emily said I was a disrupting element in the class and put me out. To avoid further exertion I got myself relegated to a defective posture and spinal curvature list, a select group who were on their honor to do corrective exercises in their rooms.

CORNELIA OTIS SKINNER AND EMILY KIMBROUGH

How to be Topp in Expression

Sometimes english masters make you *read* peoms chiz chiz chiz. You have to sa the weedy words and speke them beaitfully as if you knew what they meant. Fotherington-tomas thinks this is absolutely super and when he sa he wander lonely as a cloud you think he will flote out of the window. Some cads roters and swots love to read they beg for the chance and put their hands up saing sir sir sir please sir as if they are in agony. English masters who are always perverse then sa molesworth go on CHIZ.

SIR THE BURIAL SIR OF SIR JOHN MOORE SIR AT CORUNNA SIR
(*A titter from* 2B *they are wet and i will tuough them up after.*)

Notadrumwasheardnotafuneralnote
shut up peason larffing
As his corse
As his corse
what is a corse sir? gosh is it
to the rampart we carried
(*whisper you did not kno your voice was so lovely*)
Not a soldier discharged his farewell shot.
PING!
Shut up peason i know sir he's blowing peas at me
Oer the grave where our hero we buried.

(*A pause a grave bow i retire and Egad! peason hav placed a dainty pin upon mine seat.* Fie!)

GEOFFREY WILLANS AND RONALD SEARLE

Stop It at Once

Life at a boys' public school a half-century ago was a little short on scheduled enjoyments but at the house, one of twelve, that I was in, the housemaster did treat us all, at pleasantly recurring intervals, to sensational moral lectures of a prolonged and fascinating nature. We found them totally electrifying for he was a brilliant speaker, had obviously conscientiously prepared his material, and was quite unaware that, to young people, he was a hilarious figure. Every so often after evening prayers he would stand up and, speaking without notes, let fly. As a new boy, I couldn't always understand why he was so concerned and what had gone wrong. Had somebody, perhaps, said 'Drat' or been rude to Matron or left some gristle or smiled at a boy older or younger (you couldn't smile at a boy in another house at all, and, as I was by nature an inane smiler, I was at constant risk)? But as time went on I began to get the hang of the affair and the gist of the matter and hung upon the housemaster's words, later in the day to be so splendidly mimicked by wags as we disrobed, shrieking, for bed, and cackled ourselves into the Land of Nod.

One of the most memorable pi-jaws, delivered during a power-cut but with flickering candlelight rendering it even more, so to speak, electrifying than usual, began with the striking phrase 'This house is a midden', followed by a dramatic pause while the dimmer boys tried to work out just what a midden was and, if so, what might be the matter with it. On another occasion we were told that 'the trouble' lay neither at the top of the house, where the prefects were, nor at the bottom of the house, but in the very middle of it, and a most pious boy (later a distinguished academic and now high up, and highly respected, in the church), anxiously totting up on the house list, found that out of sixty-three boys he was the thirty-second, precisely in the middle and therefore at the very seat of the bother and deplorably culpable.

Other pleasantly recurring treats, also of a mainly moral kind, were the regular weekend visits to the school of the then Bishop of London, dear old, kindly old, indubitably wonky old Winnington Ingram, much loved by all. He preached, of course, in our chapel on Sunday and, after pronouncing the Blessing at the altar, swung round and dextrously extracted from his billowing canonicals a large gold watch and had a dekko at 'the enemy'. And indeed he was operating on a tight time schedule for as soon as the service was over he repaired to our Natural History Museum which stood close by and there, unsuitably seated among pressed grasses and cases of spreadeagled moths and the skeleton of a singularly unattractive horse, he received any boy who cared to call on him solo, and very many did, for a little moral uplift and

spiritual encouragement at two minutes flat a head, though the more personable boys could usually count on a few seconds longer. A warm, soft and somewhat clinging handshake concluded the interview. Then he was up and away to a nourishing repast with the headmaster at School House, whence a boy had once written home, 'We had beef for lunch today. The headmaster calved.' And after that, at 2.30, three school prefects appeared to make up a four at tennis with the bishop, a lively player who liked to win and whose wild rushes to the net with a loud screech of 'Mine, partner!' seemed to be in no way slowed down by the fact that he always played in enormous elastic-sided brown boots.

When this delightful cleric was not at Oundle, the newspapers kept us in touch with his doings and activities, one of which was to protest. If there was anything morally unworthy going on and ideal stuff for protesting about, there was the bishop, piping up too. He took against, for some not very clear reason, a play called *The Sacred Flame*. Doubtless the word 'sacred' upset him as the flame part meant love, of course, and the illicit love in the play was far from sacred. So protest he did, to the great profit of the newspapers and even more so of Gladys Cooper, who played the lead, and of Somerset Maugham, who had written it. Boosted by the bishop, the theatre was jammed for months with titillated playgoers and envious theatre managers pressed free seats on him, hoping that he might unearth something and be inspired to protest about *Rose Marie* or *Peter Pan* or *Where the Rainbow Ends* or *George and Margaret*.

And now, bless me, here he is again after all these years, popping up as fresh as paint and hot on the track of filth, his wails and strictures now resurrected in Edward Bristow's admirable *Vice and Vigilance*, a fine panorama of the various purity movements in Britain. I hadn't fully realized how good the bishop's track record was. In the whole thirty-eight years of his London incumbency, he never once missed a meeting of the Public Morality Council's subcommittee on brothels, the air thick with tch tchs. He kept the Home Secretary on his toes ('I took him in twenty-one filthy books', and followed them up with a cartload of saucy magazines, light reading that was probably an agreeable change from the official boxes). He spoke out, rather unfairly, against plump ladies in flesh-coloured tights displaying themselves, with not a follicle of pubic hair in sight, in music-hall *tableaux vivants*. In 1934 he announced in the Lords, muddle-headed to the last, that he would like to make a fire of all contraceptives 'and dance round it' (in those brown boots, again).

We remember Macaulay's verdict that there is no spectacle so ridiculous as the British public in one of its periodic fits of morality. Last century's fit was a longish one. There was an agitation to clothe (what with? Bloomers? Jockstraps?) some nude statues in the Strand. Sellers of obscene toothpick cases were ruthlessly tracked down and 'spoken to'. Purity workers, armed with lanterns, lurked at the doors of brothels to identify the customers, subsequently writing up their names on walls. Then the ladies were invited to leave their work awhile and come to church (male salvationists were warned 'never to kneel down with women at midnight meetings, especially behind a pew'). Tea was served, nosegays were handed out by the Bible Flower Mission, and, as soon as dawn broke, there was a group photograph ('Smile, please'), followed by breakfast.

Everybody got very worried and panicky about white-slave traffic and crateloads of drugged and insensible womanhood getting shipped abroad. Abductors, clutching hypodermic syringes, were said to haunt the most unlikely places (Barnet, Banbury, Finsbury Park) waiting to pounce and whizz servant-girls off to

Buenos Aires. Beasts in human shape were alleged to rig themselves up as clergymen and, with attractive offers, lure maidens to the capital ('Dear child, you're going to love the British Museum'). The West Ham area was apparently an unexpectedly fruitful supplier of moon-faced girls ripe for Marseilles, and even as late as 1913 the five thousand girls of London's telephone exchanges were given official warnings to watch out for drugged chocolates. Just the one violet cream or strawberry surprise and everything might go black.

ARTHUR MARSHALL

Granny Grace

Granny Grace was in fact my step-great-great-grandmother, widow of my great-great-grandfather, the tenth Lord Wemyss, whom she married in 1900 when his lordship was already eighty-two years old. Hers was the first naked female form I saw. In old age, she did not lock the bathroom door when she had a bath for fear that she should fall down or suffer a seizure. At the age of three I wandered into her bathroom on a general tour of inspection. Having studied her agitated form for a few minutes I said to her—or so she afterwards claimed: 'How beautiful you are looking today, Granny Grace.'

It was exactly the right thing to say, of course. I would like to think that the experience helped me in later years in my relations with women.

AUBERON WAUGH

Uncle Joe's Gambling Instincts Succumb to the Bow Wow

That's Uncle Joe. He was awfully stingy and so lazy that his best suit was his working clothes.

He wasn't a bad-looking man, and didn't inherit the big family mouth. He used to say that grapefruit was invented for people with big mouths who really liked oranges.

You could tell any of our family wherever you went, because their mouths looked like china closets with the doors open, and once in a while there was a gold tooth that looked like a collar button on the keyboard of a piano.

Uncle Joe had some bad habits. He would gamble on anything, dice, cards or horses. He was always going to make a big winning some day on the Honduras Lottery. He had his house papered with elapsed lottery tickets and had some left over to make rugs with.

He said that if he ever knocked off the big prize, he would save his money and have every bank in the country laying eggs for him.

But he never got within an adding machine of the prize number. Once he had 67,987 and 27,189 won and he took his ticket and tore it up slowly as if he realized that it meant just as much in pieces as it did whole.

The truth is that it did, because those Honduras people never gave any money away. Some days you would hear that George Smith, at No. 1619 Twelfth Street, won $50,000. But when you inquired at that address there wasn't no George Smith living there, and if he did he was six months behind in the rent.

Uncle Joe used to play those lotteries every month like people took baths. You couldn't convince him that it wasn't as crooked as the chimney on a shanty in a hurricane.

He would swear off the lotteries and cuss everybody in Honduras—man, woman and strangers. Then he would go right out and buy another ticket and promise to pay for it as soon as he won the prize.

Every month he would get a big sheet of paper from Honduras with a mess of numbers on it. He would read it, and then look at the number on his ticket. His head would keep bobbing back and forth from the paper to his ticket until he looked like a crow in a cornfield watching out for farmers.

But it was something like a Quaker arsenal, with nothing but blank cartridges in it.

Uncle Joe never won anything on the lottery, but he didn't stop until our Government made it illegal for any foreign country to swindle US citizens when there were so many home industries waiting for their chance.

After lotteries turned sour in the US Mails, Uncle started in to bet on the races. He made what bookmakers call laundry wagers.

Laundry wagers are something about betting on the cuff and the bookmakers used to laugh at Uncle when he would motion for them to give him fifteen to one, which would make thirty to two for two cuffs.

After that, he got discouraged and took to childish gambling like pinochle and casino. All us folks used to try to get him to stop figuring out percentages with a borrowed lead pencil, but he went right on trying to pencil his way into some money.

He got so that he and three other men would hang out in the back yard playing poker without any cards. They went through all the motions, dealing and raking in chips, and mom thought that maybe Uncle was going what they call cuckoo.

She sent me around for the doctor to look him over and after seeing the shape of Uncle's head, the doctor asked how long it had been shaped that way. Mom told the doctor that Uncle's head was that way all his life. So the doctor told her that it would never get any worse because it was that bad at the start and after a mouse was drowned it couldn't get any wetter.

What finally cured Uncle of the gambling habits was being bitten by a bulldog.

The dog bit him on the left leg.

Uncle had two legs but one of them was wooden. The right leg was the timber one and the left leg was meat.

When the dog bit him on the meat leg, Uncle got out his pencil and figured close. He hoped that for once in his life he started with an even chance. With a fifty per cent chance of being bitten on the wooden leg the dog had picked out the other.

So he quit gambling. If he couldn't win with a fifty per cent chance, he figured that he might as well quit gambling altogether.

And he did.

ARTHUR 'BUGS' BAER

A Boy's Best Bodyguard

When a fellow is faced by armed men it's my honest opinion that he should have his mother around, if the situation is not to descend into flurry and confusion.

Three times I have looked down the muzzle of a gun. On the first two occasions my mother was present, and an orderly conclusion was achieved. In her absence, the third time, I handled the business so maladroitly that even the police got it back to front. The lesson is plain.

My mother and I first started gun-slinging, as it were, in 1922. The Irish Civil War was in progress and one of its victims—or very likely to be if he didn't look slippy—was my father, then a member of the Cosgrave Government. He had returned once to our house outside Dublin with three perceptible bullet holes in the back door of his car, in no mood to share my mother's opinion, aimed at restoring his confidence, that the IRA had probably mistaken him for someone else. The shots had, apparently, been fired near Portobello Bridge. So sure was my father of their intended destination that he covered the three miles home in three minutes, and went straight to bed.

When, therefore, the thunderous banging came on the back door a few nights later it had the effect of freezing him to his armchair, in which he'd been reading the evening paper. It was my mother who went to the top of the kitchen stairs, to see what was afoot. I joined her almost immediately, a pale lad of nine, having been roused from my sleep by the noise. I'd been sleeping badly of recent weeks because it was nearly Christmas, and my whole soul was crying out to take possession of my first Hornby train.

'It's all right,' my mother said, taking her customarily steady view, 'it's only some men.'

We heard the bolts being shot on the back door, and then the voice of the cook raised in indignant surprise. She was a loyal retainer, who'd been with the family for some years. 'It's youse lot, is it?' she said. 'Janey, I thought yez wasn't comin' till half-eleven.' It was, in fact, only ten-fifteen.

A male voice said peevishly, 'Ah, don't be shoutin' . . .' and then the first of the raiders came running up the stairs. I had a brief glimpse of a gun, then a face masked with a cap and a hand-kerchief. My mother stopped him dead. 'If there's going to be any murder,' she said, 'you can get back out of that and go home.'

More masked faces and caps appeared at the bottom of the stairs. Querulous voices arose. 'What's the matther, Mick?' 'Get on with it, can't ya?' But Mick was explaining the matter to my mother.

'Nobody's gettin' shot, mum. You needn't take on. We've orders to burn down the house, that's all.' He sounded injured by the false impression.

'You're sure of that?' my mother asked him, wishing to have

the matter absolutely clear for the benefit of my father, in the event that he was still able to receive messages, in the next room.

'There'll be nobody shot,' said another raider impatiently. 'Now will you stand back owa that an' let's get on with it. We haven't all night.'

My mother remained firm. With the first matter on the agenda settled to her satisfaction, she passed to others, now of equal importance. 'What about all my lovely books?' she said. 'First editions, signed by Lawrence and Katherine Mansfield and Middleton Murry. And the pictures—Orpens, Gertlers, the little drawings by John . . .'

The raiders jammed on the stairs were getting hot and angry. An exposed youth, still stuck in the passage, was being berated by the cook. He appeared to be a cousin of hers, and was refusing to carry her trunk out into the garden.

'All right, all *right* . . .' said the first raider. The protracted conversation was causing the handkerchief to slip off his face. 'Take out anything you want, but for God's love hurry up about it.' He turned to the men behind. 'Who's got the pethrol an' the matches?' he wanted to know.

At this point my father appeared in the hall, unobtrusively, and still unsure of his welcome. The raiders appealed to him. 'Ask your missus to give us a chance, sir, will ya? Sure, we're only actin' under ordhers . . .'

He took command, in a voice slightly higher than normal, advising me to wake my sister, still peacefully asleep, and to put on some warm clothes. He then suggested to my mother that they should try to save a few personal mementoes before we all withdrew to safety in the garden.

'And leave', my mother cried passionately, 'all the children's Christmas toys behind? Certainly not!'

The possible outcome of the night struck home to me for the first time. 'Me train!' I cried. 'Don't let them burn me train!'

'Of course they won't,' said my mother. She rounded on two of the men. 'You,' she said, 'go to the cupboard in the bedroom and bring out all the parcels you can find. And look out for the doll's house. It's fragile.'

They shuffled their feet, deeply embarrassed. Several other men were throwing petrol around the hall. 'Well, go on!' my mother shouted at them. 'And leave your silly guns on the table. Nobody'll touch them.'

By the time the first whoosh of petrol flame poured out of the windows she had five of the men working for her, running out with armfuls of books and pictures, ornaments, and our Christmas toys. They'd become so deeply concerned on her behalf that they frequently paused to ask what should be salvaged next. 'Is the bit of a picture in the passage anny good, mum?' 'Is there ere a chance of gettin' the legs offa the pianna, the way we could dhrag it out . . .?'

When they disappeared into the night they left my mother,

bathed in the light of the flames, standing guard over a great heap of treasures in the middle of the lawn, with Orpen's picture under one arm and the little drawings by John under the other— a clear winner on points.

Next time it was the IRA again. My unfortunate father was now officially on the run—an appalling situation for a peaceful and dignified man—while the rest of us, being homeless, were staying with my mother's parents in Foxrock, a base that at first sight could not have been more neutral. But then, in the middle of the night, the caps and the handkerchiefs appeared again, and it turned out that we were sitting on a miniature arsenal, not, admittedly, of the first calibre, but undoubtedly containing weapons of war.

Once again it was probably the domestic staff who provided the link between the beleaguered fortress and its attackers, but— as is common in the uncertain art of espionage—they'd considerably exaggerated their report, in the interests of making it seem worthwhile.

After twenty minutes in the house the IRA were dissatisfied to find themselves in possession of two assegais, a knobkerry, a Gurkha knife, a 1914 bayonet and a pith helmet from the Boer War, trophies brought home from foreign service by my mother's numerous brothers. All these warriors, however, were now somewhere else, so that the depleted garrison put up no great struggle as the IRA ranged through the house, throwing open cupboards and peering under beds in search of the machine-guns and Mills bombs promised them by the cook.

While all this was going on I was standing on the rug beside my bed with a pillow between my knees, placed there by my mother. The burning of our house, followed by closer proximity to my grandmother, who was a fast hand with a ruler, had brought my nerves to a low state. From the first crash on the back door my knees had been knocking together so rapidly that they were now severely bruised on the inside, making each new percussion an agony. The pillow, however, eased things considerably. I was holding it in position, fore and aft, when the raider burst into the room, waving a huge Service revolver, but I dropped it immediately when he shouted, 'Hands up!' The knees started rattling again, like castanets.

My mother went into immediate action. 'How can he put his hands up?' she shouted at the raider. 'Look at his little knees!'

She slotted the pillow home again into position, and returned to the attack.

'How dare you frighten the life out of a little child!' she cried. At the age of nine I was nearly six feet tall, but the principle was right. 'Give him your gun! Let him see it isn't loaded!'

As usual, the speed and directness of her assault bouleversed the enemy. He was a lumpish youth in the regulation cap and trenchcoat, with a handkerchief over his face which looked as if it had recently been used for cleaning floors. He became placatory. 'I wouldn't frighten the little fella, mum. A'course it's not loaded. Amn't I only afther findin' it down below? . . .'

My mother pounced upon this new intelligence. 'That's Malcolm's revolver,' she cried. 'Put it back where you found it! Didn't he risk his life with it, defending you and all the other hooligans like you from the Germans?'

'Put it back, mum?' The proposition staggered him. 'I can't do that, mum. Sure, the commandant'll kill me . . .'

At this point my mother snatched the gun out of his hand. 'Let him hold it, anyway,' she cried. 'I'm not going to have any child of mine having nightmares of a filthy, silly revolver.' She thrust it into my hand.

I didn't want it at all. I only wanted to hold on to my pillow. I dropped it on the floor, with the pillow on top of it, and tried to put my hands between my knees.

In the midst of this confusion there was a hoarse shout from downstairs: 'Christy, come on owa that, willya! There's nothin' more here . . .'

Christy made a move towards the gun. My mother put her foot on it. They faced one another for a moment, with a thin, obbligato sobbing from myself. 'You'll be hearin' more of this,' said Christy unconvincingly. Then he turned and ran.

My mother put me back to bed, then she picked up the revolver by the muzzle and threw it into the bottom of the cupboard. 'I'll put it in the bank in the morning,' she said. 'Filthy, silly things. Don't you ever have anything to do with them.'

PATRICK CAMPBELL

Not Being Asked to Dance

There is a stage—or there was a stage in my youth—when a girl is glad to dance with her father; because it is better to dance with anyone than be left standing alone by the door. Not that I minded this very much. I was so interested in watching people that I soon got over the faint sense of failure at not being asked and would sit by myself completely held by the sights I saw and the developing relationships I witnessed among my friends. My pa still drew admiring glances when he whirled me around at my first dance. There was a period flavour about the way he danced. None of your 'Come Dancing', just-behind-the-beat style, he marked the beat clearly, and using up all the available floor-space navigated neatly, never bumping into other couples.

Not being asked to dance could be painful. But my people-watching activities eased the embarrassment for me. At the back of the page-a-day diaries I've been keeping for years I write in quotations I want to remember; stories I've heard and remarks made. Looking at an old diary I found this, 'On not being married—Irish voice—"When ye get over the disgrace of it, the life is more airy." ' I sometimes felt this at dances. Not being asked to dance gave me a sense of space in which I could observe and imagine. Anyway I felt invisible while I watched.

By any standard I was very green and although I looked grown-up I was immature to the point of idiocy. I knew roughly how babies came. A small contemporary, with sniggers, had told me in a Hertfordshire garden and I went straight to my mother and asked if it was true. 'Who told you?' Loyalty very nearly sealed my lips. My mother had guessed who had told me and was sad because she had wanted to tell me herself when the time came for me to ask the question. We didn't go into it very deeply. I wasn't much interested and lived on quite comfortably with hazy visions about sex and very little curiosity. So it never occurred to me even at eighteen, at my own coming-out dance, that it might be misconstrued if I said to a young man, a frequent dancing-partner and a friend, 'I know a marvellously quiet place where we can go,' and I led him up the back stairs of Aunt Nancy's London house to a top passage where the unwanted sofas and chairs from the drawing-rooms had been stacked to make room for dancing. The young man, less green than I was, made as if to kiss me. I was surprised and appalled; it spoilt everything. I got up from the sofa, pushing him away, and ran down to the cloakroom where I found my best friend Virginia Graham filling in time because no one had booked her for that dance.

'The most *terrible* thing has happened—D. tried to kiss me.'

'He *didn't*.'

'Yes, isn't it ghastly.' We were both shaken.

Going home in the taxi after the party I sat on the tip-up seat facing my parents.

'I've got something awful to tell you. D. tried to kiss me.'

My pa said something like, 'Oh—well—never mind', and my mother, pleased, I expect, that her child had done so well at her coming-out party, didn't say much. In all seriousness I said:

'Do you think I should ever speak to him again?'

My pa thumped me gently and said:

'Oh, I think I should.'

So I did.

JOYCE GRENFELL

A Few Words About Breasts

I have to begin with a few words about androgyny. In grammar school, in the fifth and sixth grades, we were all tyrannized by a rigid set of rules that supposedly determined whether we were boys or girls. The episode in *Huckleberry Finn* where Huck is disguised as a girl and gives himself away by the way he threads a needle and catches a ball—that kind of thing. We learned that the way you sat, crossed your legs, held a cigarette, and looked at your nails—the way you did these things instinctively was absolute proof of your sex. Now obviously most children did not take this literally, but I did. I thought that just one slip, just one incorrect cross of my legs or flick of an imaginary cigarette ash would turn me from whatever I was into the other thing; that would be all it took, really. Even though I was outwardly a girl and had many of the trappings generally associated with girl-dom—a girl's name, for example, and dresses, my own telephone, an autograph book—I spent the early years of my adolescence absolutely certain that I might at any point gum it up. I did not feel at all like a girl. I was boyish. I was athletic, ambitious, outspoken, competitive, noisy, rambunctious. I had scabs on my knees and my socks slid into my loafers and I could throw a football. I wanted desperately not to be that way, not to be a mixture of both things, but instead just one, a girl, a definite indisputable girl. As soft and as pink as a nursery. And nothing would do that for me, I felt, but breasts.

I was about six months younger than everyone else in my class, and so for about six months after it began, for six months after my friends had begun to develop (that was the word we used, develop), I was not particularly worried. I would sit in the bath-tub and look down at my breasts and know that any day now, any second now, they would start growing like everyone else's. They didn't. 'I want to buy a bra,' I said to my mother one night. 'What for?' she said. My mother was really hateful about bras, and by the time my third sister had gotten to the point where she was ready to want one, my mother had worked the whole busi-ness into a comedy routine. 'Why not use a Band-Aid instead?' she would say. It was a source of great pride to my mother that she had never even had to wear a brassiere until she had her fourth child, and then only because her gynecologist made her. It was incomprehensible to me that anyone could ever be proud of something like that. It was the 1950s, for God's sake. Jane Rus-sell. Cashmere sweaters. Couldn't my mother see that? '*I am too old to wear an undershirt.*' Screaming. Weeping. Shouting. 'Then don't wear an undershirt,' said my mother. 'But I want to buy a bra.' 'What for?'

I suppose that for most girls, breasts, brassieres, that entire thing, has more trauma, more to do with the coming of adoles-cence, with becoming a woman, than anything else. Certainly more than getting your period, although that, too, was traumatic,

symbolic. But you could see breasts; they were there; they were
visible. Whereas a girl could claim to have her period for months
before she actually got it and nobody would ever know the difference. Which is exactly what I did. All you had to do was make a
great fuss over having enough nickels for the Kotex machine and
walk around clutching your stomach and moaning for three to
five days a month about The Curse and you could convince anybody. There is a school of thought somewhere in the women's
lib/women's mag/gynecology establishment that claims that
menstrual cramps are purely psychological, and I lean toward it.
Not that I didn't have them finally. Agonizing cramps, heating-
pad cramps, go-down-to-the-school-nurse-and-lie-on-the-cot
cramps. But, unlike any pain I had ever suffered, I adored the pain
of cramps, welcomed it, wallowed in it, bragged about it. 'I can't
go. I have cramps.' 'I can't do that. I have cramps.' And most of
all, gigglingly, blushingly: 'I can't swim. I have cramps.' Nobody
ever used the hard-core word. Menstruation. God, what an awful
word. Never that. 'I have cramps.'

The morning I first got my period, I went into my mother's
bedroom to tell her. And my mother, my utterly-hateful-about-
bras mother, burst into tears. It was really a lovely moment, and I
remember it so clearly not just because it was one of the two

39

times I ever saw my mother cry on my account (the other was when I was caught being a six-year-old kleptomaniac), but also because the incident did not mean to me what it meant to her. Her little girl, her firstborn, had finally become a woman. That was what she was crying about. My reaction to the event, however, was that I might well be a woman in some scientific, textbook sense (and could at least stop faking every month and stop wasting all those nickels). But in another sense—in a visible sense—I was as androgynous and as liable to tip over into boyhood as ever.

I started with a 28AA bra. I don't think they made them any smaller in those days, although I gather that now you can buy bras for five-year-olds that don't have any cups whatsoever in them; trainer bras they are called. My first brassiere came from Robinson's Department Store in Beverly Hills. I went there alone, shaking, positive they would look me over and smile and tell me to come back next year. An actual fitter took me into the dressing-room and stood over me while I took off my blouse and tried the first one on. The little puffs stood out on my chest. 'Lean over,' said the fitter. (To this day, I am not sure what fitters in bra departments do except to tell you to lean over.) I leaned over, with the fleeting hope that my breasts would miraculously fall out of my body and into the puffs. Nothing.

'Don't worry about it,' said my friend Libby some months later, when things had not improved. 'You'll get them after you're married.'

'What are you talking about?' I said.

'When you get married,' Libby explained, 'your husband will touch your breasts and rub them and kiss them and they'll grow.'

That was the killer. Necking I could deal with. Intercourse I could deal with. But it had never crossed my mind that a man was going to touch my breasts, that breasts had something to do with all that, petting, my God, they never mentioned petting in my little sex manual about the fertilization of the ovum. I became dizzy. For I knew instantly—as naïve as I had been only a moment before—that only part of what she was saying was true: the touching, rubbing, kissing part, not the growing part. And I knew that no one would ever want to marry me. I had no breasts. I would never have breasts.

My best friend in school was Diana Raskob. She lived a block from me in a house full of wonders. English muffins, for instance. The Raskobs were the first people in Beverly Hills to have English muffins for breakfast. They also had an apricot tree in the back, and a badminton court, and a subscription to *Seventeen* magazine, and hundreds of games, like Sorry and Parcheesi and Treasure Hunt and Anagrams. Diana and I spent three or four afternoons a week in their den reading and playing and eating. Diana's mother's kitchen was full of the most colossal assortment of junk food I have ever been exposed to. My house was full of apples and peaches and milk and homemade chocolate-chip cookies—which were nice, and good for you, but-not-right-before-dinner-or-you'll-spoil-your-appetite. Diana's house had nothing in it that was good for you, and what's more, you could stuff it in right up until dinner and nobody cared. Bar-B-Q potato chips (they were the first in them, too), giant bottles of ginger ale, fresh popcorn with melted butter, hot fudge sauce on Baskin-Robbins jamoca ice cream, powdered-sugar doughnuts from Van de Kamp's. Diana and I had been best friends since we were seven; we were about equally popular in school (which is to say, not particularly), we had about the same success with boys (extremely intermittent), and we looked much the same. Dark. Tall. Gangly.

It is September, just before school begins. I am eleven years old, about to enter the seventh grade, and Diana and I have not seen each other all summer. I have been to camp and she has been somewhere like Banff with her parents. We are meeting, as we often do, on the street midway between our two houses, and we will walk back to Diana's and eat junk and talk about what has happened to each of us that summer. I am walking down Walden Drive in my jeans and my father's shirt hanging out and my old red loafers with the socks falling into them and coming toward me is . . . I take a deep breath . . . a young woman. Diana. Her hair is curled and she has a waist and hips and a bust and she is wearing a straight skirt, an article of clothing I have been repeatedly told I will be unable to wear until I have the hips to hold it up. My jaw drops, and suddenly I am crying, crying hysterically, can't catch my breath sobbing. My best friend has

betrayed me. She has gone ahead without me and done it. She has shaped up.

Here are some things I did to help:

Bought a Mark Eden Bust Developer.

Slept on my back for four years.

Splashed cold water on them every night because some French actress said in *Life* magazine that that was what *she* did for her perfect bustline.

Ultimately, I resigned myself to a bad toss and began to wear padded bras. I think about them now, think about all those years in high school I went around in them, my three padded bras, every single one of them with different-sized breasts. Each time I changed bras I changed sizes: one week nice perky but not too obtrusive breasts, the next medium-sized slightly pointy ones, the next week knockers, true knockers; all the time, whatever size I was, carrying around this rubberized appendage on my chest that occasionally crashed into a wall and was poked inward and had to be poked outward—I think about all that and wonder how anyone kept a straight face through it. My parents, who normally had no restraints about needling me—why did they say nothing as they watched my chest go up and down? My friends, who would periodically inspect my breasts for signs of growth and reassure me—why didn't they at least counsel consistency?

And the bathing suits. I die when I think about the bathing suits. That was the era when you could lay an uninhabited bathing suit on the beach and someone would make a pass at it. I would put one on, an absurd swimsuit with its enormous bust built into it, the bones from the suit stabbing me in the rib cage and leaving little red welts on my body, and there I would be, my chest plunging straight downward absolutely vertically from my collarbone to the top of my suit and then suddenly, wham, out came all that padding and material and wiring absolutely horizontally.

Buster Klepper was the first boy who ever touched them. He was my boyfriend my senior year of high school. There is a picture of him in my high-school yearbook that makes him look quite

42

attractive in a Jewish, horn-rimmed-glasses sort of way, but the picture does not show the pimples, which were air-brushed out, or the dumbness. Well, that isn't really fair. He wasn't dumb. He just wasn't terribly bright. His mother refused to accept it, refused to accept the relentlessly average report cards, refused to deal with her son's inevitable destiny in some junior college or other. 'He was tested', she would say to me, apropos of nothing, 'and it came out a hundred and forty-five. That's near-genius.' Had the word 'underachiever' been coined, she probably would have lobbed that one at me, too. Anyway, Buster was really very sweet—which is, I know, damning with faint praise, but there it is. I was the editor of the front page of the high-school newspaper and he was editor of the back page; we had to work together, side by side, in the print shop, and that was how it started. On our first date, we went to see *April Love*, starring Pat Boone. Then we started going together. Buster had a green coupe, a 1950 Ford with an engine he had hand-chromed until it shone, dazzled, reflected the image of anyone who looked into it, anyone usually being Buster polishing it or the gas-station attendants he constantly asked to check the oil in order for them to be overwhelmed by the sparkle on the valves. The car also had a boot stretched over the back seat for reasons I never understood; hanging from the rearview mirror, as was the custom, was a pair of angora dice. A previous girlfriend named Solange, who was famous throughout Beverly Hills High School for having no pigment in her right eyebrow, had knitted them for him. Buster and I would ride around town, the two of us seated to the left of the steering wheel. I would shift gears. It was nice.

There was necking. Terrific necking. First in the car, overlooking Los Angeles from what is now the Trousdale Estates. Then on the bed of his parents' cabana at Ocean House. Incredibly wonderful, frustrating necking, I loved it, really, but no further than necking, please don't, please, because there I was absolutely terrified of the general implications of going-a-step-further with a near-dummy and also terrified of his finding out there was next to nothing there (which he knew, of course; he wasn't that dumb).

I broke up with him at one point. I think we were apart for about two weeks. At the end of that time, I drove down to see a friend at a boarding school in Palos Verdes Estates and a disc jockey played 'April Love' on the radio four times during the trip. I took it as a sign. I drove straight back to Griffith Park to a golf tournament Buster was playing in (he was the sixth-seeded teenage golf player in southern California) and presented myself back to him on the green of the 18th hole. It was all very dramatic. That night we went to a drive-in and I let him get his hand under my protuberances and onto my breasts. He really didn't seem to mind at all.

NORA EPHRON

Two Cousins

My cousin Lady Ursula Talbot would have been a beauty but for her nose, which was so big that it seemed to enter a room long before the rest of her. Because of this defect she was painfully shy, rarely spoke and was a wallflower at every débutante dance. Eventually she could bear it no longer and, unbeknown to her parents, had it chopped off and a little *retroussé* nose took its place. After this operation she never looked back. She had three husbands and between the second and third lived with a well-known English writer for many years. Sadly she was killed in a private plane, piloted by her third husband, over the Scilly Isles.

Another cousin of mine was Dorothy Paget, daughter of Lord Queenborough. She was remarkably plain and what made it worse she had a beautiful sister, Olive, Lady Baillie, of Leeds Castle. Poor Dorothy had skin like a ploughed field, an under-hung lower lip, mousy, rather thin hair and became enormously fat. Her saving grace was that she was destined to become very rich. When she came of age she inherited a vast fortune, which made her independent. She was able to lead the eccentric life she chose, by turning night into day. Buying racehorses was her one passion, but she was seldom seen on the racecourse, except if one of her horses was running in a particularly important race. Otherwise, she relied on the wireless, as it was then called, for the results of her racing activities. She was surrounded by ruthless sycophants who, for what they could get out of her, also turned their nights into days. What they didn't know was that she was fully aware of their goings-on but put up with them because it gave her a sense of power which, in a way, compensated for her inferiority complex. Her money was in trust, so they inherited nothing. Dorothy never married and to my knowledge had no lovers, male or female. She died when she was still quite a young woman.

DAVID HERBERT

Mistresses and Murderers

Both my father and I were guilty of infidelity to the law; my mistress was writing, his was the garden. He would break off conferences to get an early train, change his clothes and do a tour of the plants he couldn't see but could only smell before the light faded and my mother would no longer be able to describe the budding of the camellias or the blowsy attraction of the dahlias. The house and garden acted like a drug on him; the place was a Circe's island from which he found it harder and harder to escape. In time I also found myself less and less willing to leave it, to cover my head with itchy horsehair and put on a stiff, winged collar, to bow to someone for whom I felt no particular respect and say 'if your Lordship pleases', and to fight, over and over again, the same battles to save some client from being treated according to his just deserts. But then, as Hamlet said, 'Use every man after his desert and who should scape whipping?'

Not, of course, that every fight was the same. The reasons for getting into trouble are the subject of infinite variation, from mere bad luck to the existence of evil. The Old Bailey was a mixture of the theatre of comedy, of tragedy, of the absurd and the macabre, and most often a drama in which these styles were alarmingly intermingled; as they were in the case of the murderous butler, a killer who, I was told, hoped to make the *Guinness Book of Records* on account of the number of persons he had done to death. In my childhood I remember my parents engaged a manservant, a tall fellow with crinkly hair who wore a grubby white mess-jacket which revealed the ends of his braces, called Tredgold. He used to ask me to go out on the common and bowl cricket balls at him, an invitation which filled me with fear. The butler in my Old Bailey case was pale, courteous and dignified. He had read a little law and discovered that in Scotland they had something which appealed to him greatly, a verdict of not proven. So he would drive his victims to Scotland, bury them on some barren heath and, if they were discovered, he hoped to take advantage of this ambiguous Scottish finding. He had been the butler of a very elderly ex-Labour MP who was no longer perfectly in his right mind. Having killed his employer's wife, the butler offered to drive the old man, who was quite unaware of the tragedy which had occurred, to the Odeon cinema in Leicester Square to see 'a nice travel film'. His victim saw no film but instead was driven to Scotland and there, beside a Highland stream, he was murdered.

Working for a county lady, the butler was recognized by her footman as someone he'd met during a spell in prison; for this the footman was killed and buried in the rose garden. Later, the lady in question wrote to the court to assure the judge that the butler was an absolute paragon who never failed to take the Labrador out each night for a run in the rose garden. I didn't act for this tailcoated assassin but for another footman who had been his accomplice. My client, I remember, complained that the butler was treated as a star in prison, enjoying the sort of deference which screws and fellow inmates accorded to such famous figures as the Kray twins, whereas he was treated with contempt and often had scalding cocoa poured over his head. At the end of the trial the judge sentenced the butler to life imprisonment from which 'you will never be released unless you are in the terminal stages of a fatal illness'. At this the perfect servant smiled faintly, bowed and left the dock as though he had been told that he might serve dinner now.

The most terrible crimes often take place in mundane surroundings and the evidence is commonplace. The story of one of the first murders I was concerned with started with a cleaning lady, employed by a very upper-class agency, let us say Dusters Ltd of Kensington. She was sent off to clean the Belgravia apartment of a family she had never met and was given the keys to let herself in. Accordingly she went to this select address, walked into the kitchen, took off her coat and hat and hung them neatly in a cupboard. She put on her overall, found the Hoover and emerged in a long passage, at the end of which she saw a young man, who was to be my client, in the act of murdering his mother with a weapon which was referred to during the trial as a 'salad knife'. Without a moment's hesitation, the cleaning lady returned to the kitchen, closed the door firmly, put away the Hoover, took off her overall, put on her hat and coat and returned to the offices of Dusters Ltd. When asked why she had come back so soon, she shook her head and said, 'No, that's not really the type of family I'd care to work for.' She told no one about the killing, which was not, in fact, discovered until a considerable time later. When the son was arrested, however, the statement he made to the police came out as a kind of lurid poetry, for he said, 'I have either buggered a prostitute or killed a peacock in paradise.' This may have been a lightning flash of lunacy or a well-contrived invention to get him to where he was destined to go, to Broadmoor.

Sometimes the plots of the dramas in which we took part might have been written, on a day when his fancy was running riot, by Joe Orton. Two young male prostitutes were standing under neighbouring lampposts in Bayswater and they struck up an acquaintance. Their names were Bob and Anthony. Bob was inclined to rob anyone who went home with him and Anthony was in the process of changing his sex. These two fell head over heels in love. Bob took his new friend, by now known as Antoinette, to live with his parents. Bob's father was a prison warder, a job which provided him with a house, and Bob's mother, overjoyed that her son had found a nice girlfriend at last, hoped for an early marriage. For a while all went well, but then Antoinette began to stray and took to visiting the Flying Saucer club in Leicester Square. One night Bob, overcome with jealousy, followed her to this resort where he found Antoinette removing her trousers whilst dancing with a young man. Enraged, Bob began to beat his friend about the head with a pink plastic piggy bank in which the club collected money for an annual children's outing. As a result of this attack Antoinette was fatally injured and the police were sent for. During the course of his questioning, Bob said to the inspector in charge of the case, 'Have you got any idea what it's like to fall in love with a bloke who changes his sex, and you take him to live with your mum and dad, and then find him undressing on the dance floor of the Flying Saucer and making you so mad you hit him with a piggy bank?' To which the inspector politely replied. 'No, sir. I can't say as I have ever had such an experience.' At the trial the judge said he was going to treat the case as a perfectly ordinary, run-of-the-mill matrimonial dispute. Bob was found guilty of manslaughter by reason of provocation and leniently treated— the reactions of judges at the Old Bailey were a source of continual surprise.

There was also a trial in which I got a startling insight into the home life of one particular his Lordship. I had a run of cases which arose from quarrels between married couples in bathrooms. Indeed, the shared bath is fraught with dangers for parties with cooling marriages; the situation in which they find themselves often gives rise to comments of a wounding and personal nature. One such dispute had led to an attempted drowning for which the husband was arrested and I was hard put to it to formulate a defence. Before the trial the judge asked us to his room for coffee and biscuits and a discussion of its probable length. He looked at me as though I was personally in the habit of drowning women in baths and said that it was a most terrible and serious case. 'Indeed it is, my Lord,' I told him. 'My client was seated at the tap end of the bath. He foolishly lost his temper when his wife adversely compared his physical prowess to that of her lover.'

'*What* did you say?' The judge looked at me aghast.

'I said she had made a comment of a personal nature which led to a violent quarrel,' I repeated, and added, 'I'm afraid the fight started when he was sitting at the tap end of the bath and—'

'The tap end!' By now the judge was seriously perturbed. 'Does the prosecution accept this evidence?'

'Yes, my Lord.' Counsel for the Crown admitted it cheerfully not being altogether sure of what was going on.

48

'How long had he been in the habit of sitting at the tap end of the bath?' the judge asked in some distress.

'Throughout the marriage. His wife required him to sit in that position so he could rinse her hair after she'd shampooed it.'

'And how long had they been married?'

'About twenty years,' I had to tell him.

'For twenty years this woman required her husband to sit at the tap end!' the judge repeated and bit quite savagely into a digestive biscuit. And so it went on, and we were bound over to keep the peace, or pleaded guilty to common assault, before a judge whose wife had always sat, apparently without complaint, with her naked shoulders pressed against the taps. Eventually I did include this incident in a story, and no one thought it other than an extravagant invention. Rewriting what went on at the Old Bailey as fiction is a constant process of calming down the truth, so that it may achieve some degree of credibility.

JOHN MORTIMER

Kitty Shipley, Aged Eleven, on Marriage

During 1771 Benjamin Franklin paid two visits to Twyford in Hampshire to stay with his friend Jonathan Shipley, the Bishop of St Asaph. In one of his thank-you letters he describes his conversation with Kitty Shipley, the youngest of the five Shipley girls, whom he was accompanying back to her school in London.

London, 12 August 1771

This is just to let you know that we arrived safe and well in Marlborough Street about six, where I delivered up my charge.

The above seems too short for a letter; so I will lengthen it by a little account of our journey. The first stage we were rather pensive. I tried several topics of conversation, but none of them would hold. But after breakfast, we began to recover spirits, and

49

had a good deal of chat. Will you hear some of it? We talked of her brother, and she wished he was married. And don't you wish your sisters married too? Yes. All but Emily; I would not have her married. Why? Because I can't spare her, I can't part with her. The rest may marry as soon as they please, so they do but get good husbands. We then took upon us to consider for 'em what sort of husbands would be fittest for every one of them. We began with Georgiana. She thought a country gentleman, that loved travelling and would take her with him, that loved books and would hear her read to him; I added, that had a good estate and was a Member of Parliament and loved to see an experiment now and then. This she agreed to; so we set him down for Georgiana, and went on to Betsy. Betsy, says I, seems of a sweet mild temper, and if we should give her a country squire, and he should happen to be of a rough, passionate turn, and be angry now and then, it might break her heart. O, none of 'em must be so; for then they would not be good husbands. To make sure of this point, however, for Betsy, shall we give her a bishop? O no, that won't do. They all declare against the Church, and against the army; not one of them will marry either a clergyman or an officer; that they are resolved upon. What can be their reason for that? Why you know, that when a clergyman or an officer dies, the income goes with 'em; and then what is there to maintain the family? There's the point. Then suppose we give her a good, honest, sensible City merchant, who will love her dearly and is very rich? I don't know but that may do. We proceeded to Emily, her dear Emily, I was afraid we should hardly find anything good

enough for Emily; but at last, after first settling that, if she did marry, Kitty was to live a good deal with her, we agreed that as Emily was very handsome we might expect an earl for her: so having fixed her, as I thought, a countess, we went on to Anna-Maria. She, says Kitty, should have a rich man that has a large family and a great many things to take care of; for she is very good at managing, helps my Mama very much, can look over bills, and order all sorts of Family business. Very well; and as there is a grace and dignity in her manner that would become the station, what do you think of giving her a duke? O no! I'll have the duke for Emily. You may give the earl to Anna-Maria if you please: but Emily shall have the duke. I contested this matter some time; but at length was forced to give up the point, leave Emily in possession of the duke, and content myself with the earl for Anna-Maria. And now what shall we do for Kitty? We have forgot her, all this time. Well, and what will you do for her? I suppose that though the rest have resolved against the army, she may not yet have made so rash a resolution. Yes, but she has: unless, now, an old one, an old general that has done fighting, and is rich, such a one as General Rufane; I like him a good deal; you must know I like an old man, indeed I do: and somehow or other all the old men take to me, all that come to our house like me better than my other sisters: I go to 'em and ask 'em how they do, and they like it mightily; and the maids take notice of it, and say when they see an old man come, there's a friend of yours, Miss Kitty. But then as you like an old general, hadn't you better take him while he's a young officer, and let him grow old upon your hands, because then you'll like him better and better every year as he grows older and older. No, that won't do. He must be an old man of seventy or eighty, and take me when I am about thirty: and then you know I may be a rich young widow. We dined at Staines, she was Mrs Shipley, cut up the chicken pretty handily (with a little direction) and helped me in a very womanly manner. Now, says she, when I commended her, my father never likes to see me or Georgiana carve, because we do it, he says, so badly: but how should we learn if we never try? We drank good Papa and Mama's health, and the health's of the dutchess, the countess, the merchant's lady, the country gentlewoman, and our Welsh brother. This brought their affairs again under consideration. I doubt, says she, we have not done right for Betsy. I don't think a merchant will do for her. She is much inclined to be a

51

fine gentlewoman; and is indeed already more of the fine gentle-woman, I think, than any of my other sisters; and therefore she shall be a vice countess.

Thus we chatted on, and she was very entertaining quite to town.

I have now made my letter as much too long as it was at first too short. The bishop would think it too trifling, therefore don't show it him. I am afraid too that you will think it so, and have a good mind not to send it. Only it tells you Kitty is well at school, and for that I let it go. My love to the whole amiable family, best respects to the bishop, and 1000 thanks for all your kindnesses, and for the happy days I enjoyed at Twyford. With the greatest esteem and respect, I am, madam, your most obedient humble servant

BENJAMIN FRANKLIN

Winning Arts

I shall not say why and how I became, at the age of fifteen, the mistress of the Earl of Craven. Whether it was love, or the sever-ity of my father, the depravity of my own heart, or the winning arts of the noble Lord, which induced me to leave my paternal roof and place myself under his protection, does not now much signify: or if it does, I am not in the humour to gratify curiosity in this matter.

I resided on the Marine Parade, at Brighton; and I remember that Lord Craven used to draw cocoa trees, and his fellows, as he called them, on the best vellum paper, for my amusement. Here stood the enemy, he would say; and here, my love, are my fel-lows: there the cocoa trees, etc. It was, in fact, a dead bore. All these cocoa trees and fellows, at past eleven o'clock at night, could have no peculiar interest for a child like myself, so lately in the habit of retiring early to rest. One night, I recollect, I fell asleep; and, as I often dream, I said, yawning, and half awake, 'Oh, Lord! Oh, Lord! Craven has got me into the West Indies again.' In short, I soon found that I had made a bad speculation by going from my father to Lord Craven. I was even more afraid of the latter than I had been of the former; not that there was any particular harm in the man, beyond his cocoa trees; but we never suited nor understood each other.

I was not depraved enough to determine immediately on a new choice, and yet I often thought about it. How, indeed, could I do otherwise, when the Honourable Frederick Lamb was my constant visitor, and talked to me of nothing else? However, in justice to myself, I must declare that the idea of the possibility of deceiving Lord Craven, while I was under his roof, never once entered into my head. Frederick was then very handsome; and certainly tried, with all his soul and with all his strength, to convince me that constancy to Lord Craven was the greatest non-sense in the world. I firmly believe that Frederick Lamb sincerely loved me, and deeply regretted that he had no fortune to invite me to share with him.

Lord Melbourne, his father, was a good man. Not one of your stiff-laced moralizing fathers, who preach chastity and forbear-ance to their children. Quite the contrary; he congratulated his son on the lucky circumstance of his friend Craven having such a girl with him. 'No such thing,' answered Frederick Lamb; 'I am unsuccessful there. Harriette will have nothing to do with me.' 'Nonsense!' rejoined Melbourne, in great surprise; 'I never heard anything half so ridiculous in all my life. The girl must be mad! She looks mad: I thought so the other day, when I met her gal-loping about, with her feathers blowing and her thick dark hair about her ears.'

'I'll speak to Harriette for you,' added His Lordship, after a long pause; and then continued repeating to himself, in an undertone, 'Not have my son, indeed! Six feet high! A fine, straight, handsome, noble young fellow! I wonder what she would have!'

In truth, I scarcely knew myself; but something I determined on: so miserably tired was I of Craven, and his cocoa trees, and his sailing boats, and his ugly cotton nightcap. Surely, I would say, all men do not wear those shocking cotton nightcaps; else all women's illusions had been destroyed on the first night of their marriage!

I wonder, thought I, what sort of a nightcap the Prince of Wales wears? Then I went on to wonder whether the Prince of Wales would think me so beautiful as Frederick Lamb did? Next I reflected that Frederick Lamb was younger than the Prince; but then, again, a Prince of Wales!!!

I was undecided: my heart began to soften. I thought of my dear mother, and wished I had never left her. It was too late, however, now. My father would not suffer me to return; and as to passing my life, or any more of it, with Craven, cotton nightcap and all, it was death! He never once made me laugh, nor said nor did anything to please me.

Thus musing, I listlessly turned over my writing-book, half in the humour to address the Prince of Wales. A sheet of paper, covered with Lord Craven's cocoa trees, decided me; and I wrote the following letter, which I addressed to the Prince.

Brighton

I am told that I am very beautiful, so, perhaps, you would like to see me; and I wish that, since so many are disposed to love me, one, for in the humility of my heart I should be quite satisfied with one, would be at the pains to make me love him. In the meantime, this is all very dull work, sir, and worse even than being at home with my father: so, if you pity me, and believe you could make me in love with you, write to me, and direct to the post-office here.

By return of post, I received an answer nearly to this effect: I believe, from Colonel Thomas.

Miss Wilson's letter has been received by the noble individual to whom it was addressed. If Miss Wilson will come to town, she may have an interview, by directing her letter as before.

I answered this note directly, addressing my letter to the Prince of Wales.

Sir,

To travel fifty-two miles, this bad weather, merely to see a man, with only the given number of legs, arms, fingers, etc., would, you must admit, be madness, in a girl like myself, surrounded by humble admirers, who are ever ready to travel any distance for the honour of kissing the tip of her little finger; but if you can prove to me that you are one bit better than any man who may be ready to attend my bidding, I'll e'en start for London directly. So, if you can do anything better, in the way of pleasing a lady, than ordinary men, write directly: if not, adieu, Monsieur le Prince.

I won't say Yours,
By day or night, or any kind of light;
Because you are too impudent.

HARRIETTE WILSON

Pleasure at the Helm

In the spring of 1912 I went with my mother for the first time to Venice, to stay with Anthony Drexel in the Palazzo Balbi Vallier. The Campanile had just been rebuilt and we watched its unveiling. The bells rang and forty thousand doves were liberated. The giant belfry dwarfed St Mark's domes and the bronze horses, and generally the new tower looked too big and too new. Again no one reproved me for making myself a cynosure by wearing an Italian officer's white cloth cloak, and on the side of my head a *bersagliere*'s hat, plumed with cocks' feathers.

That summer Lady Cunard, a new light in our lives, took a

55

small *casa* in the Via dei Catecumeni. It was with her we stayed. The fabled Louisa Casati lived in the half-built Palazzo Vanier dei Leoni. I saw her drifting down the Grand Canal under a parasol of peacocks' feathers, but this surprise was nothing to the succession of glorious shocks that were to come.

At the first of her parties she received us in her roofless palace by the light of a brazier on to which a nakedish slave for each new arrival flung a fuel that flared up into white flame. Another slave struck a reverberating gong announcing every guest while she, the Casati, tall and elegant in a lampshade skirt, seemingly growing out of a wide bowl of tuberoses, presented each of us with a waxen flower. I remember thinking with what grace the foreigners received the flower and how clumsy we poor English were, saying 'Doesn't it smell good!' when another said '*Quelle émotion—Madame!*'

The next party outshone the first and failed. It was planned that we should meet in the unbuilt palace dressed and masked as Longhis and Guardis and process in gondolas to the Piazza San Marco, there to disport ourselves—no one wondered how. The Casati wore the trousered Bakst-designed dress of an animal-tamer. On her shoulder was a 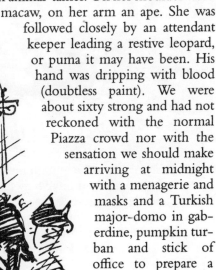 macaw, on her arm an ape. She was followed closely by an attendant keeper leading a restive leopard, or puma it may have been. His hand was dripping with blood (doubtless paint). We were about sixty strong and had not reckoned with the normal Piazza crowd nor with the sensation we should make arriving at midnight with a menagerie and masks and a Turkish major-domo in gaberdine, pumpkin turban and stick of office to prepare a way for his procession. The Piazzetta was black with Vene-

tians. The fine girls, dressed in their classical black-fringed shawls, made us the more garish. There were shouts and ribald screams and peals of laughter and we fought our way through a density that would have been impenetrable but for our leopard. Somehow we jostled our way across the immensity of the Piazza through the columned archway to the nearest embarking steps. For me it was no failure. I loved crowds and didn't mind being a spectacle, and I enjoyed madly the jostle and even the discomfiture of the elders, who must have heard the tumbrils behind the mob's howls, but the party must be written down a failure.

No longer a fledgling, I was allowed more liberty and choice after the first year. I was still forbidden to be alone with a man except by chance in the country. A married woman must bring me home from a ball. For walking and shopping and even driving in a taxi, a sister or a girl was enough protection. I could go to the Ritz but to no other London hotel. But generally there was more freedom. I was not forced to Ascot or to 'young dances' and I had more courage in choosing my friends. I desperately wanted my mother to approve of them, but she could not.

I had earned the hard name of a 'scalp-collector' and I expect the cap fitted. The more the safer. Many would save me from one. I did not want to be possessed by my heart or by another's.

Like all good mothers she planned to see me married to an Adonis reigning feudally in a palace, while I was looking for a romantic struggle with some Unknown by my side. So the tangled web of deceits grew thicker, though it barely affected my love for her. The shadow crossing her face when she saw me with an unmistakable ineligible said 'What waste of time!' This annoyed and perturbed me. The eligibles she put in my way were leprous to my eyes. Today I wonder why. I should have seen it as part of the romantic struggle instead of resenting it.

Was Tommy Bouch eligible or ineligible? I do not know in what category my mother put him. I was very fond of him, so he cannot have been eligible. Before the war he was a Master of the Belvoir Hounds. He came from a hunting world in Warwickshire and with the courage of a Siegfried braved the fiery ring of taunts and ridicule and warnings of spells without a name that encircled the Castle, to become an intimate. The Belvoir Hunt thought the air too rarefied and theatrical. Perhaps they did not know that their Master was a poet—a poet whom Maurice Baring praised to the skies. He was imaginative and generous and a benedicton to those of us in trouble with scandals, debts, love or lack of a thoroughbred mount.

Then there was George Moore—George Gordon Moore, who hailed I believe from Detroit. He was certainly not eligible. I had met him at Stanway—a most unusual man of thirty-six, Red Indian in appearance with straight black hair, flattened face and atomic energy. I understood very little of what he said, but I caught his unclear accents of admiration. I 'penetrated his consciousness', he said, and he courted me in his own exaggerated way although he had a wife and children. He gave me to understand that these hindrances could be liquidated and that his every living hour and his vast fortune would be dedicated to me—to me and to Sir John French. He moved in a shower of gold. He doled it out on the just and unjust and on his whims. His riches were evident but maybe an optical illusion, so his countrymen said. Harsh things they whispered—'Kicked out of the States', 'Just a crook', but we all believed in him, especially the Charteris family, whose protégé and patron he was. He had no snobbery. I would have liked him a lot had it not been for his infatuation for me, which frightened me into flight.

He loaded Letty and me with presents, Letty being now a Charteris and I his idol—silver foxes for Letty and an ermine coat to the ankle for me (my mother chose it from Jay's), a monstrous little monkey called Armide with a diamond waist-belt and chain, Maupassant's works in full morocco, countless *éditions de luxe*, a cream poodle called Fido cut *en papillon* with pompoms and bracelets of fluff and a heliotrope bow, and twice weekly, wherever I was, arrived a box the size of a coffin full of Madonna lilies.

It seems odd today, and no doubt seemed odd at the time, that we were allowed to accept such presents. I never thought it strange because my mother saw no harm. She liked the children to be spoilt and enjoyed nothing better than choosing gifts from wise men.

George Moore's devotion and admiration for Sir John French led him to buy a huge corner house in Lancaster Gate and there install the General. It was a ghastly house, which in the war was to be a shelter and playground for our diminishing Coterie. The dreary little parties he gave in 1913 developed under the stress of early war into uproarious ones behind barred doors which were called by our enemies the 'Dances of Death'.

A foreign eligible didn't carry the same stigma. Count Clary for instance was very eligible. He taught me the Viennese waltz and we would spin ourselves to a standstill to the strains of Cassano's band. Count Wilczeck was eligible, so was Count Hoesch, another Dream Waltzer. But the most eligible of all was Prince Felix Youssupoff. He was later to kill Rasputin, but at that time he was an innocent at Oxford and deeply in love with my sister Marjorie. A mystic, and of transcendent beauty, he sang to his guitar the Russian gypsy songs, now so hackneyed, then new to us. At the many fancy balls he wore his eighteenth-century Russian dress of gold and pearls and sables and aigrettes, with embroidered boots and jewelled scimitar. He rode in the procession with me at the revived Eglinton Tournament. . . . I prayed for Marjorie to marry Felix.

DIANA COOPER

The Worst of Me

'Mother, I have not deceived Mrs Porter; I have told her the worst of me; that I am of mean extraction; that I have no money, and that I have had an uncle hanged. She replied that she valued no one more or less for his descent; that she had no more money than myself; and that, though she had not had a relation hanged, she had fifty who deserved hanging.'

SAMUEL JOHNSON

The Fancy Dress Ball

The other boredom reliever of those last twelve months was the fancy dress ball in the Opera House. It was a predictable show—admirals dressed as pierrots, their wives as columbines. Bo-peeps were plentiful and there was a sprinkling of Old Bills and Felix the Cats among the military. Parties took boxes in the lovely tiered building and everyone tried hard to pretend that it was every bit as gay and abandoned as the Chelsea Arts Ball.

Trubshawe and I went as goats.

First we put noisome rugs on our backs. Then horns on bands were fixed to our heads and finally, between our legs, for the goat fittings, footballs swung with rubber gloves sewn on to them by the regimental cobbler. Half a pint of dry martinis apiece and we were ready for the fray.

We arrived just in time for the Grand March for the prize-giving. The judges for the best costumes were on the stage and round and round in front of them, two by two, like the animals going into the Ark, went the clowns with their red-hot pokers, the ballet dancers and the Mickey Mice. Rumblings of disapproval rose from the boxes as the two drunken goats joined in at the back of the parade.

'Trubshawe . . . Niven . . . goats! Bad show! Damn bad show!' Military moustaches and naval eyebrows bristled from every floor.

'I'm getting dizzy, old man,' said the goat behind me after we had completed several circuits.

'Left wheel!'

Obediently, I turned out of the parade towards the empty centre of the floor.

'Now squat!' commanded Trubshawe.

'What?' I asked apprehensively.

'Squat, you bloody fool.'

So there at the very hub of the wheel with a kaleidoscope of colour circling round us and the focus of hundreds of disapproving eyes I squatted. Trubshawe produced a brown paper bag from the folds of his smelly rug and sprinkled black olives on the floor directly behind me.

Except in the box that held David Kilburn and Anthony Pleydell-Bouverie, this flourish was coldly received by the ticket holders, particularly by a party of Maltese students who had a very short fuse when they thought that someone was mocking the local institutions. They jostled and shoved us as we left the floor and made threatening noises.

'Better take off, old man,' said my leader as he headed for the exit and the last I saw of Trubshawe that night he was pounding down the main street of Valletta towards the sanctuary of the Union Club pursued by the hornet students and tripping over his 'udders'.

DAVID NIVEN

Madame Glyn Lectures on 'It', with Illustrations

And this, ladies and gentlemen, is the finest day that has yet broken over the bloody and bowed head of your girlfriend. On this day there first fell into these trembling hands The Book, the Ultimate Book. There is grave doubt that I shall ever be able to talk of anything else. Certainly, I have read my last word. Print can hold for me now nothing but anticlimaxes. *It*, the chef d'œuvre of Madame Elinor Glyn,★ has come into my life. And Sherman's coming into Atlanta is but a sneaking, tiptoe performance in comparison.

I didn't know. Truly, I didn't know. Mine is a life sheltered to

★ *Elinor Glyn* (1864–1943), English author of sultry romances, is characterized by a popular jingle of the time: 'Would you like to sin/With Elinor Glyn/On a tiger skin/Or would you prefer/To err with her/On some other fur?'

the point of stuffiness. I attend no movies, for any motion-picture theater is as an enlarged and a magnificently decorated lethal chamber to me. I have read but little of Madame Glyn. I did not know that things like *It* were going on. I have misspent my days. When I think of all those hours I flung away in reading William James and Santayana, when I might have been reading of life, throbbing, beating, perfumed life, I practically break down. Where, I ask you, have I been, that no true word of Madame Glyn's literary feats has come to me?

But even those far, far better informed than I must work a bit over the opening sentence of Madame Glyn's foreword to her novel. 'This is *not*', she says, drawing her emeralds warmly about her, 'the story of the moving picture entitled *It*, but a full character study of the story *It*, which the people in the picture read and discuss.' I could go mad, in a nice way, straining to figure that out. But I shall let it stay a mystery. I shall take what comes to me, glad and grateful and unquestioning. After all, what more could one ask than a character study of a story?

Also in her foreword, Madame Glyn goes into the real meaning of 'It'. 'To have "It",' she says—and is she the girl that knows?—'the fortunate possessor must have that strange magnetism which attracts both sexes.' (Pul-ease. Madame Glyn, pul-ease!) 'He or she must be entirely unselfconscious and full of self-confidence, indifferent to the effect he or she is producing, and uninfluenced by others.' (Why, it's Levine, that's who it is, it's Levine.) 'There must be physical attraction, but beauty is unnecessary. Conceit or self-consciousness destroys "It" immediately. In the animal world, "It" demonstrates' (*sic. Sic* as a dog) 'in tigers and cats—both animals being fascinating and mysterious and quite unbiddable.'

So there you have it, in a coconut-shell. Now we can go on with the story.

Well, it seems there was this man named John Gaunt. By the time we meet him, there is iron-gray in his hair and he has twenty million dollars to go with it, but things were not always thus with him. At the age of ten, he was selling papers on the Bowery; yet he pulled himself up so sturdily that at forty he 'was a person of great cultivation'. Also, 'he had that nameless charm, with a strong magnetism that can only be called "It", and cats, as well as women, always knew when he came into a room'. Also, 'from his fifteenth year, when the saloonkeeper's wife at the corner of his street groveled before his six feet of magnificent stripling strength, to his fortieth birthday, females of all types and classes manifested ardent passion for him'. That, my friends, is living.

Then there was this girl, Ava Cleveland, and her brother Larry. Larry had It something terrible, and he also had a little way of taking opium. (Oh, please wait a minute. I think I'm going to be able to use 'opium' in a sentence. I opium mother is feeling better. No, I guess I'm not, either.) Ava was young and slender and proud. And she had It. It, hell; she had Those.

But Ava was worried. There was that big bill at the dress-maker's. And she had been unlucky at baccarat, lately. And she and Larry were but hangers-on of the rich. You see, as one of Madame Glyn's characters explains, 'Their father never brought them up to do anything, and then died.' Died happy, you gather from this succinct biography, in the knowledge of a task accomplished, and nothing more to do.

So Ava was worried. Indeed, at the end of the very first chapter, we get a sharp flash of her terrible state of mind. ' "What the H—— are we to do?" she said to herself in not very polite English.' Madame Glyn, as you see, does not flinch from plain talk. When she presents a street-Arab to us she has him cry, 'Well, I'll be d——d!' It looks to me as if, out in Hollywood, she must have been on the adjoining lot to that on which *What Price Glory?* was being filmed.

Well, anyway, Ava was worried. Oh, of course there were things she could have done. But she was one who could not Give All unless she loved. Call it her hard luck, if you will, but that's how she was. She was unapproachable, pure, sacred. She could have made any All-American team in a moment, just on her dexterity at intercepting passes. Take her, for example, when the husband of her friend pleads with her—when he says:

' "Then my moment will come—you can't do me down forever, child—I love your white skin."

'A fierce gleam now came into Ava's eyes.

' "You make me sick—you married men—it is nothing but skin—skin!" '

She did have a rich suitor,

and of honorable intent, but he had a mother fixation that belonged by rights in the Smithsonian Institution. Thus did she put him in his place:

' "I think a man is no man unless the woman he loves—the prospective mother of his children, who will carry on his name—stands above everything in his life—everything except his duty to his country and his own soil!" '

But strong as is the temptation to quote and quote and quote, we must get on with the story. We must respect Madame Glyn's duty to her own soil. Well, it turns out that Ava and John meet, and he begins promptly to 'vibrate with passion'. But she is too proud to be mastered by one not of her class; indeed, to herself she refers to him as 'this parvenue', with a convincingly aristocratic disregard for gender. And John Gaunt is one of those boys that must master his woman. Madame Glyn, in fact, has interestingly entangled his It with sadism all through the book, and maybe there is much to be said on her side. John must humble this disdainful creature; he must draw the net close.

So he gives Larry, the poppy-fancier, a job in his San Francisco office, and who would like to bet, then and there, that Larry isn't going to misappropriate funds? Then, when Ava's worries bring her to it, she seeks a position in his New York office, where he may keep his burning green eyes on her—I give you my word, she can feel them blazing through the massive oak door. She is offered a hundred dollars a week for cutting clippings out of newspapers. P.S. She got the job.

It goes on for nearly three hundred pages, with both of them vibrating away like steam launches. And then Larry comes through and steals two thousand dollars. Ava must have the money to keep Larry out of jail, where he couldn't get his hop. She goes to John's palatial residence. She will do it. She will Go Through. She will Sell Herself.

And then what do you think? She finds out it isn't the money; it isn't the principle of the thing, either. It is because she Loves. And what else do you think? He was going to marry her all the time.

Do you wonder that I am never going to read anything else?

DOROTHY PARKER

Married Life at Craigenputtoch

It was the dreariest place on the face of the earth—I lived there five years, and the only wonder is I didn't go mad; the only women that had been there before me were four farmer's wives—of that *kind* of woman, with all their own rough work about them which they were used to occupy themselves with doing, three went mad and the fourth took to drinking! . . .

Oh, there's no way of making ye understand what kind of a wretched place it was—I had seen it only once in my life, when my *grandfather* took me there, when I was quite a little child, and had always remembered it as the most dreadful, lonesome barest of places—and all thro' my childhood I used to be frightened with it—it used to be the *threat*, if ye understand, 'if ye behave so badly, ye shall go to Craigenputtoch'; and I remember once, when I must have been fourteen years old, and was self-willed about something, my mother telling me that I 'deserved to be sent to Craigenputtoch to live on a hundred a year';—and to think that I *did* live there *five* years, with not much more than a hundred a year. It was that sort of *hopeless* place, that as long as my grandfather lived, there was never anything attempted to be done with it—but when my father began to manage the property (who was the sort of man that never can have anything that belongs to him out of order) he drained it, and manured it, and planted it where it was possible—and did all else that could be done about it; but there was very little of it that ever could be made into anything but a black peat moss; have ye ever seen one?—if ye have, ye know what an ugly, dreary thing that is—and of course, they were only the hardiest trees would grow—and so all the plantation there was of Scotch firs, which make a wood fit to *hang* oneself in. But Carlyle took a strong *fancy* to it, and offered to me that we should be married and live there—it was a time when he was very much out of health, and very desponding about himself, and didn't see at all what he should do in life, and he took it in his head that if he could go

65

and live there, and have a horse to ride he was sure he should get well and get on. So I wrote him back word that I wouldn't live at Craigenputtoch with an *angel*—and how I'd been always *scared* with it, as a child etc.; and that was given up. And then my mother took a little jewel of a house for us in Edinboro', and furnished it all for us, so that it was the neatest, prettiest thing—as *pretty* as any picture, and we went into that. But we hadn't been there two months, before Carlyle grew perfectly frantic with it all, and couldn't support it any way, couldn't endure his life at all nor get on with the people that were about us—but had it all this time fixed in his head that if he were only at Craigenputtoch he should be well, and everything that *was* wrong would grow right; I might refuse before, but then, you know, it was a different matter; and there was no use refusing. But ye may imagine my— situation and how I felt it, for we'd no money, and I had to go for it to my mother—which I was *excessively* loth to do—for she was no longer well off as she had been used to being—had done a great deal for us already—and we had to take a thousand pounds from her which was *sunk*, literally *sunk* in all that was to be done to this place before we could get there as I knew it would be—in buying out the farmer who was there and persuading him to give up the rest of his lease, and then in taking down that house and building another for us, which would never be fit either for a farmer afterwards—such a house as no farmer cares to have the expense of to keep up. However it was all done, and we went; and then Mr Carlyle's brother came, and he was to manage the farm, and to pay rent to my mother. But nothing could turn out worse than that, for he was a man of the most outrageous, coarse, violent temper—(he's gone to Canada, since, and done very well there, I believe) and nobody can imagine what I went through with that man—and it had to be alone—for I could never say a word to Carlyle, that would be to drive him perfectly crazy, and 'my dear, what *can* I possibly know, or do, about all this!' So his brother was always getting into difficulties with his workmen, and everybody on the place, and all were brought to me to 'the Mistress' as they called me, to settle—(they called him 'the Master', and me 'the Mistress', and Carlyle 'the Laird')—and one day I'd have the people in declaring they'd all *leave*, at once—and then we'd trouble about *keeping* them—he wanted they should have had food so as to eat less—and I, of course, thought only to make them comfortable. In those days, no bargain was ever concluded in Scotland, without the parties *drinking* together, they always must sit down together over their whisky, or gin, or what it was—so, of course, every time he went into Dumfries on our business, he came back as drunk as a man could be—and at that time he did all the errands of the household, and got one all the things I needed from Dumfries—so ye may imagine the state they used to come in, the keg of gin broken into the bag of flour—and the powdered sugar mixed up with the *sugar-of-lead* I was goin' to say, and so forth. I had to learn to do and undo everything, and down to doctoring horses. Carlyle and his brother both lost their horses, and then mine fell sick of the same thing, and I would not let any of them touch him—I sent a boy to a sensible physician there was in Dumfries, and asked him what he would do to a person who had a severe inflammation—and then I applied the blisters and doses to my horse, only increasing the quantity according to my own ideas—and I carried him thro' so that he got well again. But I used to get up and go out to the stable to him three times in the night, while he was so sick . . .

Living at Craigenputtoch, it wasn't as if I saw anything of Carlyle; he went to his own room directly after breakfast, and worked till an hour before dinner, and always rode those two hours. And he rode *alone*, because he only galloped or walked, and it fretted him to have my horse cantering along by his side; so he rode alone and I rode alone; then he came to dinner very much *worked-up*, as bilious people always are by a ride, and he was 'dangerous' you know, and there was no freedom of communication during dinner; then he went to walk for an hour, which wasn't very wholesome, I always thought, right after eating, and to his room till tea; and afterward to his room, until about ten o'clock, and then he'd come in, quite tired out with his work, and say, 'Jane, will ye play me a few of those Scotch tunes'—and I would sit down and play Scotch tunes till he went to bed—oftenest with the tears running down my face, the while I played.

JANE CARLYLE

Love Under the Republicans
(or Democrats)

Come live with me and be my love
And we will all the pleasures prove
Of a marriage conducted with economy
In the Twentieth Century Anno Donomy.
We'll live in a dear little walk-up flat
With practically room to swing a cat
And a potted cactus to give it hauteur
And a bathtub equipped with dark brown water.
We'll eat, without undue discouragement,
Foods low in cost but high in nouragement
And quaff with pleasure, while chatting wittily,
The peculiar wine of Little Italy.
We'll remind each other it's smart to be thrifty
And buy our clothes for something-fifty.
We'll stand in line on holidays
For seats at unpopular matinees
And every Sunday we'll have a lark
And take a walk in Central Park.
And one of these days not too remote
I'll probably up and cut your throat.

OGDEN NASH

The Abominable Crime

Reporting the Assizes I was astonished at the number of men accused of making love to animals. Northants was still a rural county then and a bicycle the chief form of transport for farmworkers, so perhaps it wasn't surprising given the perversity of human nature. Some unfortunate farm labourer, wearing the labourer's uniform of thick grey flannel trousers, incongruously topped by the upper half of a double-breasted chalk-striped grey suit, and a shirt with collar stud but no collar, would stand with head bowed in the dock of the ancient Assize Court while the clerk read the charge. This was couched in the most awe-inspiring language, something like this: '. . . that you did commit and perpetrate the abominable crime, to wit BUGGERY, with a sheep, the property of Thos. Hardcastle, at Guilsborough, on April 21st 1948 . . .'

The Abominable Crime became a catchword in the office. 'Much at the Assizes?' Eric would ask and get the reply, 'Oh, only a criminal assault and a couple of abominable crimes.'

The evidence would proceed ponderously.

'As a result of a complaint by a farmer I kept watch on a field near Smith's farm, Rothersthorpe, on the night of July 5th. I saw the defendant enter the field. There was a screeching noise and he came out doing up his clothing.'

Under cross-examination: 'What was the defendant's manner when be came out?'

'Very furtive, sir.'

Inevitably a learned gentleman from the Home Office Forensic Laboratory at Nottingham travelled sixty-five miles to give evidence, and as this rarely amounted to much more than that the sheep was a sheep judges sometimes abused them for wasting public money. The animal was always destroyed. I asked a policeman why this was and he said cryptically, 'They might get a taste for it, you see.'

MICHAEL GREEN

Mr Capone, Philosopher

In Chicago the Director of the Illinois Central Bank, to whom I had been putting solemn questions on the subject of car loadings, commodity prices and the like, said moodily, 'Hell, boy, the capitalist system's on the skids anyway, let's go and get a drink.' I was glad of this attitude on his part because I had not really come to Chicago to discuss commodity prices in the Middle West, but to report the background to a murder. A couple of days before, we in New York had read the news of the killing in broad daylight of Jake Lingle, then crime reporter of the *Chicago Tribune* and —as emerged later—an important liaison officer between the Capone gang and the police department. It was one of the most spectacular and, for many reasons, looked like being one of the most revealing Chicago killings of the period when Al Capone was at approximately the height of his power. From a friend in New York who knew Chicago I learned enough of the background of the crime to make me very eager to go to Chicago myself. Hinrichs, who thought it would be a splendid story, was nevertheless hesitant. He explained to me that whenever *The Times* published a crime story from the United States somebody from the American Embassy or the English-Speaking Union or some other agency for promoting Anglo-American relations would ring up or would attack the editor at dinner, saying how much he had always previously admired *The Times*'s treatment of American affairs, and could there not be at least one British newspaper which did not represent the United States as a land dominated by gunmen and hoodlums? Hinrichs thought we had better cable London asking whether they wished me to go to Chicago.

As an assignment to report a murder the reply from *The*

Times was probably a classic. 'By all means,' it said, 'Cockburn Chicagowards. Welcome stories ex-Chicago not unduly emphasizing crime.'

By the time I was in the air over Cleveland the difficulty of carrying out this directive successfully had notably increased. Ex-Ambassador Charlie Gates Dawes had impetuously been 'drafted' or had drafted himself to act as 'strong man' of the situation, to put himself, it was stated, at the head of 'the better element' and to 'clean up' Chicago. Before I touched down at Chicago Airport he had arrested nearly six hundred people and a number of others had been wounded in indiscriminate gunplay. I drove to the Criminal Courts Building and sought the advice of the dean of Chicago crime reporters, the original, I believe, of one of the central characters in Ben Hecht's play *The Front Page*. I showed him my cable. His deep laughter shook the desk. What, he asked, did I want to do? I said I supposed the first thing to do was to interview Mr Capone. He suggested that I listen in on an extension while he telephoned Mr Capone at the Lexington Hotel where he then had his offices. Presently I heard Capone's voice on the wire asking what went on. The crime reporter explained that there was a Limey from the London *Times* who wanted to talk with him. They fixed up an appointment for the following afternoon and just before he rang off the crime reporter said, 'Listen, Al, there's just one thing. You know this bird's assignment says he's to cover all this "not unduly emphasizing crime".' Bewilderment exploded at the other end of the line. 'Not what?' Capone said. 'You heard me,' said the crime reporter. 'Not unduly emphasizing crime.'

The Lexington Hotel had once, I think, been a rather grand family hotel, but now its large and gloomy lobby was deserted except for a couple of bulging Sicilians and a reception clerk who looked at one across the counter with the expression of a speakeasy proprietor looking through the grille at a potential detective. He checked on my appointment with some superior upstairs, and as I stepped into the elevator I felt my hips and sides being gently frisked by the tapping hands of one of the lounging Sicilians. There were a couple of ante-rooms to be passed before you got to Capone's office and in the first of them I had to wait for a quarter of an hour or so, drinking whisky poured by a man who used his left hand for the bottle and kept the other in his pocket.

71

Except that there was a sub-machine gun, operated by a man called MacGurn—whom I later got to know and somewhat esteem—poking through the transom of a door behind the big desk, Capone's own room was nearly indistinguishable from that of, say, a 'newly arrived' Texan oil millionaire. Apart from the jowly young murderer on the far side of the desk, what took the eye were a number of large, flattish, solid silver bowls upon the desk, each filled with roses. They were nice to look at, and they had another purpose too, for Capone when agitated stood up and dipped the tips of his fingers in the water in which floated the roses.

I had been a little embarrassed as to how the interview was to be launched. Naturally the nub of all such interviews is somehow to get around to the question 'What makes you tick?' but in the case of this millionaire killer the approach to this central question seemed mined with dangerous impediments. However, on the way down to the Lexington Hotel I had had the good fortune to see, in I think the *Chicago Daily News*, some statistics offered by an insurance company which dealt with the average expectation of life of gangsters in Chicago. I forget exactly what the average expectation was, and also the exact age of Capone at that time—I think he was in his early thirties. The point was, however, that in any case he was four years older than the upper limit considered by the insurance company to be the proper average expectation of life for a Chicago gangster. This seemed to offer a more or less neutral and academic line of approach, and after the ordinary greetings I asked Capone whether he had read this piece of statistics in the paper. He said that he had. I asked him whether he considered the estimate reasonably accurate. He said that he thought that the insurance companies and the newspaper boys probably knew their stuff. 'In that case,' I asked him, 'how does it feel to be, say, four years over the age?'

He took the question quite seriously and spoke of the matter with neither more nor less excitement or agitation than a man would who, let us say, had been asked whether he, as the rear machine-gunner of a bomber, was aware of the average incidence of casualties in that occupation. He apparently assumed that sooner or later he would be shot despite the elaborate precautions which he regularly took. The idea that—as afterwards turned out to be the case—he would be arrested by the Federal authorities for income-tax evasion had not, I think, at that time so much as crossed his mind. And, after all, he said with a little bit of corn-and-ham somewhere at the back of his throat, supposing he had not gone into this racket? What would he have been doing? He would, he said, 'have been selling newspapers barefoot on the street in Brooklyn'.

He stood up as he spoke, cooling his fingertips in the rose bowl in front of him. He sat down again, brooding and sighing. Despite the ham-and-corn, what he said was quite probably true and I said so, sympathetically. A little bit too sympathetically, as immediately emerged, for as I spoke I saw him looking at me suspiciously, not to say censoriously. My remarks about the harsh way the world treats barefoot boys in Brooklyn were interrupted by an urgent angry waggle of his podgy hand.

'Listen,' he said, 'don't get the idea I'm one of these goddam radicals. Don't get the idea I'm knocking the American system. The American system . . .' As though an invisible chairman had called upon him for a few words, he broke into an oration upon the theme. He praised freedom, enterprise and the pioneers. He spoke of 'our heritage'. He referred with contemptuous disgust to Socialism and Anarchism. 'My rackets', he repeated several times, 'are run on strictly American lines and they're going to stay that way.' This turned out to be a reference to the fact that he had recently been elected the President of the *Unione Siciliana*, a slightly mysterious, partially criminal society which certainly had its roots in the Mafia. Its power and importance varied sharply from year to year. Sometimes there did seem to be evidence that it was a secret society of real power, and at other times it seemed more in the nature of a mutual benefit association not essentially much more menacing than, say, the Elks. Capone's complaint just now was that the *Unione* was what he called 'lousy with black-hand stuff'. 'Can you imagine', he said, 'people going in for what they call these blood feuds—some guy's grandfather was killed by some other guy's grandfather, and this guy thinks that's good enough reason to kill the other.' It was, he said, entirely unbusinesslike. His vision of the American system began to excite him profoundly and now he was on his feet again, leaning across the desk like the chairman of a board meeting, his fingers plunged in the rose bowls.

'This American system of ours,' he shouted, 'call it Americanism, call it Capitalism, call it what you like, gives to each and every one of us a great opportunity if we only seize it with both hands and make the most of it.' He held out his hand towards me, the fingers dripping a little, and stared at me sternly for a few seconds before reseating himself.

CLAUD COCKBURN

The Magistrate

Gene was a high favorite among us young reporters, for he was always good for copy, and did not hesitate to modify the course of justice in order to feed and edify us. One day an ancient German, obviously a highly respectable man, was brought in on the incredible charge of beating his wife. The testimony showed that they had been placidly married for more than forty-five years, and seldom exchanged so much as a bitter word. But the night before,

74

when the old man came home from the saloon where he played
Skat every evening, the old woman accused him of having drunk
more than his usual ration of eight beers, and in the course of the
ensuing debate he gave her a gentle slap. Astounded, she let off an
hysterical squawk, an officious neighbor rushed in, the cops came
on his heels, and so the old man stood before the bar of justice,
weeping copiously and with his wife weeping even more copiously beside him. Gene pondered the evidence with a frown on
his face, and then announced his judgement. 'The crime you are
accused of committing', he said, 'is a foul and desperate one, and
the laws of all civilized countries prohibit it under heavy penal-
ties. I could send you to prison for life, I could order you to the
whipping-post [it still exists in Maryland, and for wife-beaters
only], or I could sentence you to be hanged. [Here both parties
screamed.] But inasmuch as this is your first offense I will be
lenient. You will be taken hence to the House of Correction, and
there confined for twenty years. In addition, you are fined
$10,000.' The old couple missed the fine, for at mention of the
House of Correction both fainted. When the cops revived them,
Gene told the prisoner that, on reflection, he had decided to
strike out the sentence, and bade him go and sin no more. Husband and wife rushed out of the courtroom hand in hand, followed by a cop with the umbrella and market-basket that the old
woman had forgotten. A week or two later news came in that she
was ordering the old man about in a highly cavalier manner, and
had cut down his evenings of *Skat* to four a week.

H. L. MENCKEN

The Douglas Case, 1769

About this time was heard decisively the great cause between the
Houses of Douglas and Hamilton, by appeal to the Lords: a cause
as singular and as ambiguous as perhaps ever came before a court
of judicature.

The last Duke of Douglas, a kind of lunatic, had at various periods made different wills; at first in favour of the Hamiltons, the nearest males of his race; but latterly he had substituted as his heir the son of his sister, who having offended him by marrying a poor, elderly gentleman, had retired to France, and there, though herself past fifty, had been, or pretended to have been, delivered of two boys, of whom one only survived. A cloud of circumstances concurred to make the Hamiltons suspect that both children were supposititious, and purchased of different peasants. The Duchess of Douglas, a woman of bold and masculine spirit, and herself a Douglas, who had artfully procured to get married to the duke after the death of his sister, whom she had never seen, espoused the cause of Lady Jane's children, and prevailed on the duke, in his last days, to restore the inheritance to his rejected nephew.

The widow Duchess of Hamilton, one of the beautiful Gunnings, and of a spirit equally proud and pertinacious, though of the most delicate frame and form and outward softness, as obstinately defended the cause of her sons, particularly of the youngest, who had been named the former heir; and being incited by one Andrew Stuart, an artful and very able young man, and one of the trustees of her children, she, at immense expense to the duke, her son, had pursued the disquisition into the births of Lady Jane's children; and by the books of the police at Paris, had, at the distance of near twenty years, and by the industry of Stuart, collected such a mass of circumstantial evidence, that it seemed to many men to prove that Lady Jane had never been with child, nor ever resided long enough in one place to give even an air of probability that she had lain in; to which should be added, that Lady Jane could never fix on any consistent account of the person in whose house, or of the house in which she had been delivered, and in which she allowed she had not stayed above three or four days. Much proof appeared of Lady Jane's art and hypocrisy: on the other side, little or none that she had acted like a mother, having neglected the younger child entirely for a year; and the survivor proving to have all probable appearance of a swarthy French peasant, and no ways resembling his pretended parents, who were fair and sandy, like most Scots. The duke, Lady Jane's brother, had till near his death been persuaded of the imposture; and the cause coming before the Lords of Session in Scotland, had, after the fullest discussion, been determined in favour of the Hamiltons.

76

Mankind grew wonderfully divided in their opinions, when the cause was now brought before the English Peers. Though the cheat, if one, had its foundation and almost its detection in France, the French inclined to the legitimacy of the children; so did the generality in Scotland: and, above all, the compassion excited in favour of infants avowed by both parents, though, in truth, very equivocally by Lady Jane on her deathbed, carried the current in favour of young Douglas. He was not less eagerly patronized by the Duke and Duchess of Queensberry: the duke was his guardian; and the duchess, no less celebrated formerly by Prior, Pope and Swift, than the Duchess of Hamilton in the times of which I write, was still more singular and persevering than the two other dames of the same rank—circumstances that contributed powerfully to attract the attention of the public. Much perjury appeared on both sides, certain proof on neither; the want of which decided the suit at last in favour of the compassionate part of the question.

After a hearing of many and long days, with an attendance scarce ever known there on a cause, the House of Lords reversed the decree in favour of the Hamiltons, and restored the Douglas. The Lord Advocate Montgomery spoke for thirteen hours in three days, and with applause. Mr Charles Yorke was the least admired. The Duchess Douglas thought she had retained him; but hearing he was gone over to the other side, sent for him, and questioned him home. He could not deny that he had engaged himself to the House of Hamilton—'Then, sir,' said she, 'in the next world whose will you be, for we have all had you?' Mr Alexander Wedderburne (for the Hamiltons too), spoke with greater applause than was almost ever known. Dunning, on the same side, and Norton for the Douglas, made no great figure. The Duke of Bedford, Lord Sandwich, and Lord Gower, were the most zealous for the Hamiltons. Lord Mansfield, it had long been discovered, favoured the Douglas; but the Chancellor Camden, with dignity and decency, had concealed his opinion to the very day of the decision. The debate was opened by the Duke of Newcastle, and very poorly. He was answered by Lord Sandwich, who spoke for three hours with much humour, and scandalized the bishops, having, with his usual industry, studied even the midwifery of the case, which he retailed, with very little decency.

The Chancellor then rose, and with becoming authority and

infinite applause, told the Lords that he must now declare he thought the whole plea of the Hamiltonians a tissue of perjury, woven by Mr Andrew Stuart; and that were he sitting as judge in any other court, he would order the jury to find for Mr Douglas; and that what that jury ought to do on their oaths, their Lordships ought to do on their honours. He then went through the heads of the whole case, and without notes recapitulated even the dates of so involved a story; adding, that he was sorry to bear hard on Mr Stuart, but justice obliged him. This speech, in which it was allowed he outshone Lord Mansfield, had the most decisive effect. The latter, with still more personal severity to Stuart, spoke till he fainted with the heat and fatigue; and, at ten at night, the decree was reversed without a division—a sentence, I think, conformable to equity, as the child was owned by both parents, and the imposture not absolutely proved; yet, in my opinion, not awarded in favour of truth—a declaration I should not be so arrogant as to make, if many very able men were not as much persuaded as I am of the child being supposititious. Nor was the cause terminated at last without a duel between Andrew Stuart and Thurloe, who had poured out torrents of abuse on his antagonist in the course of the pleadings; but no mischief was done.

HORACE WALPOLE

The Serious Misconduct of Coleridge's Wife

Coleridge came to Rose* one day early, obviously in great trouble: he sat down without saying a word, and tears even began to flow down his cheeks. Rose enquired earnestly what was the matter—what was weighing upon his mind? but for some time he could get no answer. At last, Coleridge told him he was come to consult him about something relating to the conduct of his wife. Rose was startled, yet he could not think that she had been

* Hugh James Rose (1795–1838), classical scholar and theologian.

guilty of any serious misconduct, and told him so. Coleridge answered that what she had done, if he yielded to it, would embitter the rest of his life. Rose was alarmed, and besought Coleridge to tranquillize himself, and to tell him what had happened: he hinted a hope that it was nothing affecting her moral character as a wife. 'Oh no,' said Coleridge, 'nothing of that kind, but it is something that I cannot think of without the deepest pain.'—'Well,' said Rose, 'let us hear it: perhaps it is not so bad as you at this moment consider it.'—'I came to you,' added Coleridge, 'as a friend and a clergyman, to ask you what I ought under the circumstances to do.'—'Let me have the circumstances,' rejoined Rose, 'and then I may be better able to judge. Calm yourself.'

Again Coleridge wiped his 'large grey eyes', and went on to apologize for the trouble he was giving. Rose assured him that his main trouble was to see a friend so unhappy; and, after beating about the bush for some time longer, Coleridge declared that he could never live with his wife again, if she were not brought to her senses. Rose here began to fear that Mrs Coleridge had literally gone out of her mind; but Coleridge reassured him upon that head, adding, however, that a sane woman could hardly have required of her husband what she had expected from him; viz., that on the coldest mornings, even when the snow was on the ground, and icicles hanging from the eves of their cottage, she compelled him to get out of bed in his nightshirt, and light the fire, before she began to dress herself and the baby.

JOHN PAYNE COLLIER

J'Accuse

Let's have an end of all this shilly-shallying. *I* killed Rasputin. The thing has dragged on long enough, with even Mike Romanoff claiming that he did it, and my uncle claiming that it was done by the boys of his curling-club. Well, as a matter of fact, I am the one who did it, and here is how it happened.

We were sitting around in the cellar of the Winter Palace, Rasputin, Mike Romanoff, a grand duke whose name I have forgotten, and I. We had a couple of dancing bears in for the occasion, and things were beginning to get a little rowdy.

According to a pre-arranged plan between Mike Romanoff and myself, a tray of hors d'œuvres was brought in for us to dip in our vodka. Each canapé consisted of a little mound of elk-poison, covered with grated egg, and to make things safer, the egg had been poisoned, too. Four elk had been killed in the out-of-town try-out, so Mike and I were in high good humor.

Naturally, the tray was passed first to Rasputin, for, if anyone else was served first, he was one mad monk, I can tell you. He took four canapés in one hand and two in the other, and put them all in his mouth at once. I took one and palmed it, and Mike said: 'No, thanks. They're so much poison to me,' which I thought was a pretty funny crack, coming from Mike. By this time, all eyes were on Rasputin.

He wiped the crumbs from his beard, took a swig of vodka, and said: 'Those are mighty nice cookies. Where did you get them?' Then he got up and went to the window and looked out. 'It looks like snow,' he said. 'By George, it *is* snow!' And he danced up and down in delight to see the little flakes swirling down through the air. Those Russians are just like kids when it starts to snow.

I looked at Mike and he shrugged his shoulders. 'Mike,' I said, 'how about whamming old Rasputin over the head with that iron bell-clapper, just to see if he likes butter?'

Rasputin turned to see what was up, just as Mike crashed down on him with the heavy clapper we had taken from the church of St Sophia earlier that day. The hair on the Mad Monk's head went down so far that it got into the hair of his beard, but he opened up a little space in it with his fingers, and said:

'Come on, cut out this kid-ding! I've got work to do this afternoon, even if you boys haven't.'

'You try it, Bob,' said Mike, trying to dislodge the clapper. So I took out my gun, and holding Rasputin at arm's length, said: 'One to get ready— two to start—and three to  go—o!' I fired four times into him, and hit him over the head with the gun-butt for the pay-off. I have never seen a guy so sore in my life.

'Hey, what is this?' he said. 'Let somebody else be It for a while. I'm all out of breath.' So I made believe that we were friends again, and put my arm around his shoulder.

'OK, Rasputin,' I said, 'let byegones be byegones, and don't be a baby all your life. What about a little stroll down to the lake to throw firecrackers at the fish?'

He was pleased as Punch at the idea, and we walked arm in arm, down to the lake, which was frozen over, except around the edges. Rasputin tried to hypnotize me on the way, but I slapped him down. 'None of your mad monk-ey business,' I said, and, while he was laughing at my play on words, I rolled him under the edge of the ice so far, that I had to put skates on to get out to where he was.

I skated around him for a while, cutting figure eights, until Mike joined me, and then we two went fishing through the ice for him. Every time we caught him, we threw him back, until finally, tiring of our sport, we replaced the block of ice over the hole, stamped it down and left him.

Now that is the true story of how Rasputin was killed, and I don't think there's a jury in the country that would convict me. So let's have no more talk about it, please.

ROBERT BENCHLEY

Dabbling in Spiritualism

My brother and I used to play with planchette, or what the Americans call the ouija board . . . I saw quite enough of the thing to be able to testify, with complete certainty, that something happens which is not in the ordinary sense natural, or produced by the normal and conscious human will. Whether it is produced by some subconscious but still human force, or by some powers, good, bad or indifferent, which are external to humanity, I would not myself attempt to decide. The only thing I will say with complete confidence, about that mystic and invisible power, is that it tells lies. The lies may be larks or they may be lures to the imperilled soul or they may be a thousand other things; but whatever they are, they are not truths about the other world; or for that matter about this world.

I will give one or two examples. We asked planchette, in our usual random fashion, what advice it would give to an acquaintance of ours, a solid and rather dull Member of Parliament who had the misfortune to be an authority on education. Planchette wrote down with brazen promptitude (in these later times it was always very prompt, though not always very clear) the simple words, 'Get a divorce.' The wife of the politician was so respectable, and I will add so hideous, that the materials of a scandalous romance seemed to be lacking. So we sternly enquired of our familiar spirit what the devil he meant; possibly an appropriate invocation. The result was rather curious. It wrote down very rapidly an immensely and indeed incredibly long word, which was at first quite illegible. It wrote it again; it wrote it four or five times; it was always quite obviously the same word; and towards the end it was apparent that it began with the three letters 'ORR'. I said, 'This is all nonsense; there is no word in the English language beginning ORR, let alone a word as long as that.' Finally it tried again and wrote the word out quite clearly; and it ran: 'Orriblerevelationsinighlife.'

If it was our subconsciousness, our subconsciousness at least

had a simple sense of humour. But that it was our subconsciousness rather than our consciousness (if it was not something
outside both) is proved by the practical fact that we did go on
puzzling over the written word, when it was again and again
rewritten, and really never had a notion of what it was, until it
burst upon us at last. Nobody who knew us, I think, would suppose us capable of playing such a long and solemn and silly
deception on each other. We also, like our subconsciousness,
had a sense of humour. But cases of this kind fill me with wonder
and a faint alarm, when I consider the number of people who
seem to be taking spirit communications seriously, and found-
ing religions and moral philosophies upon them. There would
indeed have been some Orrible Revelations in Igh Life, and
some Orrible Revelations about our own mental state and moral
behaviour, if we had trotted off to the MP with our little message
from the higher sphere.

Here is another example of the same thing. My father, who
was present while my brother and I were playing the fool in this
fashion, had a curiosity to see whether the oracle could answer a
question about something that he knew and we did not. He
therefore asked the maiden name of the wife of an uncle of mine
in a distant country; a lady whom we of the younger generation
had never known. With the lightning decision of infallibility, the
spirit pen said, 'Manning'. With equal decision my father said,
'Nonsense'. We then approached our tutelary genius with its
lamentable romancing and its still more lamentable rashness. The
spirit, never to be beaten, wrote down the defiant explanation,
'Married before'. And to whom, we asked with some sternness,
had our remote but respected aunt been secretly married before.
The inspired instrument instantly answered, 'Cardinal Manning'.

Now I will pause here in passing to ask what exactly would
have happened to me and my social circle, what would have ultimately been the state of my mind or my general conception of
the world in which I lived, if I had taken these spiritual revelations as some spiritualists seem to take some spiritual revelations;
in short, if we had taken them seriously? Whether this sort of
thing be the pranks of some Puck or Poltergeist, or the jerks of
some subliminal sense, or the mockery of demons or anything
else, it obviously is not true in the sense of trustworthy. Anybody who had trusted it as true would have landed very near
to a lunatic asylum. And when it comes to selecting a spiritual

philosophy, among the sects and schools of the modern world, these facts can hardly be entirely forgotten. Curiously enough, as I have already recorded, Cardinal Manning had crossed my path as a sort of flaming wraith even in my childhood. Cardinal Manning's portrait hangs now at the end of my room, as a symbol of a spiritual state which many would call my second childhood. But anyone would admit that both states are rather saner than my condition would have been, had I begun to dig up The Crime of the Cardinal, by delving in the distant past of a colonial aunt.

G. K. CHESTERTON

A Comedy of Errors

A ridiculous scene marred Lady Hounde's party the other night. 'All one has to do', said the hostess, 'to stop this man Foulenough from interfering with our social engagements is to search any suspect. The so-called captain always carries a bottle of strong drink in his pocket.'

The arrival of the unfortunate Mr Augustus Cowparsleigh, who is Foulenough's double, was the signal for an outbreak of suspicion that you could have cut with a knife. Cowparsleigh's recent misadventures have, of course, made him very timid, and he entered Lady Hounde's room blushing and looking guilty.

Lady Hounde pounced like a starving jaguar. 'Have you a bottle on you?' she demanded sternly, while plunging her hand into his side pocket.

'I didn't know we were supposed to bring our own drink,' retorted Cowparsleigh.

'Don't quibble,' roared the hostess, 'where's your bottle? I know you've got one.'

'If you are as thirsty as all that,' replied the victim testily, 'why don't you get one of your own drinks?'

Taken aback, the hostess faltered. 'I do believe it's really Augustus,' she said. And everybody breathed freely.

The only other odd incident occurred half an hour later. Boubou Flaring crossed the room to speak to Cowparsleigh as he was leaving.

'I hear you were mistaken for Captain Foulenough,' she said. The reply was a wicked wink, and Boubou was surprised to see him leave with a little box full of caviare sandwiches and a bottle in each pocket, and without saying goodbye to anybody.

Ten minutes later she was amazed to see him again. She said, 'Where have you dumped the sandwiches and the booze?' Augustus Cowparsleigh flushed angrily. 'I think you're all mad here,' he said. Boubou pondered in silence.

At 7.15 the supply of drink failed—an unknown occurrence in that house. It was only then that Lady Hounde heard Boubou's story, and realized that the dreaded warrior had indeed slipped through her fingers.

J. B. MORTON, 'BEACHCOMBER'

Old Pal, Al

Chicago, Illinois, 3 Januery

Old Pal,

Al I been pretty sick ever since New Year's eve. We had a table at 1 of the swell resturunts downtown and I never seen so much wine drank in my life. I would rather of had beer but they would not sell us none so I found out that they was a certain kind that you can get for $1 a bottle and it is just as good as the kind that has got all them fancy names but this lefthander starts ordering some other kind about 11 oclock and it was $5 a bottle and the girls both says they liked it better. I could not see a hole lot of difference myself and I would of gave $0.20 for a big stine of my kind of beer. You know me Al. Well Al you know they is not

85

nobody that can drink more than your old pal and I was all OK at one oclock but I seen the girls was getting kind of sleepy so I says we better go home.

Then Marie says Oh, shut up and don't be no quiter. I says You better shut up yourself and not be telling me to shut up, and she says What will you do if I don't shut up? And I says I would bust her in the jaw. But you know Al I would not think of busting no girl. Then Florrie says You better not start nothing because you had to much to drink or you would not be talking about busting girls in the jaw. Then I says I don't care if it is a girl I bust or a lefthander. I did not mean nothing at all Al but Marie says I had insulted Allen and he gets up and slaps my face. Well Al I am not going to stand that from nobody not even if he is my brother-in-law and a lefthander that has not got enough speed to brake a pain of glass.

So I give him a good beating and the waiters butts in and puts us all out for fighting and I and Florrie comes home in a taxi and Allen and his wife don't get in till about 5 oclock so I guess she must of had to of took him to a doctor to get fixed up. I been in bed ever since till just this morning kind of sick to my stumach. I guess I must of eat something that did not agree with me. Allen come over after breakfast this morning and asked me was I all right so I guess he is not sore over the beating I give him or else he wants to make friends because he has saw that I am a bad guy to monkey with.

Florrie tells me a little while ago that she paid the hole bill at the resturunt with my money because Allen was broke so you see what kind of a cheap skate he is Al and some day I am going to bust his jaw. She won't tell me how much the bill was and I won't ask her to no more because we had a good time outside of the fight and what do I care if we spent a little money?

Yours truly,
Jack

RING LARDNER

86

Life History

When you get to be fifty you find yourself talking and thinking as much about death and money as you used to about sex. The nearness of one and the shortage of the other fill me with a sense of urgency, but urgency about what I'm not quite sure. I suppose it's a feeling of wanting to *cram* it all in; 'it' being just about everything. I used to leap out of bed at 6 a.m. and get on with the trivialities, now I wake at 6 a.m. and lie there smoking and thinking of these matters until it's time for an analgesic Smirnoff. (That time gets fractionally earlier which is worrying. Why is it perfectly OK abroad?) Anyway, today's heavyheartedness was provoked by good news I had last week. I'm going to start writing a column again for the *Sporting Life* after an absence of twelve years. It won't make me rich but it will be great fun. It seems that my passing out when I was guest speaker at the National Hunt dinner in 1971 has been forgiven. Incidentally, what was odd about that was that no one minded at all except for my boss and trainer, Bill Marshall, who always said to people, 'If you want a really good after-dinner speaker get Jeff. He's not boring because he doesn't say anything.' But as I say, the heavy heart within is weighty because of the memories of those days on the *Life* between Nijinsky's narrow defeat in the Arc and Mill Reef's victory in the Arc exactly one year later. In fact, just as we were swilling champagne after Mill Reef's victory it was none other than the champion trainer today, Henry Cecil, who told me I'd got the sack from the *Sporting Life*. He'd heard it on the grapevine.

But those 365-odd days were heady, great fun and eventually disastrous for me. To my astonishment the column took off like a rocket and became immensely popular. I wrote a lot about loss and I suppose the average reader could identify with that. There was a ghastly little picture of me at the top of the column, so complete and utter strangers recognized me at the races. They'd send me over bottles of bubbly in the Members Bar and trainers who befriended me and showed me the ropes, like Bill Marshall and Eddie Reavey, poured whisky down me like I was a drain. Of course I loved it. To be famous on any circuit in this life is fun and we all want to be loved, don't we? Typical was Ireland. I went to see a trainer called Con Collins one morning and he was on the blower. A maid brought me a tray on which was a bottle of gin, a bottle of whisky and a bottle of brandy. She said, 'Mister Collins will be with you in five minutes. If you need any more to drink ring the bell.' *Any more!* That was just after the first lot had been out, about 9 a.m.

At Newbury one day I won a fair bit on the first race and then started laying favourites to bookmakers and won a little bundle. Risky but beautifully adrenalin-filled days. And the race trains I loved. The restaurant cars filled with bookmakers, spivs, villains, mug punters and scallywags of all kinds playing cards, telling amazing anecdotes about the Turf and drinking as though there was no tomorrow. In those days I think I'm right in saying that the only train in England to sell champagne was the race train to York. We drank the buffet dry by Doncaster. Well, of course, it couldn't last. The whisky was killing me and the bouts of pancreatitis became more frequent.

As I said, the end came at the National Hunt dinner at some dreadful hotel in Kensington. It was suggested that I be the guest speaker and they should have known better. I was extremely nervous, never having spoken publicly before, and I went to the *Life* offices at 6 a.m. to try and write something, couldn't and thought a jar in a Smithfield pub might get the typewriter going. I was accompanied by one of life's and the *Life*'s real eccentrics, a greyhound correspondent called Albert Bright. He used to come out with some very odd remarks and I remember him once saying, apropos of nothing, 'Yes, Jeff, I had my first fuck when I was firewatching on the roof of the *Greyhound Express* during an air raid in 1941.' Anyway we got smashed in Smithfield and then continued in the Stab—the *Daily Mirror* pub—at opening time. Still no speech. From there I went to the Colony Room club and so it continued all day. I got to the hotel, fell asleep in the lobby and was taken upstairs and put to bed by the waiters. Here endeth the first lesson.

The next morning I flew to Paris for the Arc de Triomphe and Henry told me I'd been fired. The fact that I could never behave as I did in that year ever again doesn't diminish the depression at the memory of it all. Even at the end the lily

demanded gilding. The whisky nudged me into a nervous break-
down and I ended up in a nut house. When I came to, there was
an Irish psychiatrist sitting on my bed. Peace and saved at last, I
thought. Then he opened his mouth and said, 'What d'you think
will win the 2.30?' You just can't win, can you?

JEFFREY BERNARD

The Revd So-and-So Dismissed

During the last war I inherited Boyton Manor, after the death of
my cousin Sidney Herbert. The local clergyman was a drunkard
and the parishioners longed to get rid of him. The only possible
way would be if he were to be caught drunk in the pulpit. But he
was far too cunning to fall into that trap. As he got older I suppose he had less will-power and I received this message from our
representative when I was in Australia, where my ship was in
dock: 'Glad to inform you the Revd So-and-so dismissed. Last
Sunday he got up in the pulpit and shouted: "On your knees you
bitches and buggers." '

DAVID HERBERT

Silence Dogood on the Effects of Liquor

I cannot pretend to account for the different effects of liquor on
persons of different dispositions, who are guilty of excess in the
use of it. 'Tis strange to see men of a regular conversation become

89

rakish and profane when intoxicated with drink, and yet more surprizing to observe, that some who appear to be the most profligate wretches when sober, become mighty religious in their cups, and will then, and at no other time address their Maker, but when they are destitute of reason, and actually affronting him. Some shrink in the wetting, and others swell to such an unusual bulk in their imaginations, that they can in an instant understand all arts and sciences, by the liberal education of a little vivyfying *punch*, or a sufficient quantity of other exhilerating liquor.

And as the effects of liquor are various, so are the characters given to its devourers. It argues some shame in the drunkards themselves, in that they have invented numberless words and phrases to cover their folly, whose proper significations are harmless, or have no signification at all. They are seldom known to be *drunk*, though they are very often *boozey, cogey, tipsey, foxed, merry, mellow, fuddled, groatable, confoundedly cut, see two moons,* are *among the Philistines, in a very good humour, see the sun,* or, *the sun has shone upon them;* they *clip the King's English,* are *almost froze, feavourish, in their altitudes, pretty well entered,* etc. In short, every day produces some new word or phrase which might be added to the vocabulary of the *tiplers:* but I have chose to mention these few, because if at any time a man of sobriety and temperance happens to *cut himself confoundedly,* or is *almost froze,* or *feavourish,* or accidentally *sees the sun,* etc. he may escape the imputation of being *drunk,* when his misfortune comes to be related.

BENJAMIN FRANKLIN

Gunga Din

'There's a man called Neil on the telephone, and he says I'm to tell you Gunga Din.'

I was in the bath, washing away the sweated labour of a day in the Singapore High Court, when Penny answered the telephone. What was this, some coded message from the Workers Party? A spy from the British High Commission warning me not to endanger our diplomatic relations with Lee Kuan Yew? Then I remembered Gunga Din, a north Oxford villa into which my prep school dormitories over-flowed. You had to walk across to it in the dark from School House after supper. Desmond Neil had inhabited Gunga Din and when I acted Rich-ard II in the school play, the only unqualified success I've enjoyed, Desmond had been the Duke of York: 'See, see, King Richard doth himself appear, As doth the blush-ing, discontented sun' was what he had to say. Many years had passed since this production, but clearly the experience was fresh in our minds. Desmond Neil was now someone very important in a huge beer and soft drinks company with tentacles all over the Far East. He invited us to dinner, so we got dressed and went down to the hotel bar to await his arrival.

'Been on a salvage job. Haven't got pissed or had a white woman for three months.' The man seated unsteadily on the barstool beside us had, as I remember, ginger hair and flaming cheeks. He also had a look which was not only lean and hungry, but positively desperate. 'Can you imagine?' he asked me with considerable hostility. 'What it's like not to have had a fucking white woman for three months?'

'You've been at sea?' I tried to sound understanding.

'Fucking sea captain. Salvage. That's my business. You might as well be in sodding gaol.'

To my immense relief, I saw an elegant figure in a white suit bearing down on us. This, I profoundly hoped, was Desmond Neil, forty years on. 'I'm sorry,' I said to the sea captain. 'We're being taken out for dinner. Best of luck.'

'Ah, John. How good to see you! And you must be Penny. I've booked a table,' Desmond Neil greeted us. 'Not a fucking white woman!' the sea captain was muttering, when Desmond inter-rupted him. 'We'd better get going. Plenty to drink when we get there. Oh, and do bring your friend.'

'That's very good of you, sir. Thank you very much.' The sea captain was delighted to accept the invitation. So we all sank into the back of a long white Mercedes, driven by a uniformed chauffeur to whom Desmond spoke in Mandarin. Then he showed us a photograph of himself and E. P. Thompson, the author of *The Making of the British Working Class*, as small boys on a football field. This was rapidly followed by pictures of them both in the present. 'Don't you think', Desmond said, showing these to the sea captain, 'I've worn a great deal better than Palmer Thompson?'

'Poor bugger!' The sea captain looked at the great historian and CND protester with sympathy. 'Probably hasn't had a white woman for years.'

Dinner passed like a strange dream. The Chinese restaurant on top of a tower rotated slowly, giving us ever-changing views of the harbour. The centre part of the table also revolved, offering us a feast of dishes, a great deal of sake and many bottles of Chinese beer. Throughout this banquet, Desmond would ask questions like 'What happened to the Mitchison boys?' 'What a tragedy about Bill Mann! Did you keep up with him?' 'Or was it Winchester that Peter Tranchell went to?' With perfect courtesy he always included the sea captain in these enquiries but his unexpected, ever more intoxicated guest could only mutter, 'Any chance of a white woman around here, or are they all Chinks?' In the end he helped himself to a dish full of a sauce called Dragon's Blood, went a deep shade of purple which clashed with his ginger hair, hit himself in the chest and cried out, 'Fucking hot food they give a bloke round here!', while Desmond was asking if Mr Rety, known to us as Rats, was still teaching dancing at the Dragon School. On our way back to the hotel the white Mercedes took us on a tour of the city, during which the sea captain fell into a deep and deafening sleep. 'Interesting fellow,' Desmond Neil whispered, 'have you known him long?'

'Only about two hours,' I had to admit, 'but it seems longer.' When we stopped at the hotel, the sea captain woke with a start and staggered off into the night. I hope he found some sort of comfort. Desmond Neil never asked about him again and was always a kind host in Singapore.

JOHN MORTIMER

Life at the Pavilion

I suppose the courts or houses of princes are all alike in one thing, viz., that in attending them you lose your liberty. After one month was gone by, you fell naturally and of course into the ranks, and had to reserve your observations till you were asked for them. These royal invitations are by no means calculated to reconcile one to a court. To be sent for half an hour before dinner, or perhaps in the middle of one's own, was a little too humiliating to be very agreeable . . .

I had heard a great deal of the prince's drinking, but, during the time that I speak of, I never saw him the least drunk but once, and I was myself pretty much the occasion of it. We were dining at the Pavilion, and poor Fonblanque, a dolorous fop of a lawyer, and a member of parliament too, was one of the guests. After drinking some wine, I could not resist having some jokes at Fonblanque's expense, which the prince en-couraged greatly. I went on and invented stories about speeches Fonblanque had made in parliament, which were so pathetic as to have affected his audience to tears, all of which inventions of mine Fonblanque denied to be true with such overpowering gravity that the prince said he should die of it if I did not stop . . .

In the evening, at about ten or eleven o'clock, he said he would go to the ball at the castle, and said I should go with him. So I went in his coach, and he entered the room with his arm through mine, everybody standing and getting upon benches to see him. He was certainly tipsy, and so, of course, was I, but not much, for I well remember his taking me up to Mrs Creevey and her daughters, and telling them he had never spent a pleasanter day in his life, and that 'Creevey had been very great'. He used to drink a great quantity of wine at dinner, and was very fond of making any newcomer drunk by drinking wine with him very frequently, always recommending his strongest wines, and at last some remarkable strong old brandy which he called Diabolino.

It used to be the Duke of Norfolk's custom to come over every year from Arundel to pay his respects to the prince and to stay two days at Brighton, both of which he always dined at the Pavilion. In the year 1804, upon this annual visit, the prince had drunk so much as to be made very seriously ill by it, so that in 1805 (the year I was there) when the duke came, Mrs Fitzherbert, who was always the prince's best friend, was very much afraid of his being again made ill, and she persuaded the prince to adopt different stratagems to avoid drinking with the duke. I dined there on both days, and letters were brought in each day after dinner to the prince, which he affected to consider of great importance, and so went out to answer them, while the Duke of Clarence went on drinking with the Duke of Norfolk. But on the second day this joke was carried too far, and in the evening the Duke of Norfolk showed he was affronted. The prince took me aside and said—'Stay after everyone is gone tonight. The Jockey's got sulky, and I must give him a broiled bone to get him in good humour again.' So of course I stayed, and about one o'clock the Prince of Wales and Duke of Clarence, the Duke of Norfolk and myself sat down to a supper of broiled bones, the result of which was, having fallen asleep myself, I was awoke by the sound of the Duke of Norfolk's snoring. I found the Prince of Wales and the Duke of Clarence in a very animated discussion as to the particular shape and make of the wig worn by George II . . .

THOMAS CREEVEY

Encounter with Lord Snowdon

One evening after work, Stanley Myers and his girlfriend, and Rosalind and I, dined at a smart new restaurant in Holland Park called Chez Moi. The evening was going very well until Stanley suggested that it might be amusing if I did the trouser trick. This was a simple, and perhaps juvenile, stunt which worked only in a dignified or pretentious ambience. All that happened was that my pants fell down, apparently by accident, at a conspicuous moment. The 'trick' was that I should exhibit a high degree of embarrassment. That night, on my way back from the gents, I timed it to perfection. Barely a diner in that crowded restaurant could have missed it, and with a tremendous show of shame and apology and much bowing and shrugging I retreated to our table, where Stanley, at least, sat convulsed with laughter. Soon the maître d' was at our side, his lips to my ear. 'I am sorry, sir, but we must ask you please to leave the restaurant *immédiatement*. Lord Snowdon over zair is most offended by what just 'appen.' I had no time to protest, or even to get a view of Princess Margaret's outraged husband. Two burly waiters lifted me bodily from my chair and propelled me out the door into Addison Road, where I was obliged to loiter, undined and unwined. All I had to nibble were a few stale sponge fingers left over from my luncheon zabaglione at Bertorelli's, the kind which are sometimes known, rather suggestively, as Boudoir Fingers.

I attempted to get back into the restaurant, but the door was locked, and through a chink in a curtain I could see my wife and my friends enjoying a delicious meal as if nothing had happened; relieved, no doubt, that I was out of the way. On the corner of Addison Road was a telephone box and, after consulting a dog-eared directory, I dialled the number of the restaurant. The maître d's voice answered, ''Ullo, 'ullo?' I assumed the fluting tones of a middle-aged, upper-class Englishwoman. 'This is the Countess of Rosse speaking. My son Lord Snowdon is dining in your restaurant tonight. May I speak with him urgently please?' There was a long pause on the line and then a man's voice. 'Mother? How did you track me down here?' 'Tony, darling,' I trilled, 'there is a lovely and talented man in your restaurant tonight who has been far from well, his name is Barry Humphries and he has been accidentally locked out in the street. Please buy him and his party a large bottle of champagne and get the management to apologize.' On the other end of the line I could hear a voice cry: 'What, Mother? Who is this? *Who is this speaking?*' I rang off.

The door of Chez Moi, much to my chagrin, was not immediately thrown open, until Rosalind, Stanley and Yvonne at last emerged, but there was a sequel to this sorry incident, which will be told later.

HOUSEWIFE SUPERSTAR!

After the show had been running in the West End for several weeks, *Vogue* magazine, I was told, wished to interview me, and they were sending a photographer to meet me at the theatre. When I turned up, as usual slightly late to the appointment, I was considerably taken aback to see that the photographer was already waiting at the stage door. It was Lord Snowdon.

Remembering a distant and acutely embarrassing incident, I effusively apologized for my lateness. But he was exquisitely polite. He didn't mind in the least, he said, because it gave him a chance to think about the pictures he was planning to take. 'I'd like to take up most of your day on this job, if you can spare the time,' he said. 'Perhaps we could break somewhere for lunch?' I told him I knew a good Italian restaurant near the theatre, and would be delighted if he would be my guest. 'Oh no, thank you,' replied Lord Snowdon. 'I want you to be *my* guest. There is an excellent French restaurant I know in Addison Road, Holland Park, called Chez Moi. I wonder if you know it?'

He gave me a broad Royal Doulton smile, and I think he might have even winked. Otherwise, no subsequent reference was ever made to that evening, so long ago, when for two minutes I had been his mother.

BARRY HUMPHRIES

An Invitation to Lord Byron

Neither [Thomas] Moore nor myself had ever seen Byron when it was settled that he should dine at my house to meet Moore; nor was he known by sight to Campbell, who, happening to call upon me that morning, consented to join the party. I thought it best that I alone should be in the drawing-room when Byron entered it; and Moore and Campbell accordingly withdrew. Soon after his arrival, they returned; and I introduced them to him severally, naming them as Adam named the beasts.

When we sat down to dinner, I asked Byron if he would take soup? 'No; he never took soup.'—'Would he take some fish?'— 'No; he never took fish.' Presently I asked if he would eat some mutton? 'No; he never ate mutton.' I then asked if he would take a glass of wine? 'No; he never tasted wine.' It was now necessary to enquire what he *did* eat and drink; and the answer was, 'Nothing but hard biscuits and soda-water.' Unfortunately, neither hard biscuits nor soda-water were at hand; and he dined upon potatoes bruised down on his plate and drenched with vinegar. My guests stayed till very late, discussing the merits of Walter Scott and Joanna Baillie. Some days after, meeting Hobhouse, I said to him, 'How long will Lord Byron persevere in his present diet?' He replied, 'Just as long as you continue to notice it.' I did not then know, what I now know to be a fact—that Byron, after leaving my house, had gone to a Club in St James's Street, and eaten a hearty meat supper.

SAMUEL ROGERS

Fonthill Splendour

A distant connection of mine, who, I must presume, was a person of an enquiring mind, found himself involved in a curious adventure . . . There was one house, and that the most interesting of all, that shut its door against my inquisitive friend and everybody else. Fonthill Abbey, or Fonthill Splendour as it was sometimes called, situated a few miles from Bath, was a treasure-house of beauty. Every picture was said to be a gem, and the gardens were unequalled by any in England, the whole being guarded by a dragon in the form of Mr Beckford. 'Not only', says an authority, 'had the art-treasures of that princely place been sealed against the public, but the park itself—known by rumour as a beautiful spot—had for several years been inclosed by a most formidable wall, about seven miles in circuit, twelve feet high, and crowned by a *chevaux-de-frise*.' These formidable obstacles my distant cousin undertook to surmount, and he laid a wager of a considerable sum that he would walk in the gardens, and even penetrate into the house itself.

Having nothing better to do, he spent many an anxious hour in watching the great gate in the wall, in the hope that by some inadvertence it might be left open and unguarded; and one day the happy moment arrived. The porter was ill, and his wife opened the gate to a tradesman, who, after depositing his goods at the lodge (no butcher or baker was permitted to go to the abbey itself), retired, leaving the gate open, relying probably upon the woman's shutting it. Quick as thought my relative passed the awful portals, and made his way across the park. Guided by the high tower—called 'Beckford's Folly'—my inquisitive friend made his way to the gardens, and not being able immediately to find the entrance, was leaning on a low wall that shut the gardens from the park, and taking his fill of delight at that gorgeous

98

display—the gardens being in full beauty—when a man with a spud in his hand—perhaps the head-gardener—approached, and asked the intruder how he came there, and what he wanted.

'The fact is, I found the gate in the wall open, and having heard a great deal about this beautiful place, I thought I should like to see it.'

'Ah,' said the gardener, 'you would, would you? Well, you can't see much where you are. Do you think you could manage to jump over the wall? If you can, I will show you the gardens.'

My cousin looked over the wall, and found such a palpable obstacle—in the shape of a deep ditch—that he wondered at the proposal.

'Oh, I forgot the ditch! Well, go to the door; you will find it about a couple of hundred yards to your right, and I will admit you.'

In a very short time, to his great delight, my cousin found himself listening to the learned names of rare plants, and inhaling the perfume of lovely flowers. Then the fruit-gardens and hot-houses—'acres of them', as he afterwards declared—were submitted to his inspection. After the beauties of the gardens and grounds had been thoroughly explored, and the wager half

won, the inquisitive one's pleasure may be imagined when his guide said:

'Now, would you like to see the house and its contents? There are some rare things in it—fine pictures and so on. Do you know anything about pictures?'

'I think I do, and should, above all things, like to see those of which I have heard so much; but are you sure that you will not get yourself into a scrape with Mr Beckford? I've heard he is so very particular.'

'Oh no!' said the gardener, 'I don't think Mr Beckford will mind what I do. You see, I have known him all my life, and he lets me do pretty well what I like here.'

'Then I shall be only too much obliged.'

'Follow me, then,' said the guide.

My distant cousin was really a man of considerable taste and culture, a great lover of art, with some knowledge of the old masters and the different schools; and he often surprised his guide, who, catalogue in hand, named the different pictures and their authors, by his acute and often correct criticism . . . When the pictures had been thoroughly examined, there remained bric-à-brac of all kinds, costly suits of armour, jewellery of all ages, bridal coffers beautifully painted by Italian artists, numbers of ancient and modern musical instruments, with other treasures, all to be carefully and delightfully examined, till, the day nearing fast towards evening, the visitor prepared to depart, and was commencing a speech of thanks in his best manner, when the gardener said, looking at his watch:

'Why, bless me, it's five o'clock! Ain't you hungry? You must stop and have some dinner.'

'No, really, I couldn't think of taking such a liberty. I am sure Mr Beckford would be offended.'

'No, he wouldn't. You must stop and dine with me; I am Mr Beckford.'

My far-off cousin's state of mind may be imagined. He had won his wager, and he was asked, actually asked, to dine with the man whose name was a terror to the tourist, whose walks abroad were so rare that his personal appearance was unknown to his neighbours. What a story to relate to his circle at Bath! How Mr Beckford had been belied, to be sure! The dinner was magnificent, served on massive plates—the wines of the rarest vintage. Rarer still was Mr Beckford's conversation. He entertained his guest with stories of Italian travel, with anecdotes of the great in whose society he had mixed, till he found the shallowness of it; in short, with the outpouring of a mind of great power and thorough cultivation. My cousin was well read enough to be able to appreciate the conversation and contribute to it, and thus the evening passed delightfully away. Candles were lighted, and host and guest talked till a fine Louis Quatorze clock struck eleven. Mr Beckford rose and left the room. The guest drew his chair to the fire, and waited the return of his host. He thought he must have dozed, for he started to find the room in semi-darkness, and one of the solemn powdered footmen putting out the lights.

'Where is Mr Beckford?' said my cousin.

'Mr Beckford is gone to bed,' said the man, as he extinguished the last candle.

The dining-room door was open, and there was a dim light in the hall.

'This is very strange,' said my cousin; 'I expected Mr Beckford back again. I wished to thank him for his hospitality.'

This was said as the guest followed the footman to the front door. That functionary opened it wide and said:

'Mr Beckford ordered me to present his compliments to you, sir, and I am to say that as you found your way into Fonthill Abbey without assistance, you may find your way out again as best you can; and he hopes you will take care to avoid the bloodhounds that are let loose in the gardens every night. I wish you good-evening. No, thank you, sir: Mr Beckford never allows vails.'

My cousin climbed into the branches of the first tree that promised a safe shelter from the dogs, and there waited for daylight; and it was not till the sun showed itself that he made his way, terror attending each step, through the gardens into the park, and so to Bath. 'The wager was won,' said my relative; 'but not for fifty million times the amount would I again pass such a night as I did at Fonthill Abbey.'

W. P. FRITH

A Visit from Queen Victoria

Alas! It is but too true: the Queen is coming to pay me a visit at Stratfield Saye. I did everything I could to avoid the Subject: never mentioned the word Stratfield Saye, and kept out of Her Way. But I was summoned to Windsor last Week to attend a Chapter of the Order of the Bath; and [as I] was talking to Lady Douro in the evening, H.M. came up, was very gracious, and asked whether I was going back to Walmer Castle. I said, 'No, Madam. I left Walmer on the 15th, as I told Your Majesty, to attend the Cabinets, and have been in London ever since; and from all that I learn, I judge that I shall not be able to go out of town again till the meeting of Parliament.'

She had before said to me very graciously that she had expected to meet me at Burghley House, and was very sorry that I had not come.

In answer to my stating that I should not go out of town again, she said, 'You must permit us to pay you a visit at Stratfield Saye between this time and the meeting of Parliament.' I bowed and said that I should be highly Honoured, and added that I must go there immediately to have the preparations made for H.M.'s reception; but that I was apprehensive that H.M. would find my House, however comfortable as a Gentleman's Residence, but small and inconvenient as the Residence of H.M.'s Court. She smiled and continued to be very gracious, but did not give a Hint of postponing the Visit.

I came up on Thursday evening, was in the Cabinet all Friday, and went down to Stratfield Saye on Saturday morning to give orders about the arrangements for Her Reception.

The Difficulty under which I labour, besides the Numbers to be received in comparatively a small House, consists in my having no State apartment: H.M. and H.M. Court requiring a Sitting Room as well as the usual Lodging Rooms, and best Rooms for their attendants, not few in Number, with Bells ringing into the same from H.M. Apartments. Bells must be hung from H.M. Apartments into those for Her Attendants, Walls broken through, etc. You recollect Poor Mrs Apostles the Housekeeper. I thought that she would have burst out crying while I was talking to Her of the Honour intended and the preparations to be made. She said to me, very nearly in the Words which I had used two nights before to H.M., 'My Lord, Your House is a very comfortable Residence for yourself, your Family and your friends; but it is not fit for the Reception of the Sovereign and Her Court.' I answered, 'Very true! But H.M. coming is decided; what cannot be prevented must be borne; and we must make the best preparation in our Power.'

To say the truth, she makes the most of the Difficulties; and I am not astonished at it! She has discovered that the Steward's Room and the Housekeeper's Room are not large enough, or fit for the reception of such great Ladies as the Queen's Dressers; nor the best Bed Chambers; and she wanted to turn a Bed Chamber into a Sitting Room for the Dressers. However, she is right: the Steward's Room is small to receive at Dinner all the Attendants of the Queen [and] Prince Albert and of the Persons who will be in the House, as well as my own Servants.

Luckily I had about a year ago turned out of the House and the Offices a Wash House and Laundry; and I have been enabled to turn the old Laundry into a Dining Room for the Steward's Room. But after all, considering that the Queen will be attended by High Sheriffs, Mayors and Corporations, and Lord knows who with addresses, I certainly am at a loss to know where I can even shelter them from the Weather excepting in the Tennis Court! . . .

DUKE OF WELLINGTON

A Party at Althorp

At about ten p.m. the great cortège, led by a minion of Nick's*
driving a Volvo station wagon, departed. (Nick had promised
* Sir Nicholas Bonsor, MP for Upminster since 1983.

Raine* that we would arrive by nine-thirty p.m. and it was a forty-minute drive.) The order was Volvo wagon (Bonsor), Rolls Shadow (us), Rolls Spirit (the cheeky chappie), Range Rover (young farmers) and Mercedes 500 SEC (Dashwoods).†

Fortunately the minion in the Volvo drove extremely slowly otherwise we would never have managed the cross-country journey. I was already tight, so Jane took the wheel. Althorp itself was beautifully floodlit and looked perfect in scale, almost tiny. The arrangements for parking the cars—*endless* fleets of Shadows—were very efficient.

When we went into the Hall a magnificent sight presented itself: Barbara Cartland‡ wearing an electric pink chiffon dress, with false eyelashes, as thick as those black caterpillars that give you a rash if you handle them, was draped on the central staircase with her dress arranged like a caricature of the 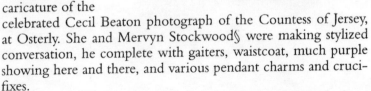 celebrated Cecil Beaton photograph of the Countess of Jersey, at Osterly. She and Mervyn Stockwood§ were making stylized conversation, he complete with gaiters, waistcoat, much purple showing here and there, and various pendant charms and crucifixes.

All very gay and glittering. Even at dinner Jane ranked no more than equal third on the carat count, although she was wearing both the leaf diamonds and Aunt Di's necklace. Some of the more mature ladies at the ball itself could hardly move, so encrustulated were they. The Princess of Wales, on the other hand, looked absolutely radiantly beautiful and was wearing not one single piece of jewellery.

ALAN CLARK

* Raine, Countess Spencer.
† Sir Francis and Lady Dashwood, owners of West Wycombe Park.
‡ Barbara Cartland, romantic novelist and Raine's mother.
§The Rt Revd Mervyn Stockwood, retired as Bishop of Southwark, 1980.

Indoor Games near Newbury

In among the silver birches winding ways of tarmac wander
  And the signs to Bussock Bottom, Tussock Wood and Windy
                                       Brake,
Gabled lodges, tile-hung churches, catch the lights of our Lagonda
  As we drive to Wendy's party, lemon curd and Christmas cake.
    Rich the makes of motor whirring,
    Past the pine-plantation purring
      Come up, Hupmobile, Delage!
    Short the way your chauffeurs travel,
    Crunching over private gravel
      Each from out his warm garáge.

Oh but Wendy, when the carpet yielded to my indoor pumps
    There you stood, your gold hair streaming,
    Handsome in the hall-light gleaming
There you looked and there you led me off into the game of
                                  clumps
    Then the new Victrola playing
    And your funny uncle saying
'Choose your partners for a fox-trot! Dance until it's *tea* o'clock!
    'Come on, young 'uns, foot it featly!'
    Was it chance that paired us neatly,
    I, who loved you so completely,
You, who pressed me closely to you, hard against your party frock?

'Meet me when you've finished eating!' So we met and no one
                                    found us.
  Oh that dark and furry cupboard while the rest played hide and
                                    seek!
Holding hands our two hearts beating in the bedroom silence
                                  round us,
  Holding hands and hardly hearing sudden footstep, thud and
                                    shriek.

Love that lay too deep for kissing—
'Where *is* Wendy? Wendy's missing!'
Love so pure it *had* to end,
Love so strong that I was frighten'd
When you gripped my fingers tight and
Hugging, whispered 'I'm your friend.'

Good-bye Wendy! Send the fairies, pinewood elf and larch tree
gnome,
Spingle-spangled stars are peeping
At the lush Lagonda creeping
Down the winding ways of tarmac to the leaded lights of home.
There, among the silver birches,
All the bells of all the churches
Sounded in the bath-waste running out into the frosty air.
Wendy speeded my undressing,
Wendy is the sheet's caressing
Wendy bending gives a blessing,
Holds me as I drift to dreamland, safe inside my slumber-wear.

JOHN BETJEMAN

King Zog's Wedding

In April 1938 I went to Albania to cover the wedding of King
Zog. There was considerable curiosity over the event in Europe.
Zog, then forty-two, was a handsome man, with blue eyes, fair
hair and a small, well-tended moustache. His father had been
hereditary chief of the Mati valley, which had been occupied
along with the rest of Albania—and indeed all of the Balkans—
by the Turks for five hundred years. In 1912, during the period
when Turkish power in Europe was ebbing fast, the Great Powers chose Prince William of Wied, one of the lesser German
royalties, to fill the unpleasant ruling chores which nobody else
could be induced to accept. He was called the Mbret, the 'M'
being silent, as in Mdivani. His later history was as undistin-

guished and depressing as his title. As for Zog, he got into Albanian politics early in the 1920s, and he did so well that by 1928 he was proclaimed king.

There were several attempts on his life, during one of which his Chamberlain was killed at his side. Albania is a land where the blood feud is accepted as the practical method of settling a dispute.

Zog made the best of things. In his tiny palace at Tirana, the capital, he installed a gymnasium where he could retain the agility desirable in one in his position. His suits were made by the finest Viennese tailors. He bought a number of sports cars, which early broke their springs on the execrable roads. He went well-armed at all times, a Lüger beneath the royal pillow on retirement being a 'must'. The favourite anecdote about Zog at that time concerned a group of British businessmen who were visiting Tirana, and who started a game of poker in a bedroom of the local hotel one night. It was warm and the blinds were left up. Soon there came a knock at their door. A hotel servant informed them that the king had been observing their game from his room at the palace through field-glasses, was feeling bored, and would they care to adjourn, bring the cards over, and cut him in?

Having duly survived for ten eventful years, it became evident that the king might consider himself sufficiently durable to contemplate marriage. His choice fell upon the twenty-two-year-old Countess Geraldine Apponyi of Hungary, a lady who proved, to the gratification of newspaper readers, to be outstandingly good-looking, and the possessor of charm and vivacity.

To the usual accoutrements which I was wont to pack for foreign jobs, I added for this special occasion my 'morning dress', i.e. cutaway coat, striped trousers, double-breasted fawn waistcoat, black shoes, four-in-hand tie and top hat. No doubt such elegance, I reflected, might seem out of place in Tirana—but I owed it to my hosts to appear as faultlessly garbed as I would have done had I been covering a similar event at home.

The last stage of the journey, which started overland across France and Italy to the Italian Adriatic port of Bari, proved inauspicious. The all-night crossing from Bari to the Albanian port of Durazzo was accomplished in a small, light vessel upon seas of unexampled commotion. All the passengers were ill and I was no exception. Durazzo in the early light looked uninviting.

The twenty-mile stretch of roadway into Tirana, supposedly the best in the country, was in pitiful condition. Great potholes and cracks yawned every few yards, and in places the car slid about in a morass of half-dried mud. It started to drizzle as I reached Tirana and the surrounding mountains swam off into a thick mist. I peered unenthusiastically at the squalid town. The minarets of mosques rose bleakly from among corrugated-iron shacks and dirty little shops and eating-places. Veiled and betrousered Moslem women were to be seen among the people trudging the muddy pavements or dodging the herds of goats and cattle being driven along the streets. (A large proportion of Albania's one million population, including Tirana's 30,000 inhabitants, were Moslems, a holdover from the Ottoman occupation.) Tall, formidable-looking men in white skull-caps, red-sashed, and wearing white baggy trousers braided with black revolvers and daggers at their waists, mingled with the townees, who wore shoddy European clothes. If you visualize the sort of old-time Wild Western film main street, on which have been superimposed a mosque and a few vintage jalopies, and where the heavily armed and handsome cowboys are wearing oriental dress instead of 'chaps', you have a fair notion of how Tirana looked. Attempts had been made to decorate the streets in preparation for the wedding; flags hung from vantage points; large photographs of Zog, frames swathed in the Albanian colours, were displayed in shop windows; and along the main street a series of rather frail-seeming triumphal arches had been put up. The hotel 'designated for the foreign journalists' proved to be cold, damp and dirty, with bare, linoleumed rooms, each containing a bed, a chair and a battered table. On the bed was a goatskin rug, dyed a bright red, and from this there emerged each night a stream of voracious bedbugs. I am particularly susceptible to insect ravages, and by the second morning my face had been worked over to such an extent that a newly arrived colleague who knew me quite well had some difficulty in recognizing me. Pitchers of cold water, drawn from some anonymous source, were brought up in the mornings by a surly manservant. None of the doors would lock, and the windows were without curtains. Perhaps the most disagreeable feature of this sombre hostelry was the room reserved for what was termed 'Turkish-style plumbing'. I was never sure whether this phrase was an intentional jest—conceivably a slap at the ancient conquerors—or was meant seriously.

Turkish-style or not, the plumbing was plain non-existent. '*Mais c'est effroyable! Mon Dieu—quel pays!*' cried a French colleague, his face almost as mottled as my own, as he emerged from this particular room after a largely sleepless night.

On the afternoon of the first day I stopped to watch an Austrian photographer taking a picture of a peasant who was driving a mule cart. The man obediently posed, holding a photograph of the king poised on his mule's head, and studying it with close attention. Afterwards I walked back to my dismal hotel, there to unpack and attempt to hang up on the single hook behind the bedroom door my wedding finery.

While I was so engaged there came a peremptory knock, and without a pause the door was flung open to reveal a small policeman dressed in shoddy grey-green, and armed with a rifle and fixed bayonet. It seemed that I was under arrest; we went out together and along the street. He followed right behind me, the bayonet pointing towards the small of my back.

At the police station I was told that there were witnesses ready to testify that I had helped to bring the king publicly into ridicule—a grave offence. I had been observed on the street, aiding and abetting another foreigner in taking photographs of the king's picture, in close juxtaposition to a beast of burden, e.g. a mule.

After a good deal of argument, I insisted on being escorted to the Foreign Office.

The press liaison officer at the Foreign Office received me with marked coolness. He had heard all about it. What principally fascinated me about his appearance (he was foppishly dressed by an extremely good tailor) was a tremendous black eye. He cut me short in the middle of my protest. 'Please remember that you are not in London now, but in Albania.' I made some rather stiff reply to that, and went on to complain about my hotel accommodation.

'It seems that you are overcritical,' he said sharply. 'You have been treated with consideration in the regrettable affair of your committal of *lèse majesté*.' We parted on glacial terms.

Wherever one ate it was almost impossible to escape a pair of peculiarly grisly visitants. These consisted of a one-eyed man, who came shuffling into the various restaurants at dinner time, accompanied by an eagle of repulsive aspect, which he led by a thick chain secured to one of its ankles. The bird had clearly led a

varied life, and it bore many scars. Its feathers were bedraggled almost beyond imagination. Its demeanour was a macabre blend of truculence and hopelessness. It walked in a way which suggested a dreadful attempt to mimic the young Chaplin, and there were angry sores on its head and torso. Despite all this, however, it could still manage a cry of distressing, and indeed haunting, intensity, and we did everything in our power to reduce the frequency of these sounds by showering its impresario with money and pointing urgently towards the door. But the eagle's owner was loath to leave the good cheer, such as it was, of the restaurant for the gloom of the ill-lit streets. He would try to get us to see as much as possible of the repertoire, which consisted mainly of inducing his charge to skip awkwardly about the floor, in response to massive tugs on its chain, punctuating this with its dreadful screams. 'Is only dancing, singing eagle to know. Ha-ha-ha! Bravo!' the owner would shout, as we watched in fascinated horror. The business would end with the man producing an unlikely-looking scrap of raw meat from some inner pocket and tossing it at the bird, which would catch and consume it with stomach-turning rapacity. Then the two would shuffle off together into the night.

My messages were taking forty-eight hours on average to reach Fleet Street. The monotony of living was broken from time to time by the appearance of Zog's three sisters, the Princesses Myzejen, Ruhije and Maxhide, wearing male military uniform, and marching about Tirana at the head of a contingent of the Albanian Women's Association. The royal sisters were sloe-eyed, raven-haired and shared a rather oriental cast of countenance. They were heavily made up, and they wore World War I steel helmets, Sam Browne belts, dark-blue waisted tunics, smart khaki riding breeches, and each carried a drawn sword.

The day before the wedding the correspondents received their official invitations on imposing pieces of pasteboard, edged with gold, I glanced casually at mine to verify what time we had to be at the annexe, which had been specially built on to the side of the tiny palace for the ceremony. Down at the bottom of the engraved invitation my eyes fell on an unwelcome announcement: 'The wearing of evening dress for those guests not in uniform is strictly enjoined.' *Evening* dress? Here was I with the wrong sort of clothes entirely. But surely I could not be the only reporter in this predicament? I walked along the corridor of the hotel, enquiring among some of my French and other colleagues. But they, Continentals to a man, had brought along evening dress—either tails, white tie and white waistcoat or tuxedo suits—as a matter of course, for formal attire for weddings in nearly every European country is indubitably evening dress; and naturally the Albanians would, on such an occasion, wish to be sticklers for the rules. What could I do to avoid committing a sad solecism? The idea of finding a Moss Bros in Tirana was laughable. Useless, too, to dream of borrowing evening clothes. Every suit in Albania would surely be on active duty on Zog's wedding day. There was only one thing to be done: swallow my pride and go to see the FO press liaison official again, to ask if he would arrange for a point to be stretched on my behalf.

It was a difficult interview. He made no secret of his lack of enthusiasm when I was at length shown into his office. But when I made clear the nature of my request his face darkened. 'Absolutely impossible!' he snapped. 'There must be a certain protocol at a ceremony of such a nature. After all, Mr MacColl, you would expect visitors to London to conform with British practice in such matters, would you not? Respect must be shown.' I made the mistake of explaining that my morning dress would be just the thing on such an occasion in London, which gave him the opportunity of repeating his earlier remark that I was in Albania now and not London. I pointed out that in its general scheme formal morning dress is not vastly dissimilar from full evening dress. Could I not perhaps borrow a white tie? Would not my fawn waistcoat do at a pinch instead of a white one? Could not my cutaway coat be smuggled inconspicuously into the annexe? He shook his head coldly. 'You have already shown grave disrespect to the person of His Majesty. You were treated leniently on that occasion. I do not intend to be any party to another gesture by you implying further lack of respect.'

I started to lose my temper. I said that I was a thousand miles from home and that I had got to get in to see the wedding. What did he suggest? He shrugged. 'That is entirely your affair. But I must make it clear that there will be no exception whatsoever to this rule. Precautions will be taken', he added, making an ostentatious note on a desk-pad, 'to ensure that anyone not properly dressed will be rigorously excluded from the palace environs.'

The situation was preposterous. And yet what was I to do? I had come all this way to cover the wedding, and now it looked very much as if I should not be allowed to watch it. An appeal to higher authority would almost certainly have been abortive. My few days in Tirana had brought home to me the futility of trying to make the direct approach in dealing with government departments in small Balkan kingdoms. And it would have taken far too long to try to explain to any other officials who might have been willing to listen to me why the liaison man designated by the Foreign Office was unprepared to help me with my problem. What was there left to do? No doubt some of my colleagues would have been ready to give me a fill-in after the ceremony; but that would have been at best a poor substitute. They, all too keenly aware of the shortcomings of the local telegraph company, would be anxious to get on with their own stories. And in any event, trying to write a colour story at secondhand is an unrewarding business.

There simply had to be a solution. But the day wore on with none in sight. I was in despair. That night I was sitting dejectedly in one of the Albanian restaurants, a bottle of wine at my side, staring dully at the eagle going through its paces. I had not even got the spirit to ask the one-eyed owner to take it away. But apparently the earlier efforts of the foreign visitors to cut short the dreadful performance had not been lost on the staff. There was a sudden commotion, a storm of argument, and then the man and bird were bundled through the door by the headwaiter. As he walked in again I turned to thank him—and my gaze froze. For it came upon me that he was wearing evening dress. It is not easy to convey the state of ill-grooming and general disrepair of the suit he had on. It may well have had a dozen earlier owners. Its surface was a crusted mass of stains. The silk facings on one of the lapels had been replaced with a piece of ordinary, and much lighter coloured, cloth. A long tear on one of the trouser legs had been inexpertly sewn up. The glazed celluloid 'dicky' which served the wearer as a shirt-front, was filthy. The buttons were missing from the sides of the coat cuffs. Perhaps worst of all, while I am six feet three inches tall, the headwaiter was quite a short man. But here indisputably was evening dress.

The equivalent of a pound sterling engineered the loan. I stayed until closing time, and then the headwaiter led me behind the scenes to a fairly noisome cubby-hole, where he took off the evening suit and handed it over. I hurried with my prize back to the hotel, obtained some water with difficulty, and did what I could to remove the worst of the stains.

The great day dawned bright and sunny. Eager crowds were out and about early. Hitler had sent a supercharged Mercedes-Benz as his wedding present. The Mayor of Tirana was to present a thirty-piece silver-backed toilet set as the gift of the municipality. Bands played in the packed and flower-strewn streets. Fierce chieftains, entering the capital at the head of their retainers, stacked their weapons to indicate that there would be no untoward incident to mar the rejoicings.

Inside the specially built palace annexe the walls were hung with scimitars, curved daggers and ancient Albanian garments. On the floor was a profusion of rich carpets. But it was the assembled company which gave the occasion a rare *panache*. 'The Hungarian contingent' (said a contemporary description)

'seemed to have stepped straight out of the Middle Ages. The men wore the most brilliant and astonishing garb—wonderful bottle-green Dolmans, fur-trimmed breeches, polished high boots, short swords in rich velvet scabbards, Hussar-like cloaks of green and blue and vermilion. One man wore a scarlet cloak and snowy white duck trousers, like those worn by some regiments of the British Army a hundred years ago. Some of the Hungarian ladies swept down the room in tight Elizabethan bodices, with high ruffles and embroidered trains, resembling sixteenth-century portraits come to gracious life. Others of the women wore the most fashionable modern gowns, with silver-fox capes and a profusion of superb jewels. The Orthodox Archimandrites, with their high black hats and noble grey beards, and the brilliantly robed Moslem Imams, added a dignified note to the picturesque scene, which might have been lifted from the fanciful pages of some fairy book. Down the middle of the hall, Army officers from élite units formed a lane, against the edges of which the kaleidoscopic company, chattering and laughing, pressed themselves.'

My thoughts, as I made for this 'story-book scene' in a fiacre, were none too sanguine. There were moments, as I dressed that morning, when I seriously doubted whether I should ever manage it. Apart from the fact that the suit was wildly small for me, the wear and tear which it had received through the years had rendered it peculiarly accident-prone. There was no question of attempting to button up the coat; the trousers ended several inches up my shins, and my wrists stuck out dolefully from my meagre sleeves. My attempts at cleaning were revealed, in the daylight, to have been no more than sketchily successful. One of the gravest problems was posed by the 'dicky'. It showed a nasty tendency to fly up suddenly and strike me beneath the chin, although I had done my best to anchor it with string tied round my waist. Looking at myself with distaste in the hall mirror of the hotel, I was reminded of a pre-war team of French comedians. One was very tall, the other short, and the tall one was always bursting out of his clothes.

In these circumstances my appearance in the doorway to the palace annexe created a sensation. An instant hush fell, and all eyes were turned incredulously on the figure of fantasy which I presented. My instinct was, naturally, to bolt up the central lane with all speed and bury myself in the anonymity of the press accommodation, which was arranged on a low dais at the far end of the chamber. But I dared not move fast. Any sudden or ill-considered move might well have provoked some fatal piece of disintegration in my costume. It was therefore with an unnatural deliberation, a blend of an invalid setting out on his first uncertain stroll after a severe illness and an old man pacing along in a funeral cortège, that I made my stately progress up the aisle. Nor could I even attempt to brazen it out, with head held high. It was the obvious course of prudence to keep my shoulders bowed as much as possible, my chest well in, and my head pressed down into my neck. One deep breath could have unshipped the 'dicky'.

The other wedding guests, therefore, had every opportunity to take in my appearance in detail; and while there was a good deal of whispering in my wake, ahead of, and alongside me, my advent occasioned only an electric silence. This, it seems to me, said much for the good manners of most of those present. But my ensemble proved too much for my colleagues of the press, and as I hove into near focus they greeted me with a burst of laughter. It was with a sense of immeasurable relief that I finally mounted the newspapermen's dais and sought cover at the rear of the sniggering group.

Thanks to the waiter, I had made it.

RENÉ MACCOLL

The Untimely Deaths of the Emperor and Empress of China

This story shows Backhouse's* style of *histoire romancée*, reminiscent of the popular writers of his time, Stanley Weyman and Anthony Hope.

According to Backhouse the events of 1908 were a crisis comparable with the crisis of 1898–1901. Now, as then, factions at

* Edmund Backhouse, the 'Hermit of Peking'.

court competed to control puppet emperors, and this time the struggle was intensified by the failing health of the empress and the prospect of a vacuum at the centre of real power. This time, also, there was a new character in the dramatis personae: for Backhouse inserts himself into the story as the empress's faithful confidant.

The story begins when the confidant receives an urgent summons from the Grand Eunuch. Backhouse, ignoring the agitated pleas of his ten servants, who apprehend disaster, boldly sets off wearing his twin-eyed peacock-feather, his yellow riding-jacket, and the rest of his court robes, and carrying the golden tablet which admits him to the Forbidden City. There he is received by the empress, 'resplendent in jewels and wearing the famous pearl jacket'. The empress describes the intrigue against her; how the dominant faction among the councillors, taking advantage of her recent illness, is scheming to end her regency and restore the Kuang-hsü Emperor to power. She herself is to be assassinated or banished to Jehol. But she protests that she is not defeated yet. Soothsayers have prophesied that she has still several years to live, and she has plans to thwart the threatened coup d'état: 'I am not one to let the grass grow under my feet, and I mean to anticipate these traitors. Consequently (and Li Lien-ying is cognizant of the plan) I feel it my bounden necessity to dispose of the emperor, because in so doing I shall deprive these treason-workers of their puppet figurehead. I shall deal with each of them later,' she added grimly. But of course, the emperor's death was to seem natural; and this is where Backhouse comes in: 'What I want is that, if you hear of the emperor's sudden passing, dragon-borne, to Heaven, you will be at pains to let your government know that it was a natural death.' Once the emperor had been disposed of, she proposed to put aside the infant P'u-i, whom she had herself designated as the next emperor, and replace him by P'u-lun, the more legitimate heir, who had been passed over in 1875 . . . Backhouse obediently agreed to misinform Sir Edward Grey, with whom, he said, he had direct connection. The empress then provided him with a cover-story for his summons to the palace. If anyone should ask the reason for his visit to the palace at such a time, he was to say that it was in order to convey an autograph birthday greeting from the empress to Queen Alexandra 'which I wish you to send direct and not through the Foreign Office'; as indeed, we are told, he then did, sending the letter via

Siberia; and it duly reached the queen 'on 2nd December, the day of her nativity'. Backhouse was, by now, according to his own account, a practised bearer of royal messages. After these arrangements had been made, the tension was relaxed in an affable conversation on more agreeable topics, and in particular, the liaison between Edward VII and Mrs Keppel.

A few days later, the empress's plan was carried out. Two eunuchs waited on the emperor, followed by a servant carrying stuffed cushions and a silken cord. They found him reclining on the k'ang 'reading the novel *Chin P'ing Mei* (not one of the most reputable Chinese novels)', and after some preliminary civilities, informed him that the empress had made new arrangements for the succession, put the noose round his neck and suffocated him slowly with the pillows.

When the news was brought to the empress she was much relieved. 'Thank God, I feel a new life within my veins,' she said: 'it's the most blessed of all events'; and she summoned the Grand Council in order to proceed to the next stage of her plan: the proclamation of a new emperor. The infant P'u-i, so recently adopted as heir-apparent, was to be set aside and the mature P'u-lun was to reign under the title of the Heng-ch'ing Emperor. All seemed to go smoothly, as planned. There were no objections. But afterwards Yüan Shih-k'ai and the Minister of War, T'ieh-liang, demanded a private audience, to submit their humble views on a matter of state:

> Yüan kotowed thrice and T'ieh followed his example. 'Your Majesty is full of years, riches and honours. You should pass your remaining years in the profound seclusion of Yi Ho Yüan and not be troubled by multitudinous state affairs . . . I ask Your Majesty, and T'ieh-liang (who nodded assent) joins me in the prayer, to issue one more decree announcing your irrevocable abdication and appointing us as Grand Imperial Preceptors, T'ai Shih, who will advise the new emperor on all governmental business as Joint Regents.'
>
> The Old Buddha's wrath kindled even as thunder. She shouted in her rage and fury, 'You traitor, nay you two traitors. After all I have done for you, is this the way you repay my benevolence? I dismiss you both from your offices and shall order that you be handed for trial to the Minister of Justice. Though you die a thousand deaths, your retribution will be

too light. The cup of your treason and iniquity is full to the brim. Leave the presence and await my orders.'

At this, Yüan drew out a six-chambered revolver and fired three shots, at point-blank range, into the empress's belly. The court apothecaries, the women of the bedchamber, the eunuchs, hearing the shots, rushed in; but it was too late. After a few dramatic last words, the empress, in a pool of blood, 'expired amidst the wailing of the eunuchs and of the household, who called upon her spirit not to leave the tenement of her body'. Once she was dead, the Council met, reversed the empress's last decrees, and reinstated the infant prince, P'u-i, on the throne left vacant by the death of the Kuang-hsü Emperor. After their successful counter-coup, the councillors declared that both deaths were natural; their statement was endorsed, out of loyalty to the empress in one instance, out of self-interest in the other, by Backhouse; and the European legations being, 'as usual, in blissful ignorance' of real events, never discovered the truth.

Such is the authentic story of the two imperial deaths of November 1908 as recounted by Backhouse from first-hand evidence: the death of the emperor from the eunuchs who carried it out; that of the empress from those who witnessed it. The only objection to this dramatic and circumstantial story is that there is not the slightest reason for believing a word of it.

HUGH TREVOR-ROPER

This Is Quite True

... So No. 3 Cmdo were very anxious to be chums with Lord Glasgow so they offered to blow up an old tree stump for him and he was very grateful and said don't spoil the plantation of young trees near it because that is the apple of my eye and they said no of course not we can blow a tree down so that it falls on a sixpence and Lord Glasgow said goodness you are clever and he asked them all to luncheon for the great explosion. So Col.

Durnford-Slater DSO said to his subaltern, have you put enough explosive in the tree. Yes, sir, 75 lbs. Is that enough? Yes sir I worked it out by mathematics it is exactly right. Well better put a bit more. Very good sir.

And when Col. D. Slater DSO had had his port he sent for the subaltern and said subaltern better put a bit more explosive in that tree. I don't want to disappoint Lord Glasgow. Very good sir.

Then they all went out to see the explosion and Col. D.S. DSO said you will see that tree fall flat at just that angle where it will hurt no young trees and Lord Glasgow said goodness you are clever.

So soon they lit the fuse and waited for the explosion and presently the tree, instead of falling quietly sideways, rose fifty feet into the air taking with it half an acre of soil and the whole of the young plantation.

And the subaltern said sir I made a mistake, it should have been 7.5 lbs not 75.

Lord Glasgow was so upset he walked in dead silence back to his castle and when they came to the turn of the drive in sight of his castle what should they find but that every pane of glass in the building was broken.

So Lord Glasgow gave a little cry and ran to hide his emotion in the lavatory and there when he pulled the plug the entire ceiling, loosened by the explosion, fell on his head.

This is quite true.

EVELYN WAUGH

The Invasion of Maidstone, 1941

Our next duty was to try and capture the town of Maidstone from the Home Guard, that civilian task force of veterans and the infirm who were supposed to harass the Germans in case of a landing, and hold vital positions until better-armed units of the army could be deployed.

We were, on this occasion, supposed to be German. As soon as the battle began, I detached myself from my unit, and advanced alone to the centre of the town by the simple expedient of knocking on people's doors. When they were opened, invariably by men in pyjamas or women in nightdresses, for it was a little before six in the morning, I would explain the vital nature of the manoeuvre, without ever revealing which side I was on. Flushed with patriotism, the good burghers of Maidstone forgot their annoyance at being woken so early, and let me through their houses, and into their gardens. Here I would climb into a neighbouring garden, and knock on the back door of another house. These people would then let me out of their front doors. Looking both ways, I would then race across the road and knock at another front door, and the process would repeat itself. It took me over two hours to penetrate into the centre of the city at right angles, as it were, to the traffic.

There, I suddenly found myself before the Home Guard headquarters. A choleric general emerged. I aimed my rifle at him, and fired. Since the rifle was empty, it only produced a click, which neither he nor the umpire, a very stout lieutenant, heard. I consequently shouted 'Bang!' and then informed the general, politely, that he was dead.

Death was the farthest thing from the general's mind, and he spluttered, 'Don't talk such tommyrot. Who are you, anyway?'

The umpire turned out to have a terrifying stammer. His face scarlet with effort and apology, he told the general that he was indeed d . . ., but the word simply would not come.

It was the delay in the verdict which more than anything seemed to enrage the general. 'Look here,' he snorted, 'it's not good enough. Fellow points a gun at me and says bang. May be a bad shot for all I know. Might have come out of the encounter unscathed, what?'

'Would you have preferred me to use ammunition?' I asked.

The general lost his head. 'Who asked your advice?' he blustered. 'Haven't you done enough harm?'

'D . . . ead!' the umpire managed at length.

'I won't accept it. Won't accept it, d'you hear? Not from a mere lieutenant.'

It was the lieutenant's turn to be annoyed. 'I am the acc . . . the . . . oh . . . acc . . .'

'I don't give a damn about all that,' ranted the general. 'I'm off to inspect the forward positions, and I'd like to see the chap who's going to stop me.'

'*Sie sind tod!*' I cried.

The general spun on me, suspicious for the first time. 'What did you say?'

'*Sie sind tod, Herr General!*'

'Are you talking some foreign language, or something?' asked the general, as though he was on the trail of something big.

'*Ich bin Deutscher.*'

'German, eh?' the general asked, his eyes narrowing.

'Acc . . . redited umpire of this exc . . . exc . . . sss,' the lieutenant declared.

Just then, some other Home Guards appeared out of headquarters.

'I've caught a German prisoner,' cried the general. 'Put him under lock and key,' and then, brushing the umpire aside, he jumped into his staff car, and told the driver to leave the scene of his humiliation as quickly as possible.

The umpire was boiling with frustration.

'I'm s . . . so . . . so . . .' he hissed.

'So am I, sir,' I said as I was led away.

A Home Guard major read all my correspondence, culled from my pockets, and then began a cross-examination.

I refused to answer in any language but German.

The major became very irritated. 'Now look here, I'm going to report you to your unit if you don't pull up your socks and answer a few questions.'

'*Dass ist mir egal*,' I rasped.

'That's your final word?' he asked, evilly.

'*Heil Hitler!*' I shouted.

'That does it.'

They chose to lock me in the armoury.

I seized a Sten gun, broke open the door, upset the staff table, smeared ink on the maps and plans of the local high command, before I was overpowered by a cohort of old gentlemen, to whom I wished no harm, and therefore allowed myself to be locked into a disused scullery. They were all very angry indeed, and I felt that the frontier between fact and fiction had become unclear. One or two of them looked at me as though indeed I were a Nazi.

In the mid-afternoon, the colonel of my battalion arrived. He was a man whose voice rarely rose above a whisper, and whose head emerged from the front of his uniform at such an extravagant angle that from the side one could read the name of his tailor inside the jacket. He had the curious prehistoric look of a bemused turtle, and I always felt that if we ever had to face actual warfare in the company of this gentleman, he might well, in a moment of difficulty, disappear into his uniform until the storm blew over.

'Now what is all this?' he asked me almost inaudibly.

I explained, as so often, my version of the truth.

'I see,' he murmured. 'But was it really necessary to confuse the issue by speaking in German?'

'It's a manner in which the Germans are likely to confuse the issue, sir, if they should ever land in Maidstone,' I suggested.

'See what you mean,' he said, 'although that's an eventuality I consider to be most unlikely, don't you?'

I was a little surprised to be consulted, but decided to suggest that if there was no likelihood of the Germans landing in Maidstone, we were all wasting our time.

'Quite, quite,' he agreed absently, then smiled briefly. 'Full marks.'

On his way out, he hesitated a moment. 'You are one of my men, are you?'

'I'm wearing the uniform, sir,' I pointed out.

'Yes, yes. I just thought you might belong to the Home Guard. But then, of course, there'd be absolutely no point in your talking German.'

Muttering confirmations of his own opinion, he left the room, and secured my release by suggesting the Home Guard should all learn German in order to know how to deal with recalcitrant prisoners if, of course, the Germans ever had the bad taste to come to Maidstone.

PETER USTINOV

Flying Visit

This was the name of an ingenious and entertaining fantasy published by Peter Fleming early in the Second World War. In it Hitler made an inadvertent forced-landing in Britain and the story retailed the embarrassment to which this event gave rise. I read it early in 1940, and forgot about it.

The great 'blitz' struck London in September. Night after night the air-raid sirens moaned their warning as darkness fell and night after night up to a thousand Londoners died. The last and perhaps the heaviest raid took place on 10–11 May 1941, and thereafter, because the Nazis had other preoccupations, there was peace in the skies over Britain until sporadic attacks began again in the early months of 1944, followed shortly afterwards by the final assault of the V Bombs.

On 10 May I was alone at 10 Downing Street. One of my colleagues had gone with the Prime Minister to Ditchley since the moon was full and at such times Chequers was believed to be vulnerable. The other two were profiting from a much needed weekend off duty. It was a warm early summer's evening and there was no immediate crisis; but the air-raid sirens sounded and I went to bed in a bunk in the somewhat rickety shelter which had been hastily constructed near the kitchen just before war broke out and which was certainly not bomb-proof.

The bombs fell; several on the Horse Guards Parade and one in Whitehall. For some inexplicable reason I awoke a few seconds before each explosion, all of them shaking the house and the shelter in which I slept. Tired and, by this time, hardened to air-raids I invariably fell asleep again immediately. Before 6 a.m. the noise of bombs and anti-aircraft fire slackened. As I lay, half awake, in my uncomfortable bunk and the fetid, badly air-conditioned atmosphere, my dozing thoughts turned to Peter Fleming's book. I remembered, too, the report I had seen in an Air Ministry Intelligence Digest that Goering was believed to fly over from time to time in a German bomber in order to gloat over the destruction which the Luftwaffe was wreaking on London. What fun it would be if he had to escape from a burning bomber by parachute! My half-waking daydreams ambled on and always they kept returning to Peter Fleming's book.

At 7.30 on that Sunday morning I dressed and went out. It was, or should have been, a perfect May morning; but a low cloud of smoke hung over the town and because a warehouse full of paper had been among the night's casualties, small flakes of paper were falling from heaven for all the world as if it were snowing. The House of Commons was a ruin; flames were bursting from the roof, William Rufus's roof, of Westminster Hall; and Westminster Abbey had received its only direct hit of the war. The Horse Guards Parade was pitted with craters; water from a ruptured main was pouring in a torrent down Whitehall. Why 10 and 11 Downing Street, fragile remnants of Sir George Downing's seventeenth-century jerry-building, had not collapsed like a pack of cards, I do not know.

I went to a service in St Faith's Chapel, crowded by those who like myself wanted to thank God for their survival through such a night. Back at No. 10 I rang up Ditchley, spoke to the Prime Minister and described the scene. 'At least', he said, 'we shot down thirty-three of the swine' (for he had been talking to the Air Ministry). The cloud of smoke evaporated; the fire engines and the ambulances proceeded with their familiar, daily duties; life returned to wartime London-Blitz normal.

At about 11 o'clock I walked over to the Foreign Office. There might perhaps be some news and, anyhow, it would be pleasant to gossip with Nicholas Lawford, an amusing and stimulating Private Secretary to Anthony Eden whom I knew to be on duty there.

When I opened the door of the large Private Secretaries' room, adjacent to that of the Secretary of State, Lawford was talking on the telephone. He saw me and said to the other party: 'Here is the man you had better speak to. Hold on a minute.' Then, placing his hand over the receiver, he whispered to me: 'This may be a lunatic. He says he is the Duke of Hamilton, that something extraordinary has happened, that he is about to fly down from Scotland to Northolt and that he wants to be met there by Alec Cadogan and the Prime Minister's Secretary. Alec is having his first day off for months and I refuse to ruin it. And he won't say what it is all about, except that it is like an E. Phillips Oppenheim thriller. Yes, I think he's a lunatic.' He handed me the receiver and the alleged duke repeated his message. Suddenly, my waking daydream came back to me. 'Has somebody arrived?' I asked. There was a long pause. 'Yes,' he said. 'Please be at Northolt to meet me.' He rang off.

I could scarcely leave No. 10 unmanned, and so I rang up Ditchley and asked for instructions.

'Well, *who* has arrived?' asked the Prime Minister.

'I don't know,' I repeated for about the fourth time; 'he wouldn't say.'

'It can't be Hitler?'

'I imagine not.'

'Well, stop imagining and have the duke, if it is the duke, sent straight here from Northolt.'

Thus it was that later that day Churchill learned from the Duke of Hamilton, who turned out to be neither an impostor nor a lunatic, that Rudolf Hess had arrived in Scotland. As for me, I make no pretence to psychic powers; but I think it strange that Peter Fleming's story, which I had read many months before and had long since forgotten, should have come flooding into my half-conscious brain that Sunday morning.

JOHN COLVILLE

Convoy to Egypt

Off Greece came a day of calm. From the top bunk one could look out in the early morning and see the line of the horizon, pale, and mingled with pale sky. An occasional welcome island slid by. Like the ancient Greeks I had little confidence in the science of navigation and preferred to stay in sight of land when at sea, and in sight of the sea when on land. Shores of one sort and another stayed visible all day; the rolling of the swell grew gentler; I began to have a secret half-allowed hope that we might even reach Egypt safely. Fear arrived as usual with nightfall. A darkened hunted vessel, we flew like a fugitive far off the normal course. My heart seemed to be holding its breath as we slid along in the gently heaving stillness of a starry night. The ship was a fast one and the danger was not great; my ignorance as usual magnified it.

The regular rhythm of the ship's engines continued. Any minute now, they were saying, any minute now, any minute now. The spent waves hissed along the side of the ship, the swishing grasping water that was waiting to get in and consume us. It would rise higher and higher in the cabin, our heads would bump along the rivets of the ceiling, the lights would all go out, we would die in terrible darkness and fear. My mother opened the Bible and I listened to the sound but not to the sense of her reading; I could not for the moment divorce myself from my fear. The rhythm of the sentences gained slowly on me. After all, they had clamped the scuttles down, so that the water could not, anyway, get in that way. The words of Isaiah flowed gradually over me like an incantation, the rocking lulling sentences were the waves of a kinder sea. My mother's low untroubled voice went on. The sound of the words rose and fell, mysteriously rhymed and chimed, dropped with certitude into their appointed places.

'Hast thou seen that which backsliding Israel hath done?'

Aware of being one who habitually backslid myself, I stopped dwelling in the sound and started to listen to the sense.

'She is gone up upon every high mountain and under every green tree, and there hath played the harlot.'

The beauty of this picture withdrew my attention from the haunting terror outside in the dark night. They had explained to me what a harlot was, but I had forgotten. Clearly, in the context, it must be some kind of musical instrument. Perhaps a mouth organ, or a guitar, or a very small harp? Anyway you played it, backslidingly or otherwise, upon every high mountain. Riding a donkey, in the bright sun, you played it; and the sound went echoing down the valley. You played it under the splashing shade of the cedars. The others can play the harp if they like, or the flute, but bags I play the harlot. The rest of you can sing.

PRISCILLA NAPIER

An Afternoon with Churchill

I arrived at the Hotel Roy-Reine,* with Malcolm Bullock, at 12 o'clock. Mary Soames met us in the hall, very pretty and charming—as always; and up we went, in the lift, to a nice room where we found Clemmie and Christopher Soames, and five dry martinis. A very warm welcome from Clemmie, who seemed somewhat relieved to see us.

Suddenly the door opened, and in walked Winston, in a blue siren suit. Bowing low to Malcolm, he came across to me. 'Ah,' he said, 'red trousers. Very nice. They match your tie. I've just been dealing with the German armour at Dunkirk, in which you are so interested. At first I was inclined to accept Halder's version, which you first told me. But that has now to be modified. These German Generals say anything that suits their book. Pownall has unearthed the official German War Diary.

* In Aix-en-Provence.

'Look. This is what happened. Kluge reported to Rundstedt that the armour was tired, and extended. He asked for two days in which to rest it. Rundstedt agreed. Then, by a piece of good luck, Hitler motored over to Rundstedt's Headquarters, and also agreed that this was necessary. In the afternoon a message came from OKW, Hitler's supreme Headquarters, ordering the armour to advance on Dunkirk. This order came from Keitel.' 'And, presumably, Halder, as Chief of Staff?' I interjected. 'Yes,' he said: 'It was disregarded by Rundstedt, despite Guderian's protests, who was fortified by Hitler's verbal agreement that the armour should be rested. That, and Calais, saved the BEF.

'I did Calais myself. I personally gave the order to stand, and fight it out to the end. I agreed to the evacuation of Boulogne with reluctance; and I think now that I ought to have ordered them to fight it out there too. But the order to Calais meant certain death for almost the entire garrison.

'It was the only time during the war that I couldn't eat. I was very nearly sick at dinner.' Tears came into his eyes. 'But, together with the Gravelines line, which was steadily flooding, it gave us two vital days; and a few of our cruiser tanks actually broke out of Calais, through the German armour, and got to the Gravelines line.

'Now look at this'—producing his proofs. 'Here is a yelp from the German Commander at Dunkirk. He says the British troops are embarking in large ships, without equipment, but unscathed. "We do not want to have to meet them again, when they have been re-equipped." Only then was the order given for the armour to move in on Dunkirk. And by then it was too late.' He put away the proofs. 'The failure to press on with their armour, and Calais, saved us. And I did Calais. Now come in to lunch.'

This was all right: langouste mayonnaise, soufflé, a couple of bottles of champagne on ice, and a bottle of Volnay, topped up with brandy.

'I find alcohol a great support in life,' he said: 'Sir Alexander Walker, who keeps me supplied with your native brew, told me that a friend of his, who died the other day, drank a bottle of whisky a day for the last ten years of his life. He was eighty-five.' 'If you ever gave it up,' I replied, 'you'd die.' Silence.

Then: 'If I become Prime Minister again, I shall give up cigars. For there will be no smoking. We cannot afford it.' 'What,' I said, 'none at all?' 'Well, only a small ration for everyone. And then a black market in coupons, organized by the Government, so that anyone who couldn't give it up would have to pay through the nose!' 'You'd better not say that before the election,' I said. 'I shan't,' he answered.

'They said', he went on, 'that I was wrong to go to Greece in 1940. But I didn't do it simply to save the Greeks. Of course, honour and all that came in. But I wanted to form a Balkan front. I wanted Yugoslavia, and I hoped for Turkey. That, with Greece, would have given us fifty divisions. A nut for the Germans to crack. Our intervention in Greece caused the revolution in Yugoslavia which drove out Prince "Palsy"; and delayed the German invasion of Russia by six weeks. Vital weeks. So it was worth it. If you back a winner it doesn't really matter much what your reasons were at the time. They now say that I went to Greece for the wrong reasons. How do they know? The point is that it was worth it.' This I knew to be nonsense. It was not worth it. It did not lead to the formation of a Balkan front. It is by no means certain that it delayed the German invasion of Russia, the date of which had already been fixed. It gave Rommel his chance, and very nearly lost us Egypt. Finally, it was a classic example of what he himself had described, in the last volume of *The World Crisis*, as the commonest of all the great military errors: 'It is the error most easy to perceive in theory and most difficult to avoid in action. There are two enemies and two theatres; the task of the commander is to choose in which he will prevail. To choose either, is to suffer grievously in the neglected theatre. To choose both, is to lose in both ... A score of good reasons can be given not only for either course, but also for the compromises which ruin them. But the path to safety nearly always lies in rejecting the compromises.' However, I had not been asked to lunch to argue, much as I would have enjoyed it. And anyway he was by now in full spate.

'My hardest time was the end of 1940, and the first six months of 1941'—with an odd look at me (it was the time of my troubles). 'I had to do eight things at once, with enough material and time for three or four. It was very exciting.'

'A bit too exciting,' I said.

'Not for me. I enjoyed it. The hornets were buzzing round my head. I like that.' I very nearly said, but didn't, that it was perhaps because everyone knew he liked it that he was no longer Prime Minister.

By this time the champagne was beginning to work. 'I see that poor Attlee has caught a cold in Ireland,' he remarked. 'I hope it's nothing worse than that.' This brought the whole party to attention, and a query from Clemmie. But he only burst into a song about colleens.

'Oliver Stanley', he went on, 'said a very clever thing the other day. He said that, to Baldwin, Europe was a bore; and to Chamberlain a bigger Birmingham. Oh, those men! I got the facts from a frantic Civil Service, whose reports were continuously disregarded. But I think there was someone in the Air Ministry who deliberately withheld information from the Cabinet.'

I said that Vansittart had told me that, when he took the Secret Service reports to Baldwin, the latter said: 'Oh, take that stuff away. It gives me nightmares. I don't want to read it.' He had not heard this; and was appalled. 'You were on the right side then. How is your constituency? How are the herrings? You seem to have persuaded a reluctant public to eat them.'

I told him that my constituency had been turned into a safe seat under the new redistribution scheme. 'You deserve it,' he said. 'You have a great record there. They must love you very much. How long have you been there? Nearly a quarter of a century!'

I said that one of my troubles in life was that I was always right about public affairs, and always wrong about my private affairs. He thought for a moment, and then said: 'No. Sometimes wrong about public affairs, and sometimes right about private affairs. That would be a fairer statement of the case.'

He got up and left the room, returning a moment later with some more papers. 'These will please you,' he said. 'It is a correspondence with Attlee about Western Union. I have put him on the spot. Max [Beaverbrook] tells me they are much upset by it. I have insisted that it be published tomorrow. You should say, at the Interlaken Conference, that you are very disappointed with the performance of the British Government about Europe, but hope for better things now—and see that it is telegraphed to London.'

The conversation then turned to the Jews. I said that they were going to win hands down in Palestine, and get more than they ever expected. 'Of course,' he said. 'The Arabs are no match for them. The Irgun people are the vilest gangsters. But, in backing the Zionists, these Labour people backed the winners; and then ran out on them. You were quite right to write to *The Times* protesting against the shelling of Jerusalem.' This brought Christopher Soames in. He said that public opinion at home was pro-Arab and anti-Jew.

'Nonsense,' said Winston. 'I could put the case for the Jews in ten minutes. We have treated them shamefully. I will never forgive the Irgun terrorists. But we should never have stopped immigration before the war.'

He went on to say that he never saw Weizmann because he found him so fascinating that, if he did, he would spend too much of his time talking to him. 'Weizmann gives a very different reason,' I replied. 'What is that?' 'Last time I saw him he said that the reason you would not see him was because, for you, he was "Conscience".' Silence.

Then back to the war.

'The Americans were not always easy to deal with. They like to concentrate on one thing. They scrap everything else—at colossal expense—to build up a single Plan. But in war nothing stands still. Everything goes on all the time. So you often lose a lot by this policy. I had the greatest difficulty in persuading them to let us capture Rome. After that, they removed nearly all Alexander's divisions for that foolish attack on the Riviera, which made no difference at all to the situation in Brittany. If they had let me have my way, we might have got to Vienna.'

This opened the way for a question I had long wanted to ask him.

'Surely', I said, 'we missed a great opportunity in Italy when Mussolini fell? If we had at once come to terms with Badoglio, we might have got the whole country without fighting. Not only Rome, but Genoa.'

He looked sombre.

'Ah,' he said, 'there is a lot in what you say. There was a plan for the capture of Rome from the air. It miscarried.'

Finally, I asked him if he knew what was going on in Berlin. 'No,' he said. 'It might be another Munich. With this difference. We shall be far stronger this time next year. The American Air Force will be three times the size, and their bombs a third bigger. And this advantage. We shall be able to have our holiday in peace!'

'Nevertheless,' he continued, 'I would have it out with them now. If we do not, war might come. I would say to them, quite

131

politely: "The day we quit Berlin, you will have to quit Moscow." I would not think it necessary to explain why. I am told that they are absolutely certain that we shall behave decently, and honourably, and do the right thing—according to their ideas of our own standards—in all circumstances. With me around, they would not be quite so sure.'

And—in conclusion—'They say I interfered during the war. I did. I interfered all the time.'

The moment then arrived for departure to Les Baux, which he remembered from fifteen years ago, and where he thought he wanted to paint a picture. I said I could not, and would not, take my car, unless they filled it up with petrol. This was accordingly done; and all the painting apparatus collected.

Winston than appeared in snakeskin shoes, and a Mexican sombrero hat; and off we set, before a wide-eyed crowd, in three cars. Winston and Clemmie and one detective in the first. The Soameses and another detective in the second. Malcolm and I in the third—mine—without a detective.

We told them they ought to see the ruins [Roman] of Saint-Rémy on the way. But they took the wrong road, so we got there first. Somewhat dazed by the combination of tremendous heat and alcohol, I found a very nice niche in a beautiful Roman arch, where I curled myself up, and went fast asleep, dreaming of centurions. I thus missed the best scene of all.

On arrival, Winston clambered out of his car, gazed for a few seconds at the ruins, and said: 'How bloody. How absolutely bloody.' 'Look at Bob asleep,' said Malcolm, hoping to divert his attention. But all he said was: 'Bloody.' Clemmie and Mary thought it was quite lovely, and decided to stay for a while. Whereupon the old boy climbed back into his car, and drove off to Les Baux; alone, except for the chauffeur and detectives.

Clemmie and Mary then looked at the ruins from every angle. Christopher confided to me, when I woke up, that he hated sightseeing; and thanked God that he and Mary were leaving the next day for a drive along the Riviera. He called it a 'pub-crawl' but, if I know Mary, it won't be that. We all then set off for Les Baux—Clemmie, Malcolm and self in my car; Soameses following.

On arrival, the detective came up to me and said: 'There's a storm on. You'd better keep clear. It'll be over in ten minutes.' It then transpired that the painting tackle was all in the Soameses' car, so he couldn't begin. He had gone off to the top of Les Baux, in a rage. The chauffeur and detectives seized the easel and paintbox and ran up the hill after him; while I looked for, and found, a bistro.

By this time all the sightseers at Les Baux had turned out to see what the hell was going on.

Presently there was an uproar. I went out and found Winston striding down the street, with the chauffeur and detectives disconsolately following him, plus all the painting apparatus. 'There's nothing to paint here,' he shouted. 'There's beer to drink here,' I shouted back. So he came into the bistro, which was almost pitch dark, and sat down.

'Were you really asleep in that arch?' he asked. And then: 'Don't you think the Calais story is very dramatic?' By that time the beer had arrived. 'It is cool, but not cold,' he said, with truth. Two pails of ice immediately appeared. Clemmie ordered a lemonade. And peace was gradually restored. 'I hate the taste of beer,' Clemmie said. 'So do most people, to begin with,' he answered: 'It is, however, a prejudice that many have been able to overcome.' The bill was then demanded. Unthinkable, said the proprietress. It was the greatest honour they had ever had. Perhaps Monsieur Churchill would sign his name in the book? Monsieur Churchill would; and did. I went out with Malcolm, wondering whether I would ever be famous enough to pay bills with my signature. 'I think', I said, 'that we can now b——r off.' 'It's more than we can do,' said a detective, who was standing immediately behind me. I had not seen him.

The sombrero and the snake-shoes reappeared. 'Let us rendezvous at the hotel later.' But I was too tired to rendezvous any more. I killed a dog on the way back. And collapsed on to my bed, with a sty in my eye. Thus ended an astonishing afternoon.

ROBERT BOOTHBY

133

Fame is the Spur

There are actors who shrink from recognition, playing a perpetual game of hide-and-seek. Alec Guinness, Paul Scofield, Elizabeth Taylor. No one, I told the latter, will know you in Leningrad; put a scarf over your hair and come for a walk, or come downstairs and dine with me in the hotel restaurant. The Russians stood on their chairs to get a better view. Miss Taylor ate very little.

No one has ever stood on a chair to see me. If there is any chance of my not being recognized, I stand on the chair. For everyone who can put a name to the face there are ten who

can't. These are the ones who ask for autographs; mine is not the most legible signature, especially when scrawled on a newspaper in pencil. I leave them to puzzle it out. Some prefer to continue guessing, and expect me to halt until they have succeeded. 'Don't tell me,' they will urge, 'I'll be there in a moment.'

'I have to be there sooner than that,' I reply, 'the name is Morley.'

'That's right,' they tell me, 'Christopher Morley,' and we part friends.

Not all my colleagues enjoy such interruptions; they have other and more serious purposes in life than being quizzed or being told by strangers that the last time he or she met them was on a plane bound for Jersey fifteen years ago. 'I don't suppose you'll remember,' they add for further identification, 'they were plumb out of gin.' It is, of course, always impossible to recall the incident, but I for one go on my way sustained by the hope that we shall meet again fifteen years from now and one of us be sufficiently impressed to recall our second meeting.

Only on race courses do I refuse to autograph. Alastair Sim, among others, always refused to give them. He would explain, at considerable length, his objections to such a foolish request. He refused to litter the world with idiotic scraps of paper. Nowadays his signature is valuable. For some reason the Germans and the Americans are the most avid autograph collectors. They write from Bremen and Minnesota in facsimile enclosing international tokens and a half-dozen blank sheets. I never sign more than one; if, as one supposes, the sender is commercially orientated one doesn't want to flood the market.

Now and again you will be shaken by the hand by someone who knows your brother in Orpington. The fact that to the best of your knowledge you haven't a brother carries little weight on such occasions. The stranger departs, convinced you are lying and that you are estranged from your relative. You depart wondering if (as in the case of a theatrical friend) your father kept the existence of an entirely separate brood a secret. My friend was tempted to investigate further the chance remark of a bookseller, and discovered he had not one but several brothers and sisters or, more correctly, half-brothers and sisters. But in my case I have been content to let sleeping dogs lie.

Occasionally I get dead rats and even more unpleasant anonymous gifts through the post. I tell myself that it is unlikely that the former were contaminated by plague, and that I have reduced the intolerable pressure of some fellow lunatic. I refuse to accept it as a judgement on my performance. The older one grows the more pleased are one's contemporaries to see one, although not necessarily performing in the theatre. They are heartened by such encounters. There is a strong geriatric bond. Some recall how well one looks; others, an occasion many years ago when they first caught sight of one across the footlights. They strive to remember the name of the piece, or the date, or where they were at the time. It is often a slow process of gradual recall. One hesitates to prompt, even if one could. The parting is delayed but pleasurable. They go on their way remembering something entirely different. How fond they were of Aunt Maud who provided the matinée treat. One is left with the name of the leading lady on the tip of the tongue.

Americans make the best fans, perhaps because they always seem to have time on their hands. The native young pound along behind, thrust a cigarette packet into one's hand, and are off back to the shop. Worst of all are the temporarily incapacitated who demand you sign the plaster on the fractured limb. I find it well nigh impossible to scratch on plaster of Paris, yet others seem to manage.

Few ask for themselves; it is usually for a child. 'My little granddaughter will be so excited,' they urge, but surely a candy bar or a toy is a more suitable present? I can hardly bear to contemplate the disappointment. 'Guess what grandpa has for you?' The small victim searching the pocket and coming up with a squashed plastic cup bearing the signature of someone of whom she is totally ignorant. 'Don't cry, dear, and Grandpa will go out right away and bring back an iced lolly.'

New Zealanders often produce passports; there is a certain satisfaction in writing on an official document. The suspicion that in so doing I may have invalidated it doesn't seem to occur to them, as it does to me. I should, I suppose, be grateful that at least people don't seem to want to write their names on me, as they do on other ancient monuments—and I am.

Heavier citizens demand that I should follow them, to be introduced to their wives on the grounds that the latter often remark on our striking resemblance. Functioning as I do as a sort of decoy duck for British Airways, I am hailed as a friendly counsellor whose advice has been accepted, and on other occasions blamed for delays at Heathrow. Sometimes asked if I ever resent being better known for performances in television advertisements than as the definitive Hamlet of my time, no, I tell them bravely, in the world of commercials everything ends happily and that is precisely what I aim to do.

Of course, it has not been so easy for the children, and now the grandchildren, who are at times appalled by my constant bonhomie. My son once summed it all up. 'There are times, Papa, when you made us cringe a little, but taking it by and large we got the service.'

ROBERT MORLEY

The Celebrated Thacker

No unusual incidents marked Thackeray's lectures in St Louis and Cincinnati,* though he was fond of relating an anecdote which had Barnum's Hotel in the former city as its setting. Dining there one day, he overheard one Irish waiter say to another:

'Do you know who that is?'

'No,' was the answer.

'That', said the first, 'is the celebrated Thacker!'

'What's *he* done?'

'D——d if I know!'

BAYARD TAYLOR

Dinner at the de la Rentas'

Another week has passed without my being invited to the de la Rentas'. Even that overstates my standing. Until I read in *The New York Times Magazine* a couple of weeks ago about the de la Rentas having become 'barometers of what constitutes fashionable society' ('Françoise and Oscar de la Renta have created a latterday salon for *le nouveau grand monde*—the very rich, very powerful and very gifted'), I wasn't even aware of what I wasn't being invited to week after week. Once I knew, of course, it hurt.

Every time the phone rang, I thought it must be Mrs de la Renta with an invitation ('Mr Trillin? Françoise de la Renta here. We're having a few very rich, very powerful and/or very gifted people over Sunday evening to celebrate Tisha B'av, and

* In 1856, when he was making his second visit to the United States.

we thought you and the missus might like to join us'). The phone rang. It was my mother calling from Kansas City to ask if I'm sure I sent a thank-you note to my Cousin Edna for the place setting of stainless Edna and six other cousins went in on for our wedding gift in 1965. The phone rang. An invitation! Fats Goldberg, the pizza baron, asked if we'd like to bring the kids to his uptown branch Sunday night to sample the sort of pizza he regularly describes as 'a gourmet tap-dance'.

'Thanks, Fat Person, but I'll have to phone you,' I said. 'We may have another engagement Sunday.'

The phone quit ringing.

'Why aren't I in *le nouveau grand monde?*' I asked my wife, Alice.

'Because you speak French with a Kansas City accent?' she asked in return.

'Not at all,' I said. 'Sam Spiegel, the Hollywood producer, is a regular at the de la Rentas', and I hear that the last time someone asked him to speak French he said "Gucci".'

'Why would you want to go there anyway?' Alice said. 'Didn't you read that the host is so phoney he added his own 'de la' to what had been plain old Oscar Renta?'

'Who can blame a man for not wanting to go through life sounding like a taxi driver?' I said. 'Family background's not important in *le nouveau grand monde*. Diana Vreeland says Henry Kissinger is the star. The Vicomtesse de Ribes says "Françoise worships intelligence." You get invited by accomplishment— taking over a perfume company, maybe, or invading Cambodia.'

'Why don't we just call Fats and tell him we'll be there for a gourmet tap-dance?' Alice said.

'Maybe it would help if you started wearing dresses designed by Oscar de la Renta,' I said. 'Some of his guests say they would feel disloyal downing Mrs d's chicken fricassee while wearing someone else's merchandise.'

Alice shook her head. 'Oscar de la Renta designs those ruffly dresses that look like what the fat girl made a bad mistake wearing to the prom,' she said.

'Things were a lot easier when fashionable society was limited to old-rich goyim, and all the rest of us didn't have to worry about being individually rejected,' I said.

'At least they knew better than to mingle socially with their dressmakers,' Alice said.

Would I be ready if the de la Rentas phoned? The novelist Jerzy Kosinski, after all, told *The Times* that evenings with them were 'intellectually demanding'. Henry Kissinger, the star himself, said that the de la Rentas set 'an interesting intellectual standard'—although, come to think of it, that phrase could also be applied to Fats Goldberg.

Alone at the kitchen table, I began to polish my dinner-table chitchat, looking first to the person I imagined being seated on my left (the Vicomtesse de Ribes, who finds it charming that her name reminds me of barbecue joints in Kansas City) and then to the person on my right (Barbara Walters, another regular, who has tried to put me at my ease by confessing that in French she doesn't do her r's terribly well). 'I was encouraged when it leaked that the Reagan Cabinet was going to be made up of successful managers from the world of business,' I say, 'but I expected them all to be Japanese.'

Barbara and the Vicomtesse smile. Alice, who had just walked into the kitchen, looked concerned.

'Listen,' Alice said. 'I read in *The Times* that Mrs de la Renta is very strict about having only one of each sort of person at a dinner party. Maybe they already have someone from Kansas City.'

Possible. Jerzy Kosinski mentioned that Mrs d is so careful about not including more than one stunning achiever from each walk of life ('she understands that every profession generates a few princes or kings') that he and Norman Mailer have never been at the de la Rentas' on the same evening ('when I arrive, I like to think that, as a novelist, I'm unique'). Only one fabulous beauty. Only one world-class clotheshorse.

Then I realized that the one-of-each rule could work to my advantage. As I envisioned it, Henry Kissinger phones Mrs d only an hour before dinner guests are to arrive. He had been scheduled to pick up fifteen grand that night for explaining SALT II to the Vinyl Manufacturers Association convention in Chicago, but the airports are snowed in. He and Nancy will be able to come to dinner after all. 'How marvelous, darling!' Mrs d says.

She hangs up and suddenly looks stricken. 'My God!' she says to Oscar. 'What are we going to do? We already have one war criminal coming!'

What to do except to phone the man who conflicts with the star and tell him the dinner had to be called off because Mr d had come down with a painful skin disease known as the Seventh Avenue Shpilkes. What to do about the one male place at the table now empty—between Vicomtesse de Ribes and Barbara Walters?

The phone rings. 'This is Françoise de la Renta,' the voice says. 'This is Calvin of the Trillin,' I say. 'I'll be right over.'

CALVIN TRILLIN

Film-Star Glamour

I had begun to get bigger parts in films, and in 1949 I appeared as the first of the gawky overgrown schoolgirl types (a folk dance enthusiast in Eric Linklater's *Poet's Pub*) that I was soon called upon to repeat in many other pictures—Miss Gossage in *The Happiest Days of Your Life*, and the unrequited policewoman, Ruby Gates, in several disguises, in three of Launder and Gilliatt's successful St Trinian's series. These films were fun to do; pleasant people worked in them, including Margaret Rutherford who read poetry better than almost anyone I ever heard, even better than she played those endearing caricatures she was so justly famed for; and Alastair Sim, with his long sad face and heavy-lidded eyes. He is an essentially non-theatrical man and I think he was probably as surprised as I was to be in the world of films.

My mother wrote to me from America wishing I would, just for *once*, just now and then, look a little less unglamorous in the films in which I acted. Picture after picture reached her local movie-house with me playing those gawky girls and failing to get my man, and she did so wish her friends could see me in a more becoming guise. On her way over to visit

140

us she told a new acquaintance at her table on board ship that I was in the film they were going to see that evening. As usual I looked plain and awkward, and my ma's heart sank. When the lights went up at the end of the picture her companion asked, 'Which was your daughter?' 'I made a mistake,' said my mother. 'She wasn't in it.' Only after she saw *The Million Pound Note*, in which I had scenes with Gregory Peck and played an Edwardian duchess in beautiful clothes designed for me by Maggie Furse, did she feel like telling her friends to go and see me in a movie.

I remember getting a letter from Carley Dawson, my childhood friend to whom I have always written since she went back to America before the war, telling me that my cameo part of the hotel proprietress in the movie *Genevieve* had been well reviewed in her local Washington paper. The short scenes had been fun to do and were filmed in half a day. The notice Carley enclosed praised my performance generously, but the critic mentioned that I had a set of teeth 'only a horse could envy'. Glamorous publicity photographs taken for a new show had just reached me, and with regrettable vanity I sent one (mouth shut) to the critic. He wrote back what was nothing less than a love letter. I had always been told never to answer critics but this unexpected result made me glad I hadn't listened to advice . . . O vanity, vanity!

I have never minded looking funny—when it was intentional. But the public doesn't always realize that one is acting, and I've met with surprised reactions from people who are familiar with my movie image but have never before seen me as myself. I startle them by being much larger than they expect and evidently less peculiar-looking. In Leeds a friendly woman in an hotel said she hoped I wouldn't mind a personal remark. I braced myself for the blow; she touched me gently on the arm and whispered: 'You look so much better since you've had your teeth fixed.' All I could think of in reply was 'I'm so glad.' At the time of writing I have not yet had my teeth fixed.

JOYCE GRENFELL

Gary Cooper's Advice to Actors

Since Mr Cooper is one of our greatest screen actors, I asked him to discuss the subject of acting with me. At first he was reluctant, but when I explained to him that many young struggling actors might benefit from his advice, he agreed to speak about it.

I reprint the interview in its entirety.

'Mr Cooper, do you believe the nobility of your vocation is that the actor remains the primary element in theatrical art although he is seldom the chief authority?'

Mr Cooper thought about this a moment and then replied: 'Yup.'

'And is it not true that actors are not just robots mouthing lines, but when called upon to play their parts they enrich the film, not because their imaginations are superior to those of the author, but because they give so much of themselves that reaches the hearts of the audience rather than the ears?'

'Yup.'

'But it is not true, as many people have maintained, that an actor ought to be able to play any part and be expected to excel at it, is it?'

'Nope.'

'An actor should recognize his limitations, because if he doesn't he will not be able to play himself, which is the only way he can give truth of character to the parts he portrays.'

'Yup.'

'Would you say the golden age of the Attic theatre, which has had no parallel except perhaps in France under the Roi Soleil, emanated from a religious seed?'

'Could be.'

'But what about Stanislavsky, Copeau, Barker and St Denis?'

'Who?'

'Would you say the actor's technique is the outward and visible sign of his inward and spiritual grace?'

'Yup.'

'Do you find the excessive cult of naturalism and the self-

142

consciousness of our newer actors has led in many cases to impoverished performances?'

'Sometimes.'

'And, once an actor learns the grammar and syntax of his business, the less he bothers about his style the better.'

'Always.'

'And we're not wrong in pointing out that if the actor exercises the same control over his histrionic actions on the screen as he does over his moral actions off it, then the actor is not only a good actor but a good man.'

'Exactly.'

'What about comedy?'

'The same thing.'

'In fact, in comedy, timing is the most important thing, is it not? That is to say, a line spoken too quickly or too slowly or too loudly will collapse without a laugh, will it not?'

'It's happened.'

'And yet, with it all, movies pay very well for a good actor, don't they?'

'Yup.'

'Would you recommend the movies, the stage or television for a young actor trying to get his foot into the door?'

'Why not?'

'Is there any other advice you have for actors?'

'Nope.'

'Do you consider the interview finished?'

'Yup.'

ART BUCHWALD

Shakespeare's Coronation

Kings must be crowned, and it is fitting that Shakespeare's belated coronation should have been held in the town of his birth.

The Stratford Jubilee (as its sponsors called it) took place, oddly, not on the bicentenary of the poet's birth in 1764 but five years later, and not, as one might expect, in April when he was born but in irrelevant September . . .

The most celebrated Shakespearean authority of the age did not attend; Johnson's absence was noted and regretted. Nor did the other intellectuals make the journey. But Boswell, delighted, was there, and as he set foot in that drowsy borough of 2,287 souls he experienced (he tells us) such emotions as stirred Cicero in Athens. On the first morning, Wednesday, 5 September, the thirty cannon roared, bells rang through all Stratford, and the serenaders—fantastically garbed actors—sang, to the accompaniment of clarinets, flutes, hautboys, and guitars:

> *Let beauty with the sun arise,*
> *To Shakespeare tribute pay.*

During the public breakfast in the Town Hall the country militia played Dibdin's 'Warwickshire', and Boswell joined in the chorus, 'The Will of all Wills was a Warwickshire Will'. Even the deer-poaching escapade made for local glory: 'The thief of all thieves was a Warwickshire thief' . . .

But the next morning the rains came, first in a drizzle, then a torrent. The procession of Shakespearean characters, with a satyr-drawn triumphal chariot containing Melpomene, Thalia, and the Graces, was called off. Cancelled too was the crowning of the Bard. There were murmurs of complaint that the managers of the Jubilee had not provided any awning or covering of some sort in anticipation of such an accident. Now two thousand revellers crowded into the Rotunda built to accommodate half that many. Dr Arne led the musicians in Garrick's 'Ode to Shakespeare'. During the encore of Mrs Baddeley's solo, 'Thou soft-flowing Avon', Garrick in a sudden gesture flung open the doors to reveal the swollen waters surging against the flimsy structure. The effect (according to one observer) was 'irresistible, electrical'. The crowd laughed, but laughter turned to tears as Mrs Baddeley, that beautiful insinuating creature, went on to sing in her haunting soprano:

> *Thou soft-flowing Avon, by thy silver stream,*
> *Of things more than mortal, sweet Shakespeare would dream . . .*

144

That night there was a masquerade, at which Corsica Boswell, resplendent in his scarlet breeches and grenadier cap embroidered with *Viva la Libertà* in gold letters, danced the minuet with water coming over his shoe-tops. Some departing merrymakers regrettably fell into flooded ditches; the more prudent stayed on until daybreak, when they retreated over planks stretching from the entrance to their waiting carriages. Several avowed that the deluge was the judgement of God on the idolatry of the Jubilee.

SAMUEL SCHOENBAUM

Miss Kitty Takes to the Road

The last time I saw the Divine Sarah, she was a ravaged and desiccated old woman with one leg. And the foot of that one was already in the grave. Indeed, she had only two months left for living. But the prospect of such an untimely taking off was never in her jaunty scheme of things, and when I went around to call upon her in that fusty and frightening museum on the Boulevard Péreire, which was her home when she was in Paris, she made it clear that her thoughts were even then at play with the witching possibility of just one more farewell tour of America—that charming America where she had always been so uncritically applauded and so handsomely paid. My French was equal to the modest task of assuring her how ravished my country would be by these glad tidings. This time, she said, she would not attempt a long tour. In the voice of one who rather hopes to be shouted down, she explained that she was now much too old for such cross-country junketing. Too old? At this suggestion I was gallantly incredulous. 'Yes, young man, much too old,' she continued sadly. 'Of course, I shall play Boston and New York and Philadelphia and Baltimore and Washington. And perhaps Buffalo and Cleveland and Detroit and Kansas City and St Louis

145

and Denver and San Francisco. But at my age I cannot attempt one of those really long tours.'

Thus, in all seriousness, the great Bernhardt when approaching her eighties. Hers was a viewpoint which seemed both alien and anachronistic in an era when there had come into possession of the New York stage a generation of players who regarded any departure from Broadway as penitential, who thought of Manhattan Transfer as a wild frontier town, and who, when induced to play three or four seacoast cities in the trial flight of a new play, would return to New York from the strain of such an exhausting expedition quite too prostrated to speak above a whisper. But Bernhardt, like all the great men and women of the theatre of her time, was a trouper. Of the younger stars now shining brightest in the theatrical firmament only one is entitled to be called by that name. That one is Katharine Cornell.

When, at the end of June, she sailed to take her well-earned ease beside the Mediterranean and brood over the prompt book of *Rosmersholm*, with which darkling tragedy she will make her first excursion into the leafy and beckoning depths of Henrik Ibsen, she had just completed an extraordinary season. With her repertory of three fine plays, her company of sixty persons—to say nothing of Flush—and her special car presided over by the only bearded porter in the entire personnel of the Pullman Company, that season had taken her on a journey of more than sixteen thousand miles and had involved her appearance in more than seventy-four cities. From Waco, Texas, to Portland, Maine, from Tacoma, Washington, to Montgomery, Alabama, she had taken to the road with such plays as the *Romeo and Juliet* of Shakespeare, the *Candida* of Mr Bernard Shaw and—most popular item in her bag of tricks—*The Barretts of Wimpole Street*, by Mr Rudolf Besier. She had taken along as fine a troupe as she could assemble, offering the country at large considerably better entertainment than had been offered it in twenty years. She had moved through sandstorms and blizzards and cloudbursts, and never failed to keep an engagement. She had come to towns where a large percentage of her eager audience had never seen a play before and were entirely unfamiliar with the idiom of the theatre. She had opened up mildewed and cobwebby opera houses which had stood dark so long that the guy ropes broke as they swung the scenery into place, the only surviving stage hands were so ancient that their palsied hands faltered at their tasks, and outraged rats ran startled along the footlight troughs during the performance. She had, incidentally, played to such huge and enthusiastic audiences that, by her unprecedented venture, she came home with a very considerable fortune . . .

Stand with me in the lobby of a West Coast theatre watching the line at the box office. One woman, puzzled by the price of the ticket, discovers only from the ticket seller himself that this is a cast of real flesh-and-blood actors who have come by train instead of by parcel post. At such a dazzling prospect, she is beside herself with excitement. She has never seen a real play before. Behind her in line is a small boy who wants to know how many bread coupons you must collect before you can get a ticket. I know not in what heathenish school of entertainment he has been brought up. Behind him a woman is hesitant because the seats offered her are so far forward. She is afraid the flicker will disturb her . . .

When you play seventy-four cities in a season, you can count on finding theatres in only a few of them, and some of those will be old opera houses so neglected that the star must give up her dream of hot water with which to remove her make-up, huddling as best she may in a community cubby-hole which has not been cleaned since last it was occupied by the late Sol Smith Russell. If no theatre is still left standing, she must dispossess a movie or make shift in a community hall or a high-school auditorium. In Oakland she must share the space with the local basketball team and, through the thin partition dividing the sheep from the goats, endure with what philosophy she can muster the pistol shots of the timekeeper on the other side of the dividing wall—strange, anachronistic gunfire sounding faintly through the swordplay which finishes Mercutio. In Memphis she must play in a temple built by a river captain who retired from the Mississippi, got religion and left as his memorial a huge auditorium which seats—in pews—a vastly profitable number of drama lovers, some of them so advantageously placed that by a little craning of their Tennessee necks they can see, over the top of the inadequate curtain, the hastily improvised dressing-room in which Robert Browning or Romeo is emerging shyly from his underclothes.

Such merely physical inconveniences lend a touch of salt to the eternal adventure of pitching one's booth in the market place, but there remains now in the path of any touring company one obstacle which only this generation has encountered. It is a commonplace that the celluloid drama has driven the flesh-and-blood companies from the one-night stands. But are you also aware that the local interests thus engaged are now stubbornly united in an instinctive conspiracy to keep such ancient rivals out of town?

Frankly, the movie houses do not welcome the advent of such a challenge as Katharine Cornell, and in one frustrated city, not a stone's throw from the Great Lakes, they pay the only feasible stage so much a month not to book any plays in the town at all. In a hundred American cities the local movie houses would not let a play be booked on any of their stages. I could name a dozen where they prevented Miss Cornell from playing in their town at all.

The viewpoint of the local management is reasonable enough. The petty lord of a movie house in which she might rear her scenery and play her play could make way for her easily enough and, with a little rehearsal, even teach its elegantly caparisoned ushers the lost art of seating an audience—the forgotten meaning of a reserved seat. But all his colleagues would regard him as a traitor to the common cause, and he himself, after he had collected his momentarily gratifying share of her enormous receipts, would discover that the neighbourhood must have been stinting itself to pay the exceptional price of her entertainment. At all events, he finds that, when he then books a film to follow her, his dependable clientele has spent all its money and his receipts for days to come are so lean that in the end he is no better off for her having passed that way.

Many of that troupe's experiences during the tour they will none of them ever want to forget. They will long remember, I suppose, the leisurely progress from Columbus to Louisville, some of the players making the jump by water, moving serenely down the Ohio, taking their ease in the rocking-chairs on the deck of perhaps the only river boat in the world which is captained by a woman. They will long remember the performance at Amarillo, where a sandstorm competed so successfully for the attention of the audience that in the tender colloquies between Elizabeth Barrett and Robert Browning neither could hear a word the other was saying and under the deafening cannonade upon the roof fell back upon the ancient art of dumb show.

And surely no one in that troupe will forget while he lives the Christmas they spent together in 1933. Christmas Eve—it was a Sunday, you remember—found them trundling through Montana. They were booked to begin a week's engagement in Seattle, and you may be sure that Mr McClintic had joined the troupe in St Paul to witness his great lady's triumph in his home town. All that Sunday there had been prodigious preparations in the purlieus of the dining car. The mere members of the public who were travelling on that train were notified to dine early, as the diner had been pre-empted from 8.30 on. Miss Cornell was giving a Christmas dinner for her company, the whole troupe—actors, electricians, everybody.

There was immense hilarity, with young Marchbanks from *Candida* cracking nuts for Juliet's nurse while Robert Browning and the hated Mr Barrett of Wimpole Street drank to each other's everlasting prosperity in thick railway tumblers of Christmas punch. But even as the last toasts were drunk and the troupe scattered to their berths with much wishing of Merry Christmas and quotations from Tiny Tim, the management was growing uneasy because of telegraphed reports that the December rains were making transit through the state of Washington slow, perilous and incalculable. It had already rained for three and twenty days and nights, and if it kept up much longer, they might have to make the rest of the trip in an ark and give their show, if at all, on the first convenient Ararat. At best, they would be later than they had hoped to be in reaching Seattle.

After they passed Spokane, it began to be doubtful whether they would get there at all. At every pause a telegram would come on board with anxious enquiries from the worried management ahead. The tickets had all been sold for the first performance. Even if the company could not arrive at the appointed time, would the management be justified in sending out word over the radio and catching the evening papers with an announcement that, however late, the troupe would at least arrive in time to give the performance at the scheduled hour? Then, as night fell, they were still proceeding at a snail's pace through rain-drenched darkness far from Seattle. The anxiety shifted to the question whether, even if the curtain could not be sent up as advertised, would they at least be there in time to make it worthwhile holding the audience fifteen minutes or half an hour? Seven o'clock, eight o'clock, nine o'clock passed, and still they crawled through the darkness, stopping even at one point while hastily mobilized bands of railroad workers flung up a new trestle, over which the train might creep breathless past the wreckage of one which had given way. By this time the company had given up hope. There could be no performance. This meant that, on the following Saturday night, one-eighth would be missing from each salary envelope. It is a rule of the theatre that such deductions can be made whenever a performance is called off through what is blasphemously known as an act of God. It was, therefore, a gloomy bunch of thespians who rode the last stretch, their noses glued to the streaming windowpanes as the train seemed to crawl over a bridge made of the very faces of the railroad workers who stood aside to let it pass, grim, rain-drenched Mongolian faces lit up in the darkness by the flare of acetylene torches, staring in cold frightening wonder at the perilous passage of these strangers whose necessity had brought them out to work in the night and the rain.

It was an exhausted and disgruntled troupe that finally climbed down on the platform in Seattle at eleven-fifteen p.m. They were just collecting their wits and their baggage when they were pounced upon and galvanized into immediate action by an astonishing piece of news. The audience was still waiting. All the best trucks in Seattle were assembled at the station to grab the scenery and costume trunks, and rush them to the theatre. Tarpaulins were stretched and a hundred umbrellas proffered to protect it as it was being put into the trucks and taken out at the other end.

A line of automobiles were waiting to carry the company to the stage door. At the theatre, or loitering in groups in the lobby of the Olympic Hotel across the street, twelve hundred people were still waiting. Most of them were in evening dress and some of them were sustaining themselves with light midnight snacks. They had waited so long. Would Miss Cornell still play for them? Would she?

But the company must have time to unpack their trunks, put on their make-up and get into the crinolines and gay, shapely pantaloons of 1855. They promised to do it in record time. Meanwhile it seemed a pity to ask that audience to wait any longer with no entertainment of any kind. So, for once in the history of the theatre, the curtain was rung up forthwith and that Seattle gathering, at midnight on Christmas Day, actually saw the stage being set and lighted, saw swing into place the walls of the Victorian prison in which the tyrant of Wimpole Street chained his frail and gifted Andromeda. Each feat of the stagehands received rounds of applause. As the windowed wall of Elizabeth Barrett's room fell into place before the distant canvas glimpses of Wimpole Street and the windows in turn were hung with the rich portieres and valances of yesteryear, the enthusiasm mounted. It grew as the trunks, in full view of the audience, were opened and the costumes doled out by the wardrobe mistress. The actors, in dripping raincoats and horn-rimmed spectacles, lined up like charity boys at a handout, each collecting his ecru pantaloons, his flowered waistcoat, his ruffled shirt and what not. There was a great round of applause for the one member of the troupe who was already in complete costume when he arrived at the theatre—Flush, the guileful and engaging cocker spaniel who has never missed a performance of *The Barretts of Wimpole Street* since the first one, in Detroit some years ago.

But the greatest interest of all, I think, attached to the mysterious and intricate process by which a stage is lighted, a carefully calculated crossplay of beams by which certain parts of the stage are bathed in radiance, and others, in which the action will be less important, are left in shadow. The focal point of *The Barretts of Wimpole Street* is the couch from which Robert Browning rescues the sleeping princess. As Elizabeth Barrett, Miss Cornell must spend the entire first act, probably the longest act in all dramatic literature, supine upon that couch, and it is a matter for

very careful calculation to have the lights which play upon it adjusted to the fraction of an inch. For this purpose, to the rapture of Seattle, Jimmy Vincent, the stage manager, stretched himself out and assumed, one after another, all the postures he knew Miss Cornell would later assume. As Mr Vincent is stocky and oriental in appearance, and as the visible gap between his trousers and his waistcoat widened horrifically with every languorous pose into which he tried to fling his arms and head, the effect was stupefying. Then the warning bell rang, the lights in the auditorium went down and the curtain fell, only to rise again with Miss Cornell at her post on the couch. The play was ready to begin.

It was five minutes past one in the morning. The entire troupe —scenery, costumes and all—had arrived in the town less than two hours before and already the curtain was rising, which is probably a record for all time. The excitement, the heady compliment paid by the audience in having waited at all, had acted like wine on the spirits of the troupe and they gave the kind of performance one hopes for on great occasions and never gets. But at the end of the first long act, Miss Cornell was visited by a kind of delayed fatigue. A postponed weariness took possession of her. She felt she must have something, anything, if she was to go on at all with what remained of the play. To Mr McClintic, hovering apprehensively in the offing, she merely said: 'Get me an egg', and rushed to her dressing-room.

Into the streets of Seattle at two o'clock in the morning rushed the faithful McClintic in quest of an egg. Nothing was open except a drug store and a lunch wagon, and the audience, in its long wait, had consumed every morsel of food in that part of town. There wasn't an egg to be had. The kitchens at the Olympic across the street were dark and inexorably locked. As a last desperate measure, McClintic began calling up such surviving citizens of Seattle as he had gone to school with years before. Finally one such appeal aroused someone. A sleepy voice asked who could be calling at such an hour in the morning. It was with some difficulty that he succeeded in identifying himself. 'You remember Guthrie, who used to live in such-and-such a street and used to go to school with you?' Oh, yes, and then what? 'Well,' the voice from the past faltered in its final task, 'can you let me have an egg?' Incidentally, she could and did.

It was a quarter of four in the morning when the final curtain fell. And that blessed audience, feeling, perhaps, that it was too late by this time to go to bed at all, stayed to give more curtain calls than the exhausted troupe had ever heard.

When the tour wound up in Brooklyn, on 23 June, Miss Kitty had played to more than half a million of her fellow countrymen. I suppose they will all remember her, but none, I am sure, more fondly than the faithful band in Seattle which, on the day after Christmas, waited until one in the morning for her first curtain to rise. They will ever have a welcoming round of applause to greet her entrance when she is an old, old actress playing the Nurse to the Juliet of some youngster as yet unthought of.

ALEXANDER WOOLLCOTT

The Secret of Miss Lillie's Success

The traditional comic formula is: Tell them what you're going to do; do it; then tell them you've done it. Miss Lillie's is: tell them what you might do; do something else; then deny having done it. Even the famous purchase of the double-damask dinner napkins embodies her basic theme: the utter futility of the English language. Nobody is a more devout anthologist of the whimpers, sighs, and twitters that the human race emits in its historic struggle against intelligibility. It is not surprising that she turns to French when delivering her demented salute to the home life of cats: '*Bonjour,* all the little kittens all over the world!' When someone in another number fails to understand a question, she tries German, brusquely demanding: '*Sprechen Sie Deutsch?*' And once, into a Cockney sketch already obscured by her inability to speak Cockney, she inserted a sudden moan of Italian. If ever a monument is erected to her, it should be modelled on the Tower of Babel. She is like Eliza Doolittle at Mrs Higgins' tea party in *Pygmalion,* using what seems to her perfectly acceptable verbal coinage but to everyone else counterfeit gibberish. In certain moods she becomes quite convinced that she is an authority on

153

bird talk. Coward once wrote for her a comic folk song that contained the line: 'And the robin sings ho! on the bough.' Every time she reached it she would pause. 'The robin', she would firmly declare, 'does *not* say ho.'

In 1954, on a trip to Japan, she visited the Kabuki Theatre and was fascinated by what she saw: the colour, the weirdness, and the elaborate stylization. The idea of using Kabuki technique in a sketch at once took hold of her mind, and she was not in the least perturbed when someone pointed out that British audiences (for whom the sketch was intended) might be slightly befuddled by a parody of something they had never seen. Following instinct, she devised a number called 'Kabuki Lil'. When it was still in the formative stage, by which I mean a condition of nightmarish inconsequence, she described it to me:

'These Kabuki plays, you see, they go on for six months with only one intermission. All the women are men, *of course*, and they're simply furious most of the time, waving swords round their heads and *hissing* at each other. They take off their boots when they come on, and kneel down on cushions. There's a lot of work done with cushions, so I shall have cushions too. And they play some kind of musical instrument that goes right round the back of my neck, only one string, but I expect I shall manage. I don't think I shall say a word of English—after all, *they* don't — but I wish I could get hold of one of those terrific rostrums they have in Tokyo that sail right down the aisle and out of the theatre. I think they have rollers underneath them, or perhaps it's men? Anyway, I think I've got the spirit of the thing . . .'

Something was dimly taking shape in the chaos of her mind,

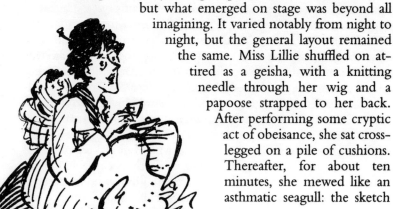

but what emerged on stage was beyond all imagining. It varied notably from night to night, but the general layout remained the same. Miss Lillie shuffled on attired as a geisha, with a knitting needle through her wig and a papoose strapped to her back. After performing some cryptic act of obeisance, she sat cross-legged on a pile of cushions. Thereafter, for about ten minutes, she mewed like an asthmatic seagull: the sketch contained not one recognizable word. Tea was served at one point, and the star produced from her sleeve a tiny bottle of Gordon's gin with which to spike it. From time to time she would grasp a hammer and savagely bang a gong, whereupon music would sound, jittery and Oriental. This seemed to placate her, until the sixth bang, which evoked from the wings a sudden, deafening amplified blast of 'Three Coins in the Fountain', sung by Frank Sinatra.

KENNETH TYNAN

Cross-Dressing

You'll *never* guess what happened next. Well, almost next, after an up and a down or three. I became a sort of paid, professional transvestite. I learned how to knot a bow tie, wear a top hat, wrestle with dress studs, swing a cane. I could toy with a cigarette like Gerald du Maurier and ogle a girl like Gilbert the Filbert, the King of the Knuts.

I was known, in fact, as the best-dressed man in London, and thereby hangs a tail that we'll get to in a minute. But beneath the starched shirt front there beat a heart emerald green in its innocence. I scarcely knew anything about *anything*, let alone the ways of the theaytah. After all, I was a *concert* artiste.

I was appearing in *A to Z* with Jack Buchanan, a tall, debonair Scot, who was making his London debut. He'd never had a singing or a dancing lesson, but with his smoky-grey eyes and dark brown wavy hair, with a look of wearing evening clothes as though he'd been poured into them, he went on to become a worldwide idol of the stage and cinema.

Backstage, I was still classified as a girl even if I hardly ever got into a skirt. We girls had dressing-rooms on one side of the theatre—the Prince of Wales's—while the men were accommodated on the other.

Jack used to kid me about my being a girl hero, decked out in tails or flannel slacks (tennis anyone?) or whatever costume was called for. 'Tell me, Beattie,' he said one day, 'how do you dress, left or right?'

I hadn't a clue to what he was talking about, not the glimmer of an idea about the meaning of the twinkle in his eyes. I still thought *flies* were something you swatted.

'Come on, Beattie. Don't be shy. On which side do you *dress*?'

Suddenly, the light dawned, or so I thought.

'Oh, yes,' I answered. 'In Number Five. Stage left.'

Jack roared with laughter; thought I was brilliant.

BEATRICE LILLIE

Isadora Duncan

Arrived at the studio we sat and drank beer, because, as Isadora remarked, there was no champagne. And, she added, one *must* drink something. Then, remembering how little I drank myself, she said:

'Though of course you and Mr Selfridge never touch wine. I can't understand it. Life only gives one glimpses of ephemeral joy, and these through love, or art, or wine.'

Isadora talked always of Mr Selfridge as she talked of Mussolini. She had met him on several occasions. Personally she liked him. But in the abstract he was her enemy. He was included in her attack on millionaires.

'Millionaires don't do anything for beauty,' she would cry. 'I ask them for a few paltry thousands for my school, and they say they have nothing to give.'

Once she told me that she would be able to run Mr Selfridge's store for him, on her own lines. I laughed. But she was serious. Recently I sat opposite Mr Selfridge in his palatial office at the very top of the still more palatial building his genius has brought into being.

'Could Isadora have helped you to run your business?' I asked him.

Mr Selfridge removed his pince-nez, shook his head.

'I admired Miss Duncan,' he said. 'I admired her great intellect. I found her conversation most interesting. But she was an artist, with all the eccentricities of an artist. I could have found no place for her in my store.'

Leaving Mr Selfridge after this interview I had the impression that he was a very tired man. Beneath the spotless perfection of his city clothes he appeared weary. As weary as Isadora herself had been. Neither of them had seemed to me to be happy. Probably Mr Selfridge is less happy than the hundreds of clerks in his store. Certainly Isadora, except when she was dancing or heard music, was more miserable than any little dancer in the back row of the ballet.

Putting down the glass out of which she had been slowly sipping her beer, Isadora suddenly decided to entertain me with an imprompru burlesque. In precisely the deferential tone of a 'society' entertainer, she said, as she walked to the middle of the room:

'Just a few impersonations. With your kind permission I will first endeavour . . .'

Then, to my utter surprise, she began to impersonate the Theory of Isadora Duncan. Several times before I had seen people, without sufficient knowledge to appreciate Isadora's art, caricature it; but never had I watched such a brilliant travesty of it as now. Nobody, except possibly Ruth Draper, could have been so completely a *diseuse* as Isadora was then, and the satire of herself might have been written by Noel Coward, so devastatingly true was every word of it.

Without warning Isadora turned herself into a conscientious mistress in one of the many schools of dancing, which, since her own first school began, have sprung up all over the world. Before her one imagined a class of ambitious, if unsuitable, girls whose fond parents were all anxious for them to learn the beauty of movement.

'Girls,' cried this teacher archly, 'I want you all to remember the words of the great Isadora. Remember, Isadora says: "Dance the sky, dance the air, dance the sea." Now, girls, I want you all, with me, to dance the sky, and the air, and the sea. Ready girls . . . ?'

Isadora then quickly became one of the 'girls' in question. How she accomplished this illusion, I do not know. Simply, I suppose, she had the art of the *diseuse* at her fingertips. For immediately there stood in the teacher's place a plump and sullen schoolgirl of eighteen. Actually a heavy-footed schoolgirl, on whose pink suety face one could count the pimples of adolescence.

This girl, with comic results, did her best to follow the teacher's instructions. While endeavouring to 'dance the air' she succeeded only in convincing the spectator that her poor feet were eternally clamped to the ground.

'*Poise*, Isadora says *poise*'—the teacher's voice, returning for a moment, cried—and watching the poise of the unfortunate girl, who reminded one of the children trying to fly in *Peter Pan*, my eyes filled with the tears of laughter. While her arms made fruitless efforts to raise her large body towards the ceiling, her feet buried themselves in the ground; and her determined expression suggested, especially about the lines of her mouth, that of a harassed goldfish. It was convulsively amusing.

'Antics like those I've just performed', said Isadora, returning, and drinking the beer left in her glass, 'are being made by schoolgirls all over the world, every day. And *I'm* blamed for it. No wonder my methods are laughed at, caricatured. But schools like these are just burlesques of my ideas. That's what I want to put right. The women who run these institutions on the shadows of my inspiration are artistic frauds. I'm told that in America there is now a woman calling herself the Crimson Mother, who supervises one of these schools. She appears each morning, just for a few moments, from behind curtains, and addresses her disciples, using a distortion of my own ideas. For that she receives an enormous income. I'm penniless. Nobody will listen to me. I started the revival of classical dancing, but now the whole thing has grown beyond me, in a hopelessly wrong direction. I feel sometimes that my art has been wasted . . .'

SEWELL STOKES

Ellen Terry in 'Macbeth'

Her appearance was magnificent: long plaits of deep red hair fell from under a purple veil over a robe of green upon which iridescent wings of beetles glittered like emeralds, and a great wine-coloured cloak, gold embroidered, swept from her shoulders.

The effect was barbaric and exactly right, though whence the wife of an ancient Scottish chieftain obtained so many oriental beetles' wings was not explained, and I remember Oscar Wilde remarking, 'Judging from the banquet, Lady Macbeth seems an economical housekeeper and evidently patronizes local industries for her husband's clothes and the servants' liveries, but she takes care to do all her own shopping in Byzantium.'

W. GRAHAM-ROBERTSON

Gwladys the Actress-Penguin

Gwladys was a *rara avis* in the true sense, for she was an actress-penguin. She had starred in a film called *To Brighton with a Bird* and it was in a film studio I had first met her, and her owner. A few months previously I had met the owner casually in the street, who expressed to me her concern at finding a home for Gwladys for two weeks whilst she went away. Gwladys hated other penguins, preferring human company, therefore a zoo was out of the question. On the spur of the moment I said I would look after her. The fish should have warned me, but having been in hospital had put it right out of my mind.

Brian's★ large enquiring eyes opened even wider when I brought Gwladys into the kitchen in my arms. He sipped his gin and said:

'I do hope, you wicked girl, you're not going to behave like your namesake Empress Theodora did with the geese!'

Gwladys wriggled when she smelt the fish, so I put her on the floor. She waddled over to the open barrel and very rapidly swallowed down several large fish.

'It'll choke,' said Peter.† 'Heavens, it's already eaten as much as I could and it's only a fraction of my size.'

They were both fascinated by the behaviour and appearance of this comical bird, although neither of them would have admitted it. Peter had put his glass on top of the unopened barrel and, after the fish, Gwladys walked over to it; in a flash the beak was in and the gin gone. She looked up at us, turned round and walked, unsteadily it seemed, out of the room. We followed her along the corridor, as unerringly she went into the bathroom, hoisted herself up on to the side of the bath and tugged at the tap with her beak. As the water gushed out she chortled, rolled and splashed about with ecstasy. Brian turned to Peter and said:

'Fancy having a mistress with a gin-drinking penguin. It's going to cost you something, my dear.'

It was a tumultuous two weeks for there were many times when, as Peter remarked, the flat looked like a second-rate lagoon. The gin (what little there was) had to be kept under lock and key as it was often broached; the bathroom door locked, for once we came back to find the place awash, the floors intricately patterned with wet webbed footmarks. There was but little painting or commercial travelling done, for she was a full-time job. Nevertheless it was worth it when she sat on my lap in the evening,

★ Brian Howard † Peter Rose

her beak nestled under my ear as I read my book. Peter liked the surrealist 'mother and child' effect, saying that it almost made him want to take photographs again, had he possessed a camera.

THEODORA FITZGIBBON

How to Name a Dog

Every few months somebody writes me and asks if I will give him a name for his dog. Several of these correspondents in the past year have wanted to know if I would mind the use of my own name for their spaniels. Spaniel owners seem to have the notion that a person could sue for invasion of privacy or defamation of character if his name is applied to a cocker without written permission, and one gentleman even insisted that we conduct our correspondence in the matter through a notary public. I have a way of letting communications of this sort fall behind my roll-top desk, but it has recently occurred to me that this is an act of evasion, if not, indeed, of plain cowardice. I have therefore decided to come straight out with the simple truth that it is as hard for me to think up a name for a dog as it is for anybody else. The idea that I was an expert in the business is probably the outcome of a piece I wrote several years ago, incautiously revealing the fact that I have owned forty or more dogs in my life. This is true, but it is also deceptive. All but five or six of my dogs were disposed of when they were puppies, and I had not gone to the trouble of giving to these impermanent residents of my house any names at all except Hey, You! and Cut That Out! and Let Go!

Names of dogs end up in 176th place in the list of things that amaze and fascinate me. Canine cognomens should be designed to impinge on the ears of the dogs and not to amuse neighbours, tradespeople, and casual visitors. I remember a few dogs from the past with a faint but lingering pleasure: a farm hound named Rain, a roving Airedale named Marco Polo, a female bull terrier known as Stephanie Brody because she liked to jump from moving motorcars and second-storey windows, and a Peke

161

called Darien; but that's about all. The only animals whose naming demands concentration, hard work, and ingenuity are the seeing-eye dogs. They have to be given unusual names because passers-by like to call to seeing-eyers—'Here, Sport', or 'Yuh, Rags', or 'Don't take any wooden nickels, Rin Tin Tin'. A blind man's dog with an ordinary name would continually be distracted from its work. A tyro at naming these dogs might make the mistake of picking Durocher of Teeftallow. The former is too much like Rover and the latter could easily sound like 'Here, fellow' to a dog.

Speaking of puppies, as I was a while back, I feel that I should warn inexperienced dog owners who have discovered to their surprise and dismay a dozen puppies in a hall closet or under the floors of the barn, not to give them away. Sell them or keep them, but don't give them away. Sixty per cent of persons who are given a dog for nothing bring him back sooner or later and plump him into the reluctant and unprepared lap of his former owner. The people say that they are going to Florida and can't take the dog, or that he doesn't want to go; or they point out that he eats first editions or lace curtains or spinets, or that he doesn't see eye to eye with them in the matter of housebreaking, or that he makes disparaging remarks under his breath about their friends. Anyway, they bring him back and you are stuck with him—and maybe six others. But if you charge ten or even five dollars for pups, the new owners don't dare return them. They are afraid to ask for their money back because they believe you might think they are hard up and need the five or ten dollars. Furthermore, when a mischievous puppy is returned to its former owner it invariably behaves beautifully, and the person who brought it back is likely to be regarded as an imbecile or a dog hater or both.

Names of dogs, to get back to our subject, have a range almost as wide as that of the violin. They run from such plain and simple names as Spot, Sport, Rex, Brownie, and Rover—all originated by small boys—to such effete and fancy appellations as Prince Rudolph Hertenberg Gratzheim of Darndorf-Putzelhorst, and Darling Mist o' Love III of Heather-Light-Holyrood—names originated by adults, all of whom in every other way, I am told, have made a normal adjustment to life. In addition to the plain and the fancy categories, there are the Cynical and the Coy. Cynical names are given by people who do not like dogs too much. The most popular cynical names during the war were Mussolini, Tojo, and Adolf. I never have been able to get very far in my exploration of the minds of people who call their dogs Mussolini, Tojo, and Adolf, and I suspect the reason is that I am unable to associate with them long enough to examine what goes on in their heads. I nod, and I tell them the time of day, if they ask, and that is all. I never vote for them or ask them to have a drink. The great Coy category is perhaps the largest. The Coy people call their pets Bubbles and Boggles and Sparkles and Twinkles and Doodles and Puffy and Lovums and Sweetums and Itsy-Bitsy and Betsy-Bye-Bye and Sugarkins. I pass these dog owners at a dog-trot, wearing a horrible fixed grin.

There is a special subdivision of the Coys that is not quite so awful, but awful enough. These people, whom we will call the Wits, own two dogs, which they name Pitter and Patter, Willy and Nilly, Helter and Skelter, Namby and Pamby, Hugger and Mugger, Hokery and Pokery, and even Wishy and Washy, Ups and Daisy, Fitz and Startz, Fetch and Carrie, and Pro and Connie. Then there is the Cryptic category. These people select names for some private reason or for no reason at all—except perhaps to arouse the visitor's curiosity, so that he will exclaim, 'Why in the world do you call your dog *that*?' The Cryptics name their dogs October, Bennett's Aunt, Three Fifteen, Doc Knows, Tuesday, Home Fried, Opus 38, Ask Leslie, and Thanks for the Home Run, Emil. I make it a point simply to pat these unfortunate dogs on the head, ask no questions of their owners, and go about my business.

This article has degenerated into a piece that properly should be entitled 'How Not to Name a Dog'. I was afraid it would. It seems only fair to make up for this by confessing a few of the names I have given my own dogs, with the considerable help, if not, indeed, the insistence, of their mistress. Most of my dogs have been females, and they have answered, with apparent gladness, to such names as Jeannie, Tessa, Julie, and Sophie. Sophie is a black French poodle whose kennel name was Christabel, but she never answered to Christabel, which she considers as foolish a name for a dog as Pamela, Jennifer, Clarissa, Jacqueline, Guinevere, and Shelmerdine. Sophie is opposed, and I am also, to Ida, Cora, Blanche, and Myrtle.

About six years ago, when I was looking for a house to buy in Connecticut, I knocked on the front door of an attractive home whose owner, my real estate agent had told me, wanted to sell it and go back to Iowa to live. The lady agent who escorted me around had informed me that the owner of this place was a man named Strong, but a few minutes after arriving at the house, I was having a drink in the living-room with Phil Stong, for it was he. We went out into the yard after a while and I saw Mr Stong's spaniel. I called to the dog and snapped my fingers but he seemed curiously embarrassed, like his master. 'What's his name?' I asked the latter. He was cornered and there was no way out of it. 'Thurber,' he said, in a small frightened voice. Thurber and I shook hands, and he didn't seem to me any more depressed than any other spaniel I have met. He had, however, the expression of a bachelor on his way to a party he has tried in vain to get out of, and I think it must have been this cast of countenance that had reminded Mr Stong of the dog I draw. The dog I draw is, to be sure, much larger than a spaniel and not so shaggy, but I confess, though I am not a spaniel man, that there are certain basic resemblances between my dog and all other dogs with long ears and troubled eyes.

The late Hendrik Van Loon was privy to the secret that the dog of my drawings was originally intended to look more like a bloodhound than anything else, but that he turned up by accident with legs too short to be an authentic member of this breed. This flaw was brought about by the fact that the dog was first drawn on a telephone memo pad which was not large enough to accommodate him. Mr Van Loon laboured under the unfortunate delusion that an actual bloodhound would fit as unobstrusively into the Van Loon living-room as the drawn dog does in the pictures. He learned his mistake in a few weeks. He discovered that an actual bloodhound regards a residence as a series of men's rooms and that it is interested only in tracing things. Once, when Mr Van Loon had been wandering around his yard for an hour or more, he called to his bloodhound and was dismayed when, instead of coming directly to him, the dog proceeded to follow every criss-cross of the maze its master had made in wandering about. 'That dog didn't care a damn about where I was,' Mr Van Loon told me. 'All he was interested in was how I got there.'

Perhaps I should suggest at least one name for a dog, if only to justify the title of this piece. All right, then, what's the matter with Stong? It's a good name for a dog, short, firm, and effective.

I recommend it to all those who have written to me for suggestions and to all those who may be at this very moment turning over in their minds the idea of asking my advice in this difficult and perplexing field of nomenclature.

JAMES THURBER

Our Cat

Our cat is growing positively tyrannical. If she finds herself alone anywhere she emits bloodcurdling yells until somebody comes running. She sleeps on a table in the service porch and now demands to be lifted up and down from it. She gets warm milk about eight o'clock at night and starts yelling for it about seven-thirty. When she gets it she drinks a little, goes off and sits under a chair, then comes and yells all over again for someone to stand beside her while she has another go at the milk. When we have company she looks them over and decides almost instantly if she likes them. If she does she strolls over and plops down on the floor just far enough away to make it a chore to pet her. If she doesn't like them she sits in the middle of the living-room, casts a contemptuous glance around, and proceeds to wash her backside.

In the middle of this engaging performance she will stop dead, lift her head without any other change of position (one leg pointing straight at the ceiling), stares off into space while thinking out some abstruse problem, then resumes her rear-end-job. This work is always done in the most public manner. When she was younger she always celebrated the departure of visitors by tearing wildly through the house and ending up with a good claw on the davenport, the one that is covered with brocatelle and makes superb clawing, and it comes off in strips. But she is lazy now. Won't even play with her catnip mouse unless it is dangled in such a position that she can play with it lying down. I'm going to send you her picture. It has me in it, but you'll have to overlook that. I believe I told you how she used to catch all sorts of very breakable living things and bring them in the house quite unhurt as a rule. I'm sure she never hurt them intentionally. Cats are very interesting. They have a terrific sense of humor and, unlike dogs, cannot be embarrassed or humiliated by being laughed at. There is nothing in nature worse than seeing a cat trying to provoke a few more hopeless attempts to escape out of a half-dead mouse. My enormous respect for our cat is largely based on a complete lack in her of this diabolical sadism. When she used to catch mice—we haven't had any for years—she brought them alive and undamaged and let me take them out of her mouth. Her attitude seemed to be, 'Well, here's this damn mouse. Had to catch it, but it's really your problem. Remove it at once.' Periodically she goes through all the closets and cupboards on a regular mouse-inspection. Never finds any, but she realizes it's part of her job.

RAYMOND CHANDLER

Titty Bitty Little Kitty

To return to Lady Cunard, one evening a group of us were sitting on the piazza in Venice, including her and Sir Thomas Beecham. Sir Thomas was holding forth on the amount of mangy cats to be found in the streets of that city. He said that they should all be exterminated. Suddenly he was interrupted by a young American, whom no one knew, who had joined our table. He, in a falsetto voice, said: 'Do you mean, Sir Thomas, that if you saw a little titty bitty, little kitty drowning in the Grand Canal you wouldn't jump in and save it?' Sir Thomas, scarlet in the face, said: 'Young man, if I saw a titty bitty little kitty . . .' He got no further as Emerald, putting up her lorgnette, said: 'Oh my dear, who asked this young man on to the piazza?'

DAVID HERBERT

How Long, O Lord? . . .

And God said unto Noah, Make thee an ark of gopher wood; rooms shalt thou make in the ark, and the length of the ark shall be 300 cubits.

And of every living thing of all flesh, two of every sort shalt thou bring into the ark, to keep them alive with thee.

And Noah said, Sign here, and leavest Thou a deposit.

And the Lord signed here, and left a deposit.

And Noah was 600 years old when the flood of waters was upon the Earth.

And the Lord said unto Noah, Where is the ark, which I commanded thee to build?

And Noah said unto the Lord, Verily, I have had three carpenters off ill.

The gopher-wood supplier hath let me down—yea, even though the gopher wood hath been on order for nigh upon twelve months. The damp-course specialist hath not turned up. What can I do, O Lord?

And God said unto Noah, I want that ark finished even after seven days and seven nights.

And Noah said, It will be so.

And it was not so.

And the Lord said unto Noah, What seemeth to be the trouble this time?

And Noah said unto the Lord, Mine subcontractor hath gone bankrupt. The pitch which Thou commandest me to put on the outside and on the inside of the ark hath not arrived. The plumber hath gone on strike.

Noah rent his garments and said, The glazier departeth on holiday in Majorca—yea, even though I offerest him double time. Shem, my son, who helpeth me on the ark side of the business, hath formed a pop group with his brothers Ham and Japeth. Lord, I am undone.

And God said in his wrath, Noah, do not thou mucketh Me about.

The end of all flesh is come before me; for Earth is filled with violence through them; and behold, I will destroy them with the Earth. Art thou incapable of completing the job that thou was contracted to do?

And Noah said, Lo, the contract will be fulfilled.

And lo, it was not fulfilled.

And Noah said unto the Lord, The gopher wood is definitely in the warehouse. Verily, and the gopher-wood supplier waiteth only upon his servant to find the invoices before he delivereth the gopher wood unto me.

And the Lord grew angry and said, Scrubbeth thou round the gopher wood. What about the animals?

Of fowls after their kind and of cattle after their kind, of every sort have I ordered to come unto thee, to keep them alive.

Where, for example, are the giraffes?

And Noah said unto the Lord, They are expected today.

And the Lord said unto Noah, And where are the clean beasts, the male and the female, to keep their seed alive upon the face of all the Earth?

And Noah said, The van cometh on Tuesday; yea and yea it will be so.

And the Lord said unto Noah, How about the unicorns?

And Noah wrung his hands and wept, saying, Lord, Lord, they are a discontinued line. Thou canst not get unicorns for love nor money.

And God said, Come thou, Noah, I have left with thee a deposit, and thou hast signed a contract.

Where are the monkeys, and the bears, and the hippopotami, and the elephants, and the zebras and the hartebeests, two of each kind; and, of fowls also of the air by sevens, the male and the female?

And Noah said unto the Lord, They have been delivered unto the wrong address, but should arriveth on Friday, all save the fowls of the air by sevens, for it hath just been told unto me that fowls of the air are sold in half-dozens.

And God said unto Noah, Thou hast not made an ark of gopher wood, nor hast thou lined it with pitch within and without; and of every living thing of all flesh, two of every sort hast thou failed to bring into the ark. What sayest thou, Noah?

And Noah kissed the Earth and said, Lord, Lord, thou knowest in thy wisdom what it is like with delivery dates.

And the Lord in his wisdom said, Noah, my son, I knowest. Why else dost thou think I have caused a flood to descend upon the Earth?

KEITH WATERHOUSE

How an Old Geyser Fell on Hard Times

An elderly widowed lady of whom I am rather fond was notified some time ago that she was about to undergo the full horrors of conversion to Natural Gas. Resigning herself to a future of uncontrollably fluctuating gas-pressures, burnt saucepans and higher bills, she awaited the coming of the converters. The day dawned. Two men came; they converted her stove, her kitchen water-heater, her refrigerator and her gas fires. She also has, however, in her bathroom, a geyser of ancient design and dilapidated condition (I suppose we had better pause here for the one that goes 'Mornin' lady; 'ave you got an old geyser 'ere what won't work?'—'Yes, 'e's just gone down to the Labour Exchange to draw the dole'), but which—mark these words, and mark them well—has operated adequately and served her well.

Obstinate in its faith, the geyser resisted conversion. The two gas men explained that it needed a device that they did not have with them, but which they would bring; meanwhile, the geyser was out of action. The lady bore her bathless state with as much fortitude as she could muster, and awaited their return.

They did not return, of course. Nor, of course, did she hear from anybody at all on the subject. So she telephoned the office from which the men had come; they had left a form with its address and telephone number. (It was the Conversion Report Centre, Oakington Road, London W9, telephone 349 3171, and I put these details in so that whoever is in what is laughably

known as charge shall know exactly where the finger is pointing.) She explained that she had now been without a bath for a
week, that a promise had been made and broken, and what was
going to be done about it? The reply was that action would be
taken. About a week later (nobody, of course, had told her anything at all in the interim) two more men turned up. They, too,
tinkered with the geyser; they, too, said that it needed an extra
device that they had not got with them; they, too, said that they
would return with it; they, too, of course, did no such thing.
Nor, of course, did anybody at all get in touch with her.

The lady in question, I will have you know, likes to bath regularly and often; moreover, she is not accustomed, or for that
matter able, to take a bath in a kettle. So when another week had
gone by, she telephoned the Gas Board. The office for the district in which she lives is North Thames Gas Board Area 5,
telephone number 328 1717, address not given in the telephone
book (I suppose they are afraid of violence from their customers,
and well they might be). An official of the Gas Board came round
(she cannot remember how long after her call, though she doubts
if it was immediately, and so, by God, do I); he explained that the
Gas Board and the conversion programme are independently run
(if 'run' is the right word, and my own opinion is that it is most
emphatically not the right word), but that he would inspect
the geyser. He did so, told her that he knew exactly what was
needed, and left with the memorable words, 'Leave it to me, Mrs
Levin.' The reason he addressed her thus was that Levin is her
name, and this seems as good a moment as any to reveal that the
fact that it is the same name as mine is not a coincidence; she is
my mother.

She did indeed leave it to him; she is a patient and trusting
soul, and—rather more to the point—she had no option. He
did not return, of course; nor, of course, did anybody get in
touch with her. So she rang the Gas Board again. She was assured
that action would be taken. It was: another man arrived (this
made six she had actually seen, plus several more she had spoken
to on the telephone). Had he, she asked, brought the necessary
device? 'I have brought nothing,' he replied with candour; nor
had he. (He also explained that he knew nothing of any extra
and needed part.) He would, however, go back to the office and
report the situation. He went; that was on Monday. Not long
after he left an official (female) telephoned from the Gas Board to

ask if he had been. Yes, said my mother, grinding her teeth, he had; but he had not brought the magic device, and had therefore gone away. In that case, said the official, I will see what the situation is, and ring you back and let you know. She didn't, of course, and at the time of writing this (Wednesday afternoon), my mother had heard nothing more from anybody.

I now want three things to happen. First, I want my mother's bathroom water-heater fixed, and at once. Second, I want a written apology to my mother to be sent from both the Natural Gas Conversion office and from the Gas Board.

That will satisfy my mother. But I also want a third thing on my own behalf; or rather, on behalf of the public in general, who have to put up with the kind of behaviour I have just described. I want a public answer to this question: what is wrong with a national organization which gives its customers not the service they pay for but, instead, incompetence and a string of broken promises?

Later:
The nation, I gather, is agog to know whether my mother is clean. This is not, I take it, a matter into which a well-bred nation would normally seek to enquire. But since I sang the saga of my mother's bathroom water-heater and the North Thames Gas Board, recounting how she was without hot water from her geyser for over three weeks, its normally copious supply being replaced only by a flow of broken promises from officials of the North Thames Gas Board, I have had virtually uncountable numbers of letters wishing to know whether my words have had the desired results.

All in good time. But first, about those letters in general. To begin with, their number exceeded, by a very considerable margin, those I have received on any single topic arising out of this column since I began writing it two and a half years ago. Next, in the overwhelming majority, the writer recounted experiences, at the hands of the North Thames Gas Board, that were undoubtedly at least as bad as, and in a substantial number of cases very much worse than, those undergone by my mother. Finally, the pattern of behaviour on the part of the North Thames Gas Board was the same in almost all the accounts: promises of action unfulfilled, and no coordination whatever between any two people in that organization, so that the men who supposedly come to fit a part which a previous visitor has declared necessary and promised will be sent, come without either the part or any knowledge of a previous visit or the conclusions formed by the previous visitor. (My mother had four sets of such visitors: one correspondent had nineteen.) Several sufferers, incidentally, seeing the advantage of being my mother, offered to adopt me; one asked if I would adopt *her*.

I am also informed by *The Times* Business News that the subject on which they regularly receive the largest number of letters is the North Thames Gas Board and its incompetence, though incompetence, to judge by my postbag on the subject, is too mild a word; the organization seems to be putrescent from top to bottom, its officials leaving letters unanswered, phone calls ignored, and customers offered nothing but false assurances of action.

Which brings me to the question of my mother and her bath. The first conclusion to be drawn from the affair is that top officials of the North Thames Gas Board read *The Times*. Not long after breakfast on the morning the article appeared, my mother's flat was filled from wall to wall with North Thames officials—eventually, at least seven. There were engineers, and fitters, and executives, and one man who, from my mother's account, appears to have been the apologizer. Anyway, just as the place was about to collapse from the weight of Gas Board men (some of them even arrived from outside, by ladder) they finished the job and left. My mother, exhausted by the weeks of battle, and no doubt in addition emotionally drained by the abrupt discovery that she was the owner of the most famous bathroom geyser in the world, immediately went away on holiday, pausing only to take a bath.

When she returned (she got her written apology, incidentally) she found that North Thames had, while doing the work, apparently installed a fascinating and novel system. Whenever she takes a bath, and much of the time now even when she does not, water pours out of the ceiling in the room next door. This, of course, enables her to offer a visitor, in addition to tea and cakes, an informal shower in the kitchen, but she cannot help feeling that the degree of informality in the arrangement is excessive, and the bucket she puts underneath does tend to fill rather quickly, besides adding little if anything to the kitchen's appearance. ('It seems', she says—she is a woman long accustomed to seeing into the heart of a problem—'that they must have knocked a hole in something.') Unless the Gas Board, feeling that it has done its final duty by the tribe of Levin, has now given up *The Times*, perhaps any senior official reading this might care to indicate to his colleagues that something in the nature of a return to square one is urgently needed.

BERNARD LEVIN

Sailing to America

We have eighty-six passengers; and such a strange collection of beasts never was got together upon the sea, since the days of the Ark. I have never been in the saloon since the first day; the noise, the smell, and the closeness being quite intolerable. I have only been on deck *once!*—and then I was surprised and disappointed at the smallness of the panorama. The sea, running as it does and has done, is very stupendous, and viewed from the air or some great height would be grand no doubt. But seen from the wet and rolling decks, in this weather and these circumstances, it only impresses one giddily and painfully. I was very glad to turn away, and come below again.

I have established myself, from the first, in the ladies' cabin—you remember it? I'll describe its other occupants, and our way of passing the time, to you.

First, for the occupants. Kate, and I, and Anne—when she is out of bed, which is not often. A queer little Scotch body, a Mrs P——,whose husband is a silversmith in New York. He married her at Glasgow three years ago, and bolted the day after the wedding; being (which he had not told her) heavily in debt. Since then she has been living with her mother; and she is now going out under the protection of a male cousin, to give him a year's

173

trial. If she is not comfortable at the expiration of that time, she means to go back to Scotland again. A Mrs B——, about twenty years old, whose husband is on board with her. He is a young Englishman domiciled in New York, and by trade (as well as I can make out) a woollen-draper. They have been married a fortnight. A Mr and Mrs C——, marvellously fond of each other, complete the catalogue. Mrs C——, I have settled, is a publican's daughter, and Mr C——is running away with her, the till, the time-piece off the bar mantelshelf, the mother's gold watch from the pocket at the head of the bed; and other miscellaneous property. The women are all pretty; unusually pretty. I never saw such good faces together, anywhere . . .

As for news, we have more of that than you would think for. One man lost fourteen pounds at vingt-un in the saloon yesterday, or another got drunk before dinner was over, or another was blinded with lobster sauce spilt over him by the steward, or another had a fall on deck and fainted. The ship's cook was drunk yesterday morning (having got at some salt-water-damaged whiskey), and the captain ordered the boatswain to play upon him with the hose of the fire engine until he roared for mercy—which he didn't get; for he was sentenced to look out, for four hours at a stretch for four nights running, without a great coat, and to have his grog stopped. Four dozen plates were broken at dinner. One steward fell down the cabin stairs with a round of beef, and injured his foot severely. Another steward fell down after him, and cut his eye open. The baker's taken ill: so is the pastry-cook. A new man, sick to death, has been required to fill the place of the latter officer, and has been dragged out of bed and propped up in a little house upon deck, between two casks, and ordered (the captain standing over him) to make and roll out pie-crust; which he protests, with tears in his eyes, it is death to him in his bilious state to look at. Twelve dozen of bottled porter has got loose upon deck, and the bottles are rolling about distractedly, overhead. Lord Mulgrave (a handsome fellow, by the bye, to look at, and nothing but a good 'un to go) laid a wager with twenty-five other men last night, whose berths, like his, are in the fore-cabin, which can only be got at by crossing the deck, that he would reach his cabin first. Watches were set by the captain's, and they sallied forth, wrapped up in coats and storm caps. The sea broke over the ship so violently, that they were *five-and-twenty minutes* holding on by the handrail at the starboard paddle-box, drenched to the skin by every wave, and not daring to go on or come back, lest they should be washed overboard. News! A dozen murders in town wouldn't interest us half as much.

CHARLES DICKENS

A Deception

You may remember that I lectured lately for the young gentlemen of the Clayonian Society? During the afternoon of that day I was talking with one of the young gentlemen referred to, and he said he had an uncle who, from some cause or other, seemed to have grown permanently bereft of all emotion. And with tears in his eyes this young man said:

'Oh, if I could only see him laugh once more! Oh, if I could only see him weep!'

I was touched. I could never withstand distress. I said:

'Bring him to my lecture. I'll start him for you.'

'Oh, if you could but do it! If you could but do it, all our family would bless you for evermore; for he is very dear to us. Oh, my benefactor, can you make him laugh? Can you bring soothing tears to those parched orbs?'

I was profoundly moved. I said:

'My son, bring the old party round. I have got some jokes in my lecture that will make him laugh, if there is any laugh in him; and, if they miss fire, I have got some others that'll make him cry or kill him, one or the other.'

Then the young man wept on my neck, and presently spread both hands on my head and looked up towards heaven, mumbling something reverently; and then he went after his uncle. He placed him in full view, in the second row of benches, that night, and I began on him. I tried him with mild jokes—then with severe ones; I dosed him with bad jokes, and riddled him with good ones; I fired old, stale jokes on him, and peppered him fore and aft with red-hot new ones. I warmed up to my work, and assaulted him on the right and left, in front and behind; I fumed, and charged, and ranted, till I was hoarse and sick, and frantic and furious; but I never moved him once—I never started a smile or a tear! Never a ghost of a smile, and never a suspicion of moisture! I was astounded. I closed the lecture at last with one despairing shriek—with one wild burst of humor—and hurled a joke of supernatural atrocity full at him. It never phased him! Then I sat down bewildered and exhausted.

The president of the society came up and bathed my head with cold water, and said:

'What made you carry on so towards the last?'

I said, 'I was trying to make that confounded old idiot laugh in the second row.'

And he said, 'Well, you were wasting your time; because he is deaf and dumb, and as blind as a badger.'

Now was that any way for that old man's nephew to impose on a stranger and an orphan like me?

MARK TWAIN

Out in Front

Audiences are funny.

I once saw Marie Löhr, as Calpurnia, fall through a chaise longue in an earnest modern play about Julius Caesar. It got a laugh that Victor Borge would have given his ears for. But even that was topped when Gielgud, playing Caesar in a grey flannel suit, moved elegantly to the up left entrance to receive the replacement chair, which was brought on behind him, down right, by a stage hand who had difficulty in catching his attention. The roof came in on that one, and they had to drop the curtain for a minute while the house recovered.

My heart, probably the only one, went out to a repertory actor in Mary Hayley Bell's *Duet for Two Hands*. He had a chilling scene, alone on the silent stage, affecting to hear supernatural music. Flesh was satisfactorily creeping when the rest of us heard it. Well, not it, exactly. The local Boys Brigade band, distant at first, perhaps a couple of streets off, struck up with bugles and drums. It drew near, was nigh, banged and blasted its way past the stage door, dwindled, and all too slowly died. The audience rolled in the aisles. Why not? They'd come for entertainment, and didn't mind how they got it.

Like actors, the speaker soon learns how generously the audience will rise to unrehearsed effects. His own may fail. They're always a gamble. But never the crockery crash from the kitchens, or a bout of loud sneezes by a man at the back.

One of Sheridan's characters in *The Critic* says, 'I open with a clock striking, to beget an awful attention in the audience.' It's not bad. The danger is that they'll all start comparing and winding watches. Even if not, all you need is a police siren passing the windows and they won't even notice the clock striking.

By an odd chance, just about the time when the Queen was once speaking in Calgary, putting in a good word for Canada's underprivileged Indians and having it obliterated by a low-flying jet, I was telling a luncheon of Adjustable Shelving executives the one about W. C. Fields and the Chinese laundry: or possibly Austen Chamberlain and the Grand Union Canal: it's not important. On the punchline somebody knocked a bowl of geraniums off its decorative plinth.

Granted, the incidents aren't quite on a par and not only because of the status discrepancy. The Frank Whittle effect can blot you out for a full minute, and when it's over the audience has broken up into discussion groups on aircraft recognition. All the same, you'd be surprised how long it took even to get a shattered bowl of geraniums out of earshot, what with the management running hotfoot, the laughter, ironic cheers, people

177

saying 'Are you all right?' (but not to me), helping to pick up the bits, and not facing my way again until the last speck of diversion had been moaned into the vacuum-cleaner.

I hadn't been going too badly up to then, though perhaps Fields and Chamberlain weren't the best people to chime in with adjustable shelving. No one will ever know. I abandoned them, and unlike Royal speeches mine don't get circulated in advance for the benefit of those who wonder what they missed when the plane went over, or the geraniums fell. But if I'd been Fields or Chamberlain in person, or Marshall Hall and F. E. Smith rolled into one, I couldn't have recaptured that audience in under ten minutes. Their attention was divided. They were half waiting for something else amusing. The chairman might faint, or a dog get in.

Interruptions from British Rail are always well received, and it's a consideration, when engagements come up, to make sure they aren't at railway hotels. Even without that, you can get trains, as I found last autumn on a sultry evening in Colchester. I'd been mildly distracted for some time by the sight of three hundred ladies fanning themselves with the dinner menus, but it was only when I tugged my tie and came away with damp fingers that it seemed sensible to ask for windows to be opened.

I've been on the other end of window-opening before now, notably when standing in for a non-starter once at a local literary circle. I don't know what disaster had overtaken the man who was supposed to be there, but it had left things pretty late. It was after lunch on the day of the event that they came on the phone with the SOS.

It's one solution, in such emergencies, to say that you can't make a speech at four hours' notice (which astounds them: call yourself a speaker?). You offer instead to fill the gap by just answering questions. If they can't see the difference between ten thousand unaided words for solo voice and a series of short displays as the audience keeps lighting the blue paper and retiring immediately, well, you can't help that. It means, inevitably, being introduced as 'our one-man brains trust', but you've sat through worse preambles than that and sustained your death's-head grin. It also means making sure that some questions are asked, and you beg the organizers to look to it. They see the force of this, but usually want to know what kind of questions.

Unreasonably, no doubt, you feel that if they've thought of

getting you, they ought to have a rough idea of what they're getting you for. All is vanity. For all they know, having had your name from another possible stand-in, who turned them down but threw you in as a sop, your speciality is the Life-Cycle of the Beaver, or Transport Through the Ages. In fact, though, the questions don't matter much. They can usually be got round, and if you get the old chestnut about the difference between British and American humour, and you only come back with James Thurber's claim, when his eyesight was failing, that he'd once seen a cat rolling across Broadway in a striped tub, at least the Q and A form is preserved.

This time something went wrong. There weren't any Qs. Either the chairman hadn't been able to think of any. Or he couldn't find volunteers to ask them. Or the volunteers had said they would, and then couldn't bring themselves. I don't know. When question-time after a speech yields no questions it isn't too bad. They've had their pound of flesh, and an alert chairman will quickly suggest that the dummies out front should, in that case, signify their appreciation in the usual way. This isn't good, because they've just signified it after the speech. But it's better than having made no speech at all, and the dummies still sitting there. Tonight they sat for a full minute. Novelists are always using that 'full minute'. Tick it off on your second-hand to see how long it takes.

'Oh, come now,' said the chairman. And a woman at the back, yes, really at the back, rose up nobly at last. 'I was wondering', she said, 'if we could have a window open?'

'Certainly, madam,' I said. And I hopped off the platform nimbly and personally ran to the back and opened one. Or tried to. They were tall, louvred windows worked with strings. You won't need to be told, in this advanced stage of our acquaintance, that I worked the wrong string, broke it, and sat down in a metal wastepaper bin.

It was one way of breaking the ice, and the questions came in quite well after that. There was one, I fancy, about the difference between British and American humour, which enabled me to tell them about W. C. Fields and the Chinese laundry. Or possibly Austen Chamberlain and the Grand Union Canal.

Nothing is wasted, as Alan Herbert used to say. Speaking to a Young Wives' Fellowship some time later, I told them, on what pretext I can't imagine, about the time I'd hopped from a platform to open a window and sat down in a waste-bin. Some wild impulse made me embark on a demonstration. But the literary circle's platform had been low. The Young Wives' was higher. And this was the occasion when the floor had been french-polished for dancing.

Just as it was mad to give that demonstration, so it was, at Colchester, to originate the idea of opening windows. For one thing, the windows thought most suitable, behind the top table, had heavy double-glazing to be lifted out, and though speakers should at all times strive for a superior detachment from the spoken to, it seemed wrong to stand idly by while Mesdames President and Hon. Tombola Secretary struggled unaided, and I returned to the microphone damper than ever. The other thing was that a commendably frequent train service, connecting Liverpool Street with Ipswich and vice versa, now roared past the seat of my trousers, or so it seemed, whistling its two-tone diesels. This was a wrecker. One gag falling under a train you can cover with an ad lib: 'Didn't Beeching ever get to work on this line?' (It needn't be good.) After half a dozen, all you want is to catch the next train out of there.

When events of this kind conspire against you, their timing is a lesson to us all. I can't remember now the exactly judged point where the waiter pushed over the plinth, but I wouldn't be surprised to learn that I'd just said, 'Mr Fields was paying this laundry bill when he dropped his wallet . . .' Or, 'Mr Chamberlain thumped the dispatch-box . . .' (Crash! Dead on cue.) Sometimes it's the human voice, and this is a bitter thing, when it picks its moment perfectly—as you, a student of these skills, so often don't.

'I think the time has now come', I once said to a concourse of diners, 'to bring these remarks to a close.' 'So long, then, Audrey,' cried a girl in a headscarf and white boots, leaving the kitchens for the staff exit—'You've had me for tonight.' It was a big hit. Nobody could talk about anything else afterwards.

Drunks are difficult. Separate tables, increasingly a feature of public dining, encourage the gathering of like minds. At first the disturbance is hard to identify. Someone, you suspect, has brought in a transistor, not wishing to miss tonight's instalment of 'Study on 3'. But there are bouts of laughter where none was due. Singing can begin. All becomes clear during your pause after, 'But seriously, Mr Chairman', when this gathers form as

'Lloyd George Knew My Father'. There's no way out of this one. Even an appealing glance at Mr Chairman isn't always wise. You can catch him on the point of joining in. Sit down, is all. You're only spoiling their evening.

I've only once had to rise above a fight, I'll say that. It was during the fateful evening at Pentonville, and at least a couple of friendly warders took my side and restored order. You can't rely on that kind of support at Service reunions. You're on your own.

Strictly, if you lose your audience to rival attractions, you've only yourself to blame. Let the trains, drunks, jets and geraniums do their worst. All you have to do is turn them to advantage with a witty impromptu. If you can. I can't, myself, though I often see afterwards how I could. Too late. Like so many good ideas.

Such as staying at home.

BASIL BOOTHROYD

The Ethics of Art in Leadville

From Salt Lake City one travels over the great plains of Colorado and up the Rocky Mountains, on the top of which is Leadville, the richest city in the world. It has also got the reputation of being the roughest, and every man carries a revolver. I was told that if I went there they would be sure to shoot me or my travelling manager. I wrote and told them that nothing that they could do to my travelling manager would intimidate me. They are miners—men working in metals, so I lectured to them on the Ethics of Art. I read them passages from the autobiography of Benvenuto Cellini and they seemed much delighted: I was reproved by my hearers for not having brought him with me. I explained that he had been dead for some little time which elicited the enquiry, 'Who shot him?' They afterwards took me to a dancing-saloon where I saw the only rational method of art criticism I have ever come across. Over the piano was printed a notice:

> PLEASE DO NOT SHOOT
> THE PIANIST.
> HE IS DOING HIS BEST.

The mortality among pianists in that place is marvellous. Then they asked me to supper, and having accepted, I had to descend a mine in a rickety bucket in which it was impossible to be graceful. Having got into the heart of the mountain I had supper, the first course being whisky, the second whisky and the third whisky.

I went to the theatre to lecture and I was informed that just before I went there two men had been seized for committing a murder, and in that theatre they had been brought on to the stage at eight o'clock in the evening, and then and there tried and executed before a crowded audience. But I found these miners very charming and not at all rough.

Among the more elderly inhabitants of the South I found a melancholy tendency to date every event of importance by the late war. 'How beautiful the moon is tonight,' I once remarked to a gentleman who was standing next to me. 'Yes,' was his reply, 'but you should have seen it before the war.'

So infinitesimal did I find the knowledge of Art, west of the Rocky Mountains, that an art patron—one who in his day had been a miner—actually sued the railroad company for damages because the plaster cast of Venus of Milo, which he had imported from Paris, had been delivered minus the arms. And, what is more surprising still, he gained his case and the damages.

OSCAR WILDE

'The Fighting Téméraire'

A man, with five shillings to spare, may at this present moment half-kill himself with pleasure in London town, and in the neighbourhood of Pall Mall, by going from one picture gallery to another, and examining the beauties and absurdities which are to be found in each. There is first the National Gallery (entrance, nothing), in one wing of the little gin-shop of a building so styled near St Martin's Church; in another wing is the exhibition of the Royal Academy (entrance, one shilling; catalogue, one ditto). After having seen this, you come to the Water-Colour Exhibition in Pall Mall East; then to the gallery in Suffolk Street; and, finally, to the New Water-Colour Society in Pall Mall—a pretty room, which formerly used to be a gambling-house, where many a bout of seven's-the-main, and iced champagne, has been had by the dissipated in former days. All these collections (all the modern ones, that is) deserve to be noticed, and contain a deal of good, bad, and indifferent wares, as is the way with all other institutions in this wicked world.

Commençons donc avec le commencement—with the exhibition of the Royal Academy, which consists, as everybody knows, of thirty-eight knight and esquire Academicians, and nineteen simple and ungenteel Associates, who have not so much as a shabby Mister before their names. I recollect last year facetiously ranging these gentlemen in rank according to what I conceived to be their merits—King Mulready, Prince Maclise, Lord Landseer, Archbishop Eastlake (according to the best of my memory, for Jack Straw, strange to say, does not take in *Fraser's Magazine*), and so on. At present, a great number of newcomers, not Associates even, ought to be elevated to these aristocratic dignities; and, perhaps, the order ought to be somewhat changed. There are many more good pictures (here and elsewhere) than there were last year. A great stride has been taken in matters of art, my dear friend. The young painters are stepping forward. Let the old fogies look to it; let the Academic Olympians beware, for there are fellows among the rising race who bid fair to oust them from sovereignty. They have not yet arrived at the throne, to be sure, but they are near it. The lads are not so good as the best of the Academicians; but many of the Academicians are infinitely worse than the lads, and are old, stupid, and cannot improve, as the younger and more active painters will.

If you are particularly anxious to know what is the best picture in the room, not the biggest (Sir David Wilkie's is the biggest, and exactly contrary to the best), I must request you to turn your attention to a noble river-piece by J. W. M. Turner, Esquire, RA,

'The Fighting *Téméraire*'—as grand a painting as ever figured on the walls of any academy, or came from the easel of any painter. The old *Téméraire* is dragged to her last home by a little, spiteful, diabolical steamer. A mighty red sun, amidst a host of flaring clouds, sinks to rest on one side of the picture, and illumines a river that seems interminable, and a countless navy that fades away into such a wonderful distance as never was painted before. The little demon of a steamer is belching out a volume (why do I say a volume? not a hundred volumes could express it) of foul, lurid, red-hot, malignant smoke, paddling furiously, and lashing up the water round about it; while behind it (a cold grey moon looking down on it), slow, sad, and majestic, follows the brave old ship, with death, as it were, written on her. I think, my dear Bricabrac (although, to be sure, your nation would be somewhat offended by such a collection of trophies), that we ought not, in common gratitude, to sacrifice entirely these noble old champions of ours, but that we should have somewhere a museum of their skeletons, which our children might visit, and think of the brave deeds which were done in them. The bones of the *Agamemnon*, and the *Captain*, the *Vanguard*, the *Culloden*, and the *Victory* ought to be sacred relics, for Englishmen to worship almost. Think of them when alive, and braving the battle and the breeze, they carried Nelson and his heroes victorious by the Cape of Saint Vincent, in the dark water of Aboukir, and through the fatal conflict of Trafalgar. All these things, my dear Bricabrac, are, you will say, absurd, and not to the purpose. Be it so; but Bowbellites as we are, we Cockneys feel our hearts leap up when we recall them to memory; and every clerk in Threadneedle Street feels the strength of a Nelson, when he thinks of the mighty actions performed by him.

It is absurd you will say (and with a great deal of reason), for Titmarsh, or any other Briton, to grow so poetically enthusiastic about a four-foot canvas, representing a ship, a steamer, a river, and a sunset. But herein surely lies the power of the great artist. He makes you see and think of a great deal more than the objects before you; he knows how to soothe or intoxicate, to fire or to depress, by a few notes, or forms, or colours, of which we cannot trace the effect to the source, but only acknowledge the power. I recollect some years ago, at the theatre at Weimar, hearing Beethoven's 'Battle of Vittoria', in which, amidst a storm of glorious music, the air of 'God save the King' was introduced. The very

184

instant it began, every Englishman in the house was bolt upright, and so stood reverently until the air was played out. Why so? From some such thrill of excitement as makes us glow and rejoice over Mr Turner and his 'Fighting Téméraire'; which I am sure, when the art of translating colours into music or poetry shall be discovered, will be found to be a magnificent national ode or piece of music.

I must tell you, however, that Mr Turner's performances are for the most part quite incomprehensible to me; and that his other pictures, which he is pleased to call 'Cicero at his Villa', 'Agrippina with the Ashes of Germanicus', 'Pluto carrying off Proserpina', or what you will, are not a whit more natural, or less mad, than they used to be in former years, since he has forsaken nature, or attempted (like your French barbers) to embellish it. *On n'embellit pas la nature*, my dear Bricabrac; one may make pert caricatures of it, or mad exaggerations like Mr Turner in his fancy pieces. O ye gods! why will he not stick to copying her majestical countenance, instead of daubing it with some absurd antics and fard of his own? Fancy pea-green skies, crimson-lake trees, and orange and purple grass—fancy cataracts, rainbows, suns, moons and thunderbolts—shake them well up, with a quantity of gamboge, and you will have an idea of a fancy picture by Turner. It is worth a shilling alone to go and see 'Pluto and Proserpina'. Such a landscape! such figures! such a little red-hot coal-scuttle of a chariot! As Nat Lee sings—

> *Methought I saw a hieroglyphic bat*
> *Skim o'er the surface of a slipshod hat;*
> *While, to increase the tumult of the skies,*
> *A damned potato o'er the whirlwind flies.*

If you can understand these lines, you can understand one of Turner's landscapes; and I recommend them to him, as a pretty subject for a piece for next year.

WILLIAM MAKEPEACE THACKERAY

Hearst Castle

Hearst's four-hundred-thousand-acre ranch at San Simeon extended thirty miles along the Pacific Coast. The living quarters were set back on a plateau like a citadel, five hundred feet above sea level and four miles from the ocean. The main château was built from several castles shipped over in crates from Europe. The façade looked like a combination of Rheims Cathedral and a gigantic Swiss chalet. Surrounding it like vanguards were five Italian villas, set in on the edge of the plateau, each housing six guests. They were furnished in Italian style with baroque ceilings from which carved seraphs and cherubs smiled down at you. In the main château were rooms for thirty more guests. The reception room was about ninety by fifty feet, hung with Gobelin tapestries, some genuine, others faked. In this baronial atmosphere were backgammon tables and pinball games at each end of the room. The dining-room was a small replica of the nave of Westminster Abbey and seated comfortably eighty guests. The house personnel numbered sixty.

Within hearing distance of the château was a zoo, containing lions, tigers, bears, apes, orang-outangs, birds and reptiles. From the lodge gates to the château was a five-mile drive flanked with notices: 'Animals have the right of way.' One waited in one's car while a brace of ostriches made up their minds to get off the roads. Ewes, deer, elks and buffaloes roamed the estate in herds and impeded one's progress.

There were cars to meet the guests at the railway station, or, if you came by plane, there was a private landing field. If you happened to arrive between meals, you were shown your quarters and instructed that dinner was at eight and cocktails would be served in the main hall at seven-thirty.

For amusement, there was swimming, horseback riding, tennis and games of every description, or a visit to the zoo. Hearst made a rigid rule that no one could get a cocktail until six in the evening. But Marion would gather her friends in her quarters, where cocktails were served surreptitiously.

The dinners were elaborate; the menu read like a Charles the First banquet. There was game of the season: pheasant, wild duck, partridge and venison. Yet amidst this opulence we were served paper napkins, and it was only when Mrs Hearst was in residence that the guests were given linen ones.

Mrs Hearst visited San Simeon annually, and nothing conflicted. The co-existence between Marion and Mrs Hearst was mutually understood: when it was nearing time for Mrs Hearst's arrival, Marion and the rest of us would discreetly leave or return to Marion's Santa Monica beach-house. I had known Millicent Hearst since 1916 and we were very good friends, so I had a visa to both establishments. When ensconced at the ranch with her San Francisco society friends, she would ask me for the weekend and I would show up as though it were my first visit of the season. But Millicent had no illusions. Although feigning ignorance of the recent exodus, she had a sense of humour about it. 'If it weren't Marion it would be someone else,' she said. She often talked confidentially with me about the relationship of Marion and W.R., but never with bitterness. 'He still acts as though nothing had ever happened between us and as if Marion doesn't exist,' she said. 'When I arrive he is always sweet and charming, but never stays more than a few hours. And it's always the same routine: in the middle of dinner the butler hands him a note, then he excuses himself and leaves the table. When he returns, he sheepishly mentions that some urgent business matter needs his immediate attention in Los Angeles, and we all pretend to believe him. And of course we all know he returns to join Marion.'

One evening after dinner I accompanied Millicent on a walk about the grounds. The château was drenched in moonlight, looking wondrous and ghostly against the wild setting of the seven mountain tops; the stars pierced an intensely clear sky. We stood a moment taking in the panoramic beauty. From the zoo the occasional roar of a lion could be heard and the continual scream of an enormous orang-outang, that echoed and bounced about the mountain tops. It was eerie and terrifying, for each evening at sundown the orang-outang would start, quietly at first, then working up to horrific screaming, which lasted on into the night.

'That wretched animal must be insane,' I said.

'The whole place is crazy. Look at it!' she said, viewing the château. 'The creation of mad Otto . . . and he'll go on building and adding to it till the day he dies. Then what use will it be? No one can afford to keep it up. As an hotel it's useless, and if he leaves it to the State I doubt whether they could make any use of it—even as a university . . .'

One evening when I arrived at San Simeon for a weekend, Marion met me, nervous and excited. One of the guests had been attacked with a razor as he was crossing the grounds.

Marion stuttered whenever excited, which added to her charm and gave her a lady-in-distress quality. 'We d-d-don't know yet who did it,' she whispered, 'but W.R. has several detectives searching the grounds, and we're trying to keep the news away from the other guests. Some think that the attacker was a Filipino, so W.R. has had every Filipino put off the ranch until a proper investigation is made.'

'Who is the man that's been attacked?' I asked.

'You'll see him this evening at dinner,' she said.

At dinner I sat opposite a young man whose face was swathed in bandages; all that could be seen were his gleaming eyes and white teeth, which he bared in a perpetual smile.

Marion nudged me under the table. 'That's him,' she whispered.

He seemed none the worse for the attack and had a very good appetite. To all enquiries about the matter he just shrugged and grinned.

After dinner Marion showed me where the assault had taken place. 'It was behind that statue,' she said, pointing to a marble replica of 'Winged Victory'. 'Here are the bloodstains.'

'What was he doing behind the statue?' I asked.

'T-t-trying to get away from the a-t-t-tacker,' she answered.

Suddenly out of the night our guest appeared again, his face dripping with blood, as he staggered past us. Marion screamed and I jumped three feet. In a moment twenty men from nowhere surrounded him. 'I've been attacked again,' he moaned. He was borne on the arms of two detectives and taken back to his room, where they questioned him. Marion disappeared, but I saw her in the main hall an hour later. 'What happened?' I asked.

She looked sceptical. 'They say he did it himself. He's a nut and just wants attention.' Without further compunction the eccentric was bundled off the hill that night and the poor Filipinos returned to their work in the morning.

CHARLES CHAPLIN

How 'A Night in Casablanca' Kept Its Name

When the Marx Brothers were about to make a movie called 'A Night in Casablanca', there were threats of legal action from the Warner Brothers, who, five years before, had made a picture called, simply, 'Casablanca' (with Humphrey Bogart and Ingrid Bergman as stars). Whereupon Groucho, speaking for his brothers and himself, immediately despatched the following letters:

Dear Warner Brothers

Apparently there is more than one way of conquering a city and holding it as your own. For example, up to the time that we contemplated making this picture, I had no idea that the city of Casablanca belonged exclusively to Warner Brothers. However, it was only a few days after our announcement appeared that we received your long, ominous legal document warning us not to use the name Casablanca.

It seems that in 1471, Ferdinand Balboa Warner, your great-great-grandfather, while looking for a shortcut to the city of Burbank, had stumbled on the shores of Africa and, raising his alpenstock (which he later turned in for a hundred shares of the common), named it Casablanca.

I just don't understand your attitude. Even if you plan on re-releasing your picture, I am sure that the average movie fan could learn in time to distinguish between Ingrid Bergman and Harpo. I don't know whether I could, but I certainly would like to try.

You claim you own Casablanca and that no one else can use that name without your permission. What about 'Warner Brothers'? Do you own that, too? You probably have the right to use the name Warner, but what about Brothers? Professionally, we were brothers long before you were. We were touring the sticks as The Marx Brothers when Vitaphone was still a gleam in the inventor's eye, and even before us there had been other brothers—the Smith Brothers; the Brothers Karamazov; Dan Brothers, an outfielder with Detroit; and 'Brother, Can You Spare a Dime?' (This was originally 'Brothers, Can You Spare a Dime?' but this was spreading a dime pretty thin, so they threw out one brother, gave all the money to the other one and whittled it down to, 'Brother, Can You Spare a Dime?')

Now Jack, how about you? Do you maintain that yours is an original name? Well, it's not. It was used long before you were born. Offhand, I can think of two Jacks—there was Jack of 'Jack and the Beanstalk', and Jack the Ripper, who cut quite a figure in his day.

As for you, Harry, you probably sign your checks, sure in the belief that you are the first Harry of all time and that all other Harrys are imposters. I can think of two Harrys that preceded you. There was Light-house Harry of Revolutionary fame and a Harry Appelbaum who lived on the corner of 93rd Street and Lexington Avenue. Unfortunately, Appelbaum wasn't too well known. The last I heard of him, he was selling neckties at Weber and Heilbroner.

Now about the Burbank studio. I believe this is what you brothers call your place. Old man Burbank is gone. Perhaps you remember him. He was a great man in a garden. His wife often said Luther had ten green thumbs. What a witty woman she must have been! Burbank was the wizard who crossed all those fruits and vegetables until he had the poor plants in such a confused and jittery condition that they could never decide whether to enter the dining-room on the meat platter or the dessert dish.

This is pure conjecture, of course, but who knows—perhaps Burbank's survivors aren't too happy with the fact that a plant that grinds out pictures on a quota settled in their town, appropriated Burbank's name and uses it as a front for their films. It is even possible that the Burbank family is prouder of the potato produced by the old man than they are of the fact that from your studio emerged 'Casablanca' or even 'Gold Diggers of 1931'.

This all seems to add up to a pretty bitter tirade, but I assure you it's not meant to. I love Warners. Some of my best friends are Warner Brothers. It is even possible that I am doing you an injustice and that you, yourselves, know nothing at all about this dog-in-the-Wanger attitude. It wouldn't surprise me at all to discover that the heads of your legal department are unaware of this absurd dispute, for I am acquainted with many of them and they are fine fellows with curly black hair, double-breasted suits and a love of their fellow man that out-Saroyans Saroyan.

I have a hunch that this attempt to prevent us from using the title is the brainchild of some ferret-faced shyster, serving a brief apprenticeship in your legal department. I know the type well— hot out of law school, hungry for success and too ambitious to follow the natural laws of promotion. This bar sinister probably needled your attorneys, most of whom are fine fellows with curly black hair, double-breasted suits, etc., into attempting to enjoin us. Well, he won't get away with it! We'll fight him to the highest court! No pasty-faced legal adventurer is going to cause bad blood between the Warners and the Marxes. We are all brothers under the skin and we'll remain friends till the last reel of 'A Night in Casablanca' goes tumbling over the spool.

Sincerely,
Groucho Marx

191

For some curious reason, this letter seemed to puzzle the Warner Brothers' legal department. They wrote—in all seriousness—and asked if the Marxes could give them some idea of what their story was about. They felt that something might be worked out. So Groucho replied:

Dear Warners

There isn't much I can tell you about the story. In it I play a Doctor of Divinity who ministers to the natives and, as a sideline, hawks can openers and pea jackets to the savages along the Gold Coast of Africa.

When I first meet Chico, he is working in a saloon, selling sponges to barflies who are unable to carry their liquor. Harpo is an Arabian caddie who lives in a small Grecian urn on the outskirts of the city.

As the picture opens, Porridge, a mealy-mouthed native girl, is sharpening some arrows for the hunt. Paul Hangover, our hero, is constantly lighting two cigarettes simultaneously. He apparently is unaware of the cigarette shortage.

There are many scenes of splendor and fierce antagonisms, and Color, an Abyssinian messenger boy, runs Riot. Riot, in case you have never been there, is a small night club on the edge of town.

There's a lot more I could tell you, but I don't want to spoil it for you. All this has been okayed by the Hays Office, *Good Housekeeping* and the survivors of the Haymarket Riots; and if the times are ripe, this picture can be the opening gun in a new worldwide disaster.

Cordially,
Groucho Marx

Instead of mollifying them, this note seemed to puzzle the attorneys even more; they wrote back and said they still didn't understand the story line and they would appreciate it if Mr Marx would explain the plot in more detail. So Groucho obliged with the following:

Dear Brothers

Since I last wrote you, I regret to say there have been some changes in the plot of our new picture, 'A Night in Casablanca'. In the new version I play Bordello, the sweetheart of Humphrey Bogart. Harpo and Chico are itinerant rug peddlers who are weary of laying rugs and enter a monastery just for a lark. This is a good joke on them, as there hasn't been a lark in the place for fifteen years.

Across from this monastery, hard by a jetty, is a waterfront hotel, chockfull of apple-cheeked damsels, most of whom have been barred by the Hays Office for soliciting. In the fifth reel, Gladstone makes a speech that sets the House of Commons in an uproar and the King promptly asks for his resignation. Harpo marries a hotel detective; Chico operates an ostrich farm. Humphrey Bogart's girl, Bordello, spends her last years in a Bacall house.

This, as you can see, is a very skimpy outline. The only thing that can save us from extinction is a continuation of the film shortage.

Fondly,
Groucho Marx

After that, the Marxes heard no more from the Warner Brothers' legal department.

The Early Life of 'Waiting for Godot'

It was a remarkable thing to come on in the first act and feel a bungful house, only to return in the second to find a certain percentage of gaps in the theatre and the audience shrunk in size.

193

Not that it was a great surprise, because those who had left did not attempt to cover up their movements. It was not just the banging of seats and slamming of exit doors, but quite often they would take the trouble to come right down to the foot-lights, glare at the actors and make their egress into outer space, snorting the while. Incidents were numerous and cries of 'Rubbish', 'It's a disgrace', 'Take it off', 'Disgusting', and I regret to say on one occasion 'Balls', floated through the auditorium. There was one unforgettable night when, during the second act, the two tramps are alone on the stage cogitating about life as they were apt to do and one says: 'I am happy', to which the other replies, 'I am happy too', after which a gent in Row F shouted: 'Well, I'm bloody well not.' At this point there was a certain amount of shushing, but the man would not be shushed and stood up and yelled at the audience: 'And nor are you. You've been hoaxed like me.' A free fight ensued (well, fairly free; 15s. 6d. a head actually) and during a lull Hugh Burden observed quietly: 'I think it's Godot,' which brought the house down.

PETER BULL

An Expedition to Debra Lebanos

It was during our third week in Addis Ababa, when the official celebrations were over and the delegations were being packed off to the coast as fast as the Franco-Ethiopian Railway's supply of sleeping cars would allow, that Professor W. suggested to me that we should make an expedition together to Debra Lebanos.

This monastery has for four centuries been the centre of Abyssinian spiritual life. It is built round a spring where the waters of Jordan, conveyed subterraneously down the Red Sea, are believed to well up endowed with curative properties; pilgrims go there from all parts of the country, and it is a popular burial-ground for those who can afford it, since all found there at

the Last Trump are assured of unimpeded entry into Paradise . . .

The expedition consisted simply of ourselves, a bullet-headed Armenian chauffeur, and a small native boy, who attached himself to us without invitation. At first we were a little resentful of this, but he firmly refused to understand our attempts at dismissal, and later we were devoutly grateful for his presence. The car, which did things I should have thought no car could possibly do, was an American make which is rarely seen in Europe. When we had packed it with our overcoats, rugs, tins of petrol, and provisions, there was just room for ourselves. The hotel supplied beer and sandwiches and olives and oranges, and Irene gave us a hamper of tinned and truffled foods from Fortnum & Mason. We were just starting, rather later than we had hoped, when Professor W. remembered something. 'Do you mind if we go back to my hotel for a minute? There's just one thing I've forgotten.' We drove round to the Imperial.

The thing he had forgotten was a dozen empty Vichy bottles. 'I thought it would be courteous', he explained, 'to take some holy water back to Ras Kassa and the Abuna. I'm sure they would appreciate it.'

'Yes, but need we take quite so much?'

'Well, there's the patriarchal legate, I should like to give him some, and Belatingeta Herui, and the Coptic patriarch at Cairo . . . I thought it was a nice opportunity to repay some of the kindness I have received.'

I suggested that this purpose could be more conveniently

achieved by giving them *tedj*, and that from what I had seen of Abyssinians they would much prefer it. Professor W. gave a little nervous laugh and looked anxiously out of the window.

'Well, why not fill my empty beer-bottles?'

'No, no, I don't think that would be quite suitable. I don't really like using Vichy bottles. I wish I had had time to scrape off the labels,' he mused. 'I don't *quite* like the idea of holy water in Vichy bottles. Perhaps the boy could do it tomorrow—before they are filled, of course.'

A new aspect of the professor's character was thus revealed. My acquaintance with him until that day was limited to half a dozen more or less casual encounters at the various parties and shows. I had found him full of agreeably ironical criticism of our companions, very punctilious, and very enthusiastic about things which seemed to me unexceptionable. 'Look,' he would say with purest Boston intonation, 'look at the exquisite grace of the basket that woman is carrying. There is the whole character of the people in that plaited straw. Ah, why do we waste our time looking at crowns and canons? I could study that basket all day.' And a wistful, faraway look would come into his eyes as he spoke.

Remarks of that kind went down very well with some people, and I regarded them as being, perhaps, one of the normal manifestations of American scholarship. They were compensated for by such sound maxims as 'Never carry binoculars; you only have to hand them over to some wretched woman as soon as there is anything worth seeing.' But this worldly good sense was a mere mask over the essentially mystical nature of the professor's mind; one touch of church furniture, and he became suddenly transfused with reverence and an almost neurotic eagerness to do all that could be expected of him, with an impulsive and demonstrative devotion that added a great deal to the glamour of our expedition together.

Those bottles, however, were an infernal nuisance. They clinked about the floor, making all the difference between tolerable ease and acute discomfort. There was nowhere to rest our feet except on their unstable, rolling surface. We drew up our knees and resigned ourselves to cramp and pins and needles.

Debra Lebanos is practically due north of Addis Ababa. For the first mile or two there was a clearly marked track which led out of the town, right over the summit of Entoto. It was extremely steep and narrow, composed of loose stones and boulders; on the top of the hill was a little church and parsonage, the ground all round them broken by deep ravines and outcrops of stone. 'Whatever happens,' we decided, 'we must make quite certain of coming over here by daylight.'

From Entoto the way led down to a wide plain, watered by six or seven shallow streams which flowed between deep banks at right angles to our road. Caravans of mules were coming into the town laden with skins. Professor W. saluted them with bows and blessings; the hillmen answered him with blank stares or broad incredulous grins. A few, more sophisticated than their companions, bellowed, 'Baksheesh!' Professor W. shook his head sadly and remarked that the people were already getting spoiled by foreign intrusion.

It took two or three hours to cross the plain; we drove, for the most part, parallel to the track, rather than on it, finding the rough ground more comfortable than the prepared surface. We crossed numerous dry water-courses and several streams. At some of these there had been rough attempts at bridge-building, usually a heap of rocks and a few pieces of timber; in rare cases a culvert ran underneath. It was in negotiating these that we first realized the astonishing powers of our car. It would plunge nose first into a precipitous gully, shiver and stagger a little, churn up dust and stones, roar, and skid, bump and sway until we began to climb out, and then it would suddenly start forward and mount very deliberately up the other side as though endowed with some peculiar prehensile quality in its tyres. Occasionally, in conditions of scarcely conceivable asperity, the engine would stop. Professor W. would sigh, and open the door, allowing two or three of his empty bottles to roll out on to the running-board.

'*Ah, ça n'a pas d'importance,*' said the driver, prodding the boy, who jumped out, restored the bottles, and then leant his shoulder against the back of the car. This infinitesimal contribution of weight seemed to be all the car needed; up it would go out of the river-bed, and over the crest of the bank, gaining speed as it reached level ground; the child would race after us and clamber in as we bumped along, a triumphant smile on his little black face.

At about eleven we stopped for luncheon by the side of the last stream. The boy busied himself by filling up the radiator by the use of a small cup. I ate sandwiches and drank beer rendered volatile by the motion of the car. The professor turned out to be a vegetarian; he unwrapped a little segment of cheese from its silver paper and nibbled it delicately and made a very neat job of an orange. The sun was very powerful, and the professor advanced what seemed, and still seems, to me the radically unsound theory that you must wear thick woollen underclothes if you wish to keep cool in the tropics.

After leaving the plain we drove for three hours or so across grassy downland. There was now no track of any kind, but occasional boundary-stones hinted at the way we should follow. There were herds grazing, usually in charge of small naked children. At first the professor politely raised his hat and bowed to them, but the effect was so disturbing that after he had sent three or four out of sight, wailing in terror, he remarked that it was agreeable to find people who had a proper sense of the menace of motor transport, and relapsed into meditation, pondering, perhaps, the advisability of presenting a little holy water to the emperor. The route was uneventful, broken only by occasional clusters of *tukals*, surrounded by high hedges of euphorbia. It was very hot, and after a time, in spite of the jangle of the bottles and the constriction of space, I fell into a light doze.

I awoke as we stopped on the top of a hill; all round us were empty undulations of grass. '*Nous sommes perdus?*' asked the professor. '*Ça n'a pas d'importance,*' replied the driver, lighting a cigarette. The boy was despatched, like the dove from Noah's ark, to find direction in the void. We waited for half an hour before he returned. Meanwhile three native women appeared from nowhere, peering at us from under straw sunshades. The professor took off his hat and bowed. The women huddled together and giggled. Presently fascination overcame their shyness and they approached closer; one touched the radiator and burned her fingers. They asked for cigarettes and were repelled, with some very forceful language, by the driver.

At last the child returned and made some explanations. We turned off at right angles and drove on, and the professor and I fell asleep once more.

When I next woke, the landscape had changed dramatically. About half a mile from us, and obliquely to the line of our path, the ground fell away suddenly into a great canyon. I do not know how deep it was, but I should think at least two thousand feet, descending abruptly in tiers of sheer cliff, broken by strips and

198

patches of timber. At the bottom a river ran between green banks, to swell the Blue Nile far in the south; it was practically dry at this season except for a few shining channels of water which split and reunited on the sandy bed in delicate threads of light. Poised among trees, two-thirds of the way down on a semi-circular shelf of land, we could discern the roofs of Debra Lebanos. A cleft path led down the face of the cliff and it was for this that we were clearly making. It looked hopelessly unsafe, but our Armenian plunged down with fine intrepidity.

Sometimes we lurched along a narrow track with cliffs rising on one side and a precipice falling away on the other; sometimes we picked our way on broad ledges among great volcanic boulders; sometimes we grated between narrow rock walls. At last we reached a defile which even our driver admitted to be impassable. We climbed out along the running-boards and finished the descent on foot. Professor W. was clearly already enchanted by the sanctity of the place.

'Look,' he said, pointing to some columns of smoke that rose from the cliffs above us, 'the cells of the solitary anchorites.'

'Are you sure there are solitary anchorites here? I never heard of any.'

'It would be a good place for them,' he said wistfully.

The Armenian strode on in front of us, a gallant little figure with his cropped head and rotund, gaitered legs; the boy staggered behind, carrying overcoats, blankets, provisions, and a good half-dozen of the empty bottles. Suddenly the Armenian stopped and, with his finger on his lips, drew our attention to the rocks just below us. Twenty or thirty baboons of both sexes and all ages were huddled up in the shade.

'Ah,' said Professor W., 'sacred monkeys. How very interesting!'

'Why do you think they are sacred? They seem perfectly wild.'

'It is a common thing to find sacred monkeys in monasteries,' he explained gently. 'I have seen them in Ceylon and in many parts of India . . . Oh, why did he do that? How very thoughtless!' For our driver had thrown a stone into their midst and scattered them barking in all directions, to the great delight of the small boy behind us.

It was hot walking. We passed one or two *tukals* with women and children staring curiously at us, and eventually emerged on

199

to an open green ledge littered with enormous rocks and a variety of unimposing buildings. A mob of ragged boys, mostly infected with disagreeable skin diseases, surrounded us and were repelled by the Armenian. (These, we learned later, were the deacons.) We sent the boy forward to find someone more responsible, and soon a fine-looking, bearded monk carrying a yellow sunshade, came out of the shadow of a tree and advanced to greet us. We gave him our letter of introduction from the Abuna, and after he had scrutinized both sides of the envelope with some closeness, he agreed, through our Armenian, who from now on acted as interpreter, to fetch the head of the monastery. He was away some time and eventually returned with an old priest, who wore a brown cloak, a very large white turban, steel-rimmed spectacles, and carried in one hand an old black umbrella and in the other a horsehair flywhisk. Professor W. darted forward and kissed the cross which swung from the old man's neck. This was received rather well, but I felt too shy to follow his lead and contented myself with shaking hands. The monk then handed his superior our letter, which was tucked away in his pocket unopened. They then explained that they would be ready to receive us shortly, and went off to wake up the other priests and prepare the chapter house.

We waited about half an hour, sitting in the shade near the church, and gradually forming round us a circle of inquisitive ecclesiastics of all ages. The Armenian went off to see about his car. Professor W. replied to the questions that were put to us, with bows, shakes of the head, and little sympathetic

moans. Presently one monk came up and, squatting beside us, began to write on the back of his hand with a white pencil in a regular, finely formed Amharic script. One of the letters was in the form of a cross. Professor W., anxious to inform them all that we were good Christians, pointed to this mark, then to me and to himself, bowed in the direction of the church, and crossed himself. This time he made a less happy impression. Everyone looked bewildered and rather scared; the scribe spat on his hand, and hastily erasing the text, fell back some paces. There was an air of tension and embarrassment, which was fortunately disturbed by our Armenian with the announcement that the council of the monastery were now ready to receive us.

Apart from the two churches, the most prominent building was a tall, square house of stone, with a thatched roof and a single row of windows set high up under the eaves; it was here that we were led. A small crowd had collected round the door, which was covered with a double curtain of heavy sackcloth. The windows also were heavily screened, so that we stepped from the brilliant sunshine into a gloom which was at first completely baffling. One of the priests raised the door-curtain a little to show us our way. A single lofty room constituted the entire house; the walls were of undisguised stone and rubble, no ceiling covered the rafters and thatch. Preparations had clearly been made for us; carpets had been spread on the earthen floor, and in the centre stood two low stools covered with rugs; twelve priests stood ranged against the wall, the head of the monastery in their centre; between them and our seats stood a table covered with a shawl; the only other furniture was a cupboard in the far corner, roughly built of irregularly stained white wood, the doors secured with a staple and padlock. We sat down and our chauffeur-interpreter stood beside us jauntily twirling his cap. When we were settled, the head of the monastery, who apparently also bore the title of abuna, brought our letter of introduction out of his pocket and, for the first time, opened it. He read it first to himself and then aloud to the company, who scratched their beards, nodded, and grunted. Then he addressed us, asking us what we wanted. Professor W. explained that we had heard from afar of the sanctity of the place and the wisdom and piety of the monks, and that we had come to do reverence at their shrine, pay our duty and respect to them, and take away some account of the glories of the monastery of which all the

201

world stood in awe. This pretty speech was condensed by our chauffeur into three or four harsh vocables, and greeted with further nods and grunts from the assembly.

One of them asked whether we were Mohammedans. It seemed sad that this question was necessary after all Professor W.'s protestations. We assured him that we were not. Another asked where we had come from. Addis Ababa? They asked about the coronation, and Professor W. began a graphic outline of the liturgical significance of the ceremony. I do not think, however, that our chauffeur was at very great pains to translate this faithfully. The response, anyway, was a general outburst of chuckling, and from then onwards, for about ten minutes, he took the burden of conversation from our shoulders and speedily established relations of the utmost geniality. Presently he began shaking hands with them all and explained that they would like us to do the same, a social duty which Professor W. decorated with many graceful genuflections and reverences.

The professor then asked whether we might visit the library of which the world stood in awe. Why, certainly; there it was in the corner. The abuna produced a small key from his pocket and directed one of the priests to open the cupboard. They brought out five or six bundles wrapped in silk shawls, and, placing them with great care on the table, drew back the door-curtain to admit a shaft of white light. The abuna lifted the corners of the shawls one after another and revealed two pieces of board clumsily hinged together in the form of a diptych. Professor W. kissed them eagerly; they were then opened, revealing two coloured lithographs, apparently cut from a religious almanac printed in Germany some time towards the end of the last century, representing the Crucifixion and the Assumption, pasted on to the inner surfaces of the wood. The professor was clearly a little taken aback. 'Dear, dear, how remarkably ugly they are,' he remarked as he bent down to kiss them.

The other bundles contained manuscripts of the Gospels, lives of the saints, and missals, written in Ghiz* and brightly illuminated. The painting was of the same kind as the frescos, reduced to miniature. Sometimes faces and figures had been cut out of prints and stuck into the page with a discomposing effect on their highly stylized surroundings. They told us with great pride

* The ecclesiastical language, unintelligible to all the laity and most of the priesthood. It is written in Amharic characters.

that the artist had been employed at Addis Ababa on some work for the late empress. Professor W. asked whether there were not some older manuscripts we might see, but they affected not to understand. I remembered hearing from George Herui that it was only after very considerable difficulties that Professor Mercer had unearthed his Ecclesiastes. No doubt there were still reserves hidden from us.

It was then suggested that we should visit the sacred spring. Our Armenian here sidled unobtrusively out of the way; he had had enough exercise for one day. Professor W. and I set out with a guide up the hillside. It was a stiff climb; the sun was still strong and the stones all radiated a fierce heat. 'I think, perhaps, we ought to take off our hats,' said the professor; 'we are on very holy ground.'

I removed my topi and exposed myself to sunstroke, trusting in divine protection; but, just as he spoke, it so happened that our guide stopped on the path and accommodated himself in a way which made me think that his reverence for the spot was far from fanatical.

On our way we passed a place where overhanging cliffs formed a shallow cave. Water oozed and dripped all round, and the path was soft and slippery. It is here that the bodies of the faithful are brought; they lay all about, some in packing-cases, others in hollow treetrunks, battened down with planks, piled and tumbled on top of each other without order; many were partially submerged in falls of damp earth; a few of these rough coffins had broken apart, revealing their contents. There were similar heaps, we were told, on the other parts of the hillside.

We had a fine view of the valley; our guide pointed out a group of buildings on the far side. 'That is the convent for the women,' he explained. 'You see it is quite untrue that we live together. The houses are entirely separate. We do not cross the valley to them, and they do not cross to us. Never. It is all a lie.' He wanted to make this point quite clear.

At last we reached the spring, which fell in a pretty cascade to join the river far below at the bottom of the valley. Most of the water, however, had been tapped, and was conveyed in two iron pipes to bathing-places near the monastery. We climbed down again to see them. One, built especially for Menelik, was a little brick house with a corrugated iron roof. The old empress had frequently come here, and since her death it had not been used.

We peered through the window and saw a plain kitchen-chair. There was a rusty spout in the ceiling from which a trickle of water fell on to the brick floor and drained away through the waste-pipe in one corner. The other bath was for public use. The pipe was fitted with a double spout, directing two streams of water on to either side of a brick wall. One side was for men and the other for women, and a three-sided screen was built round each. The floor was made of cement. A boy was in there at the time of our visit, swilling himself down with as much puffing and spluttering as if he were under any purely secular shower-bath.

As we turned back, our Armenian and a monk met us with a message from the abuna—should they kill a goat, a sheep, or a calf for our dinner? We explained that we had full provision for our food. All we required was shelter for the night and water to wash in. The Armenian explained that it was usual to accept something. We suggested some eggs, but were told that they had none. They urged a goat very strongly. Meat is a rare luxury in the monastery, and they were, no doubt, eager to take the opportunity of our visit for a feast. The professor's vegetarian scruples, however, were unconquerable. At last they suggested honey, which he accepted readily. The question of our accommodation was then discussed. There was a hut or a tent. The Armenian warned us that if we slept in the hut we should certainly contract some repulsive disease, and if in the tent, we might be killed by hyenas. He had already made up his own mind, he said, to sleep in the car. We returned to the monastery, and the abuna led us in person to see the hut. It was some time before the key could be found; when the door was at last wrenched open, an emaciated she-goat ran out. The interior was windowless and fetid. It appeared to have been used as a kind of lumber-room; heaps of old rags and broken furniture encumbered the floor. A swarm of bees buzzed in the roof. It was not quite ready, the abuna explained; he had not expected guests. It could, of course, be prepared, or would we think it inhospitable if he offered us the tent? We declared that the tent would be wholly satisfactory, and so, with evident relief, the abuna gave instructions for its erection. It was now nearly sunset. A spot of ground was chosen near the house where we had been received, and a very decent bell-tent pitched. (It was the property of the old empress, we learned. She had often slept there on her visits to the spring.) The floor was covered with hay and the hay with rugs. A little boat-shaped oil-lamp was hung from the tent-pole; our rugs, provisions, and bottles were brought in and laid on one side. We were then invited to enter. We sat down cross-legged and the abuna sat beside us. He looked enormous in the tiny light; the shadow from his great turban seemed to fill the whole tent. The chauffeur squatted opposite us. The abuna smiled with the greatest geniality and expressed his best wishes for our comfort; we thanked him heartily. Conversation lapsed and we all three sat smiling rather vacantly. Presently the flap was lifted and a monk came in wearing a heavy brown burnous and carrying an antiquated rifle. He bowed to us and retired. He was a guard, the abuna explained, who would sleep outside across the door. Another smiling pause. At last supper arrived; first a basket containing half a dozen great rounds of native bread, a tough, clammy substance closely resembling crêpe rubber in appearance; then two earthenware jugs, one of water, the other of *talla*—a kind of thin, bitter beer; then two horns of honey, but not of honey as it is understood at Thame; this was the product of wild bees, scraped straight from the trees; it was a greyish colour, full of bits of stick and mud, bird dung, dead bees, and grubs. Everything was first carried to the abuna for his approval, then to us. We expressed our delight with nods and more extravagant smiles. The food was laid before us and the bearers retired. At this moment the Armenian shamelessly deserted us, saying that he must go and see after his boy.

The three of us were left alone, smiling over our food in the half darkness.

In the corner lay our hamper packed with Irene's European delicacies. We clearly could not approach them until our host left us. Gradually the frightful truth became evident that he was proposing to dine with us. I tore off a little rag of bread and attempted to eat it. 'This is a very difficult situation,' said the professor; 'I think, perhaps, it would be well to simulate ill-health,' and, holding his hands to his forehead, he began to rock gently from side to side, emitting painfully subdued moans. It was admirably done; the abuna watched him with the greatest concern; presently the professor held his stomach and retched a little; then he lay on his back, breathing heavily with closed eyes; then he sat up on his elbow and explained in eloquent dumb show that he wished to rest. The abuna understood perfectly, and, with every gesture of sympathy, rose to his feet and left us.

In five minutes, when I had opened a tinned grouse and a

bottle of lager and the professor was happily mumbling a handful of ripe olives, the Armenian returned. With a comprehensive wink, he picked up the jug of native beer, threw back his head, and, without pausing to breathe, drank a quart or two. He then spread out two rounds of bread, emptied a large quantity of honey into each of them, wrapped them together, and put them in his pocket. '*Moi, je puis manger comme abyssin,*' he remarked cheerfully, winked at the grouse, wished us goodnight, and left us.

EVELYN WAUGH

A Welcome Party in Borneo

We were very tired. It was all too confusing; the river seemed to have spun cat's-cradles of pain out of all the muscle fibres in my calves and back; and the monitor-lizard's tail was still gently whisking, from side to side, in my stomach. I took a long pull at the arak-can and lay down on the floor of the chief's room. The huge cross-beams of the roof bucked and twisted and stuck fast on some celestial river floating over my head: I fell asleep.

'Come on,' shouted James, 'get up! There's going to be a welcome party.'

Staggering out, wanting to sleep as never before, I looked around, and wished I was somewhere else. The gallery was packed. The lamps had been lit. Tuak was being drunk. A long, uninviting space had been cleared in front of part of the line of long-house doors; and around its three sides sat an expectant audience.

Leon and Inghai, looking fresh and eager, beckoned us to the back row. Dana was nowhere to be seen. He was, as Leon explained, as befitted his high and kingly status, drinking with the deputy chief of all the Kenyah on the Baleh, and was not to be disturbed, because, being Absolute Chief of all the Iban of Kapit District, he had many cares, and would soon be taking a sleeps.

We were given a glass of tuak. A tray of huge cone-shaped cheroots of Kenyah tobacco wrapped in leaves and each tied with a bow of leaf-strips was passed round; a sinuous young girl put ours in our mouths and lit them with a taper. I noticed that Leon was wearing his large and flashy, supposedly waterproof, digital watch. After its first celebratory dive with Leon into the depths of the Rajang this watch had ceased to tell the time, but it would still, if shaken violently enough, and to Leon's unvarying delight, sound its alarm.

The musicians sat in front of us. An old man held a keluri, a dried gourd shaped like a chemical retort but held upwards, and with six bamboo pipes projecting in a bundle from its bulb; a group of young men sat ready with a bamboo harp (a tube of bamboo with raised strips cut from its surface), a bamboo xylophone, a bamboo flute, and a single stringed instrument, a dugout-canoe-like sounding box carved from a single block of wood, the string so heavy it had to be pulled with an iron hook.

The chief's son entered, transformed. On his head he wore a war-helmet, a woven rattan cap set with black and yellow and crimson beads, topped with six long black and white plumes from the tail of the helmeted hornbill. He was dressed in a war-coat, made from the skin of the largest cat in Borneo, the clouded leopard. His head placed through an opening at the front of the skin, the bulk stretched down his back, and on to it were fastened row upon row of rhinoceros hornbill feathers. Around his waist, slung on a silver belt and sheathed in a silver scabbard, was a parang to outshine all other parangs, its hilt intricately carved in horn from the antler of the kijang, the big Borneo deer. In his left hand, his arm crooked behind it, he carried a long shield, pointed at both ends, and from the centre of which a huge mask regarded us implacably, its eyes red, its teeth the painted tusks of the wild boar. Thick black tufts of hair hung in neat lines down either edge and across the top and bottom, tufts of hair which, we were led to believe, had long ago been taken from the scalps of heads cut off in battle.

Laying the ancient, and presumably fragile, shield carefully against the wall, the warrior took up his position at the centre of the floor. He crouched down and, at a nod from the man on the bass string, a hollow, complicated, urgent, rhythmic music began. With exaggerated movements, his thigh muscles bunching and loosening, his tendons taut, a fierce concentration on his face, the chief's son turned slowly in time with the music, first on one foot and then on another, rising, inch by inch, to his own height, apparently peering over some imaginary cover. Sighting the enemy, he crouched again, and then, as the music quickened, he drew his bright parang and leapt violently forward, weaving and dodging, with immense exertion, cutting and striking, parrying unseen blows with his mimed shield. For a small second, his ghostly foe was off-guard, tripped on the shingle, and the heir to the Lordship of all the Kenyah of Nanga Sinyut claimed his victory with one malicious blow.

Everyone clapped and cheered, and so did I. Five young girls rushed forward to take off the hero's hornbill helmet, and war-coat, and parang. It was wonderful. The girls were very beautiful. All was right with the world. And then I realized, as a Rajah Brooke's birdwing took a flap around my duodenum, that the beautiful girls, in a troop, were coming, watched by all the long-house, for me.

'You'll be all right,' said James, full of tuak. 'Just do your thing. Whatever it is.'

Strapped into the war-coat and the parang, the hornbill feathers on my head, I had a good idea. It would be a simple procedure to copy the basic steps that the chief's son had just shown us. There really was not much to it, after all. The music struck up, sounding just a little bit stranger than it had before.

I began the slow crouch on one leg, turning slightly. Perhaps, actually, this was a mistake, I decided. Ghastly pains ran up my thighs. Terminal cramp hit both buttocks at once. Some silly girl began to titter. A paraplegic wobble spread down my back. The silly girl began to laugh. Very slowly, the floor came up to say hello, and I lay down on it. There was uproar in the longhouse. How very funny, indeed.

Standing up, I reasoned that phase two would be easier. Peering over the imaginary boulder, I found myself looking straight into the eyes of an old man on the far side of the verandah. The old fool was crying with laughter, his ridiculous long ears waggling about. Drawing the parang, which was so badly aligned that it stuck in the belt and nearly took my fingers off, I advanced upon the foe, jumping this way and that, feeling dangerous. The old man fell off his seat. There was so much misplaced mirth, so much plain howling, that I could not hear the music, and so perhaps my rhythm was not quite right.

'Redsi!' came an unmistakable shout, 'why don't you improvise?'

Stabbed in the back just as I was about to take my very first head, I spun round violently to glare at the Fenton. I never actually saw him, because the cord of the war-helmet, not used to such movements, slipped up over the back of my head, and the helmet itself, flying forward, jammed fast over my face. Involuntarily, I took a deep gasp of its sweat-smooth rattan interior, of the hair of generations of Kenyah warriors who had each been desperate to impress the girls of their choice. It was an old and acrid smell.

The boards were shaking. The audience was out of control. And then, just in time, before suffocation set in, the five girls, grossly amused, set me free.

'Go and get James,' I spluttered, 'you go and get James.'

'Now you sing song,' shouted Leon.

'No, no—James sing songs.'

'Jams!' shouted Leon, remembering his mission.

'Jams!' The longhouse reverberated. 'Jams! Jams!' Leon had done his work well.

With great theatrical presence, offering almost no resistance to the five young girls, James processed on to the stage. The Kenyah fell silent. T. D. Freeman, in his work on Iban augury, tells us that the King of the Gods, Singalang Burong, may well be encountered in dreams. There is no mistaking him. He is almost as old as the trees, awe-inspiring, massive of body, and, a characteristic which puts his identity beyond doubt, completely bald. Judging by the slightly uneasy, deferential, expectant faces around me, Bali Penyalong, the High God of the Kenyah, was but a different name for the same deity.

The attendants withdrew. James, resplendent in leopard skin and hornbill feathers, looked even more solemn than is his habit. With the accumulated experience of many thousands of evenings at the theatre, of years of drama criticism, he regarded his audience; his huge brown eyes appeared to fix on everyone in turn. There was some backward shuffling in the front row. A dog whimpered.

The music began, a little shakily. James, in time with the music, began to mime. He was hunting something, in a perfunctory way; he made rootling movements with his head, and grunted. He was hunting a pig. Evidently successful, he butchered his quarry, selected the joint he had in mind, hung the carcase from a hook in the roof and betook himself to his ideal kitchen. Passion entered the show; James began to concentrate; his gestures quickened and the mesmerized musicians increased their tempo. He scored the pork; he basted it; he tied it with string; he made extraordinarily complex sauces; he cooked potatoes and sprouts and peas and beans and broccoli and *zucchini*, I think, until they were *fritti*. After many a tasting and many an alchemical manoeuvre with a *batterie de cuisine* decidedly better than Magny's, James deemed the gravy to be perfect. The apple sauce was plentiful. The decanted Burgundy was poured into a glass. James looked fondly at his creation and began to eat. The crackling crackled between his teeth. The warriors of the Kenyah, as if they had been present at a feast of the Gods, rose to their feet and burped. Everybody cheered.

REDMOND O'HANLON

The Revd Sydney Smith Deals with a Bore

During his Edinburgh days, the reigning bore was Leslie, the Scottish philosopher, whose favourite subject was the North Pole. Sooner or later, whatever the topic, the North Pole crept into the conversation. No one could escape him or it; Sydney had serious thoughts of inventing a 'slip-button' for such occasions; Jeffrey simply fled when he came in sight. One day Leslie called on the editor of the *Edinburgh Review* and found him just about to set out for a ride. They had not been talking for more than a minute when the North Pole was introduced by Leslie. 'Oh, damn the North Pole!' shouted Jeffrey in a rage, spurring his horse and galloping off. Shortly afterwards Leslie met Sydney and seriously complained of Jeffrey's behaviour. 'Oh, my dear fellow, never mind,' said Sydney consolingly, 'no one cares what Jeffrey says; he is a privileged person; he respects nothing, absolutely nothing. Why, you will scarcely credit it, but, strictly between ourselves, it is not more than a week ago that I heard him speak disrespectfully of the Equator!'

HESKETH PEARSON

A Hotel in Guadalajara

At Guadalajara we were met by Anthony. He was wearing a green seersucker suit and a large Mexican hat.

'I've laid on a car for you,' he said.

Later, when we were rolling through long handsome streets in a Studebaker, he said, 'I've been hanging round this bus terminal since noon.'

'When did you get in?' said I.

'11 a.m. On this plane from Mex City.'

'How long did it take you?' said E.

'Couple of hours.'

'Indeed,' said E.

'Did you enjoy yourself?' said I.

'Oh, fine. They didn't serve breakfast though. Lousy little plane.'

'I meant in Mexico City.'

'Oh, that was fine.'

Anthony is a second cousin of E.'s, and one of the best-looking young men I've ever set eyes on. We are all very fond of him.

Later he said, 'That was quite a rat-race you led me. I ought to be mad. I could have saved time and flown out to this Guadala-jara straight from Baltimore.' He smiled sweetly. Anthony is the kind of boy whose radiant looks make him content with the world that gives him such a warm reception, rather than with himself.

We pulled up in front of a large and beautiful sixteenth-century palace. 'Hotel Guzman,' said Anthony. 'Don't worry, it's all fixed up new inside. You've never seen such bathrooms. Solid black marble.'

We all shot up in a small, fast lift. The manager flung open a door and ushered us into a splendid apartment full of divan beds and somebody's clothes.

'Why that's *my* room,' said Anthony.

'Yes, sir. I had beds for the ladies moved in while you were absent.'

'Now, see here . . .' said Anthony.

E. took over. 'We do not want to be three in a room,' she said gently.

'No room for three? But the gentleman said he was expecting two ladies.'

'Yes, and here we are. But you see we don't want all three to share one room.'

'That is all right, señora. It is a large room. In Holy Week when there are many travellers we would have a family of seven, nine persons in such a room. And their servants in the bathroom.'

'But this isn't Holy Week.'

'It is not, señora. In Holy Week there would be a family and servants in every room, now it is only one gentleman and two ladies. It costs more in Holy Week, too.'

'Look here,' I said, 'we have strange habits and we want two, or at least one other room. Have you got them?'

'Yes, yes, many rooms. We are the newest hotel in Guadala-jara.'

'Well, can we see them?'

'They are very new, señora. More new than this room. We are still working on the newness.'

After a good deal more of this, a bed for Anthony was moved into a cupboard leading out of our room. The cupboard had a window, but it opened into a corridor. Ours had an open view over red-tiled rooftops and a brilliant nocturnal sky. The night was warmer than it had been in Morelia. We were very hungry.

A cry of distress from E. in the bathroom. 'My dear, I can't make the water run. Do try.'

Indeed: hot tap, cold tap, tub and basin, not a drop. There was a telephone on the wall, I picked it up.

'There doesn't seem to be any water in our bathroom.'

'Of course not, señora. It has not been laid on. One thing after another. Perhaps next year? Yes, certainly next year. If we do well. You will recommend us?'

Ready first, I proceeded to go downstairs. I walked up the corridor, none too well lit, then saw, caught myself, and knees buckling reeled a step backward, collapsed against a wall and howled for Anthony.

He came running. 'What's the matter?'

'THERE ARE NO STAIRS.'

'Well, what d'you want stairs for?'

'I was about to go down.'

'What's wrong with the elevator?'

'Oh God, Anthony, don't be so yourself. And don't let's have a Mexican conversation. Go and see . . . No, don't go! Be careful!'

Anthony went a few steps up the corridor. 'Jesus Christ,' he said.

The corridor ended in space. Seventy feet below, at the bottom of the crater left by flights of marble recently ripped out, lay visible in a dim pool of light the reception desk, the leather armchairs and the spittoons of the entrance hall. Between, a void. They had begun working on the newness on the top floor. Anthony and I fetched E. from the room and we all went down in the lift.

SYBILLE BEDFORD

Observations in a Harrogate Hotel

I was conceived in a strange bedroom. My birthday, like my brother's, is in May, and, though three years separate us, we were both born on the same date. Counting back the months, I realize we must both have been conceived during the old August Bank Holiday, in a boarding-house bedroom in Morecambe, or Flamborough, or Filey—oilcloth on the floor, jug and basin on the wash-hand stand, the bathroom on the next landing. Nowhere like this, anyway, a bedroom in the Crown Hotel, Harrogate.

That said, though, I might be expected to feel at home in rented accommodation, but for years nowhere filled me with the same unease as did a hotel.

Nowadays I like hotels, at any rate in small doses; they're a setting where you see people trying to behave, which is always more interesting than them just behaving. When people are on

213

their best behaviour they aren't always at their best. But I wasn't always so relaxed. For years, hotels and restaurants were for me theatres of humiliation, and the business of eating in public every bit as fraught with risk and shame as taking one's clothes off.

What it was—when I was little my parents didn't have much money, and when we went into cafés the drill was for my Mam and Dad to order a pot of tea for two, and maybe  a token cake and my brother and me would be given sips of tea from their cup, while under the table my mother unwrapped a parcel of bread and butter that she'd brought from home, and she smuggled pieces to my brother and me, which we had to eat while the waitress wasn't looking.

The fear of discovery, exposure and ignominious expulsion that this procedure involved stayed with me well into my twenties, and memories of that and similar embarrassments come back whenever I stay in a hotel. Not that this is an intimidating establishment at all: it's comfortable and straightforward and caters for what the marketing men call 'a good social mix'. Once, visitors came to take the waters; now it's a 'Leisure Break' or a conference, a mecca for businessmen.

I always carry my bags myself—avoids the tip. It's not the money: like catching the barman's eye, tipping is a skill I've never mastered. But then my parents graduated from boarding-house to hotels when I was in my teens and at my most thin-skinned, and, when, because of the tip, arriving at the hotel, like leaving it, was always fraught with anxiety.

Dad would probably have his shilling ready before he'd even signed the register, and when the porter had shown them up to their room would give it to him, as often as not misjudging the moment, not waiting till his final departure but slipping it to him while he was still demonstrating what facilities the room had to offer—the commodious wardrobe, the luxurious bathroom—so the tip came as an unwelcome interruption. Once the potentially dangerous procedure of arrival had been got through, the luggage fetched up, the porter endowed with his shilling, and the door finally closed, my parents' apprehension gave way to huge relief—it was as if they'd bluffed their way into the enemy camp, and relief gave way to giggles as they explored the delights of the place. 'Come look in here, Dad. It's a spanking place—there's umpteen towels.'

In a new refinement of gentility, the maids these days plait the ends of the toilet roll. It's a good job they didn't do this when I was a child or I'd have imagined this was standard practice throughout the land, our family's toilet roll unique in its ragged and inconsequent termination.

This was long before the days of trouser presses and hairdryers, and even kettles in the rooms came in just too late for my parents. That would have been the ultimate, though. With a kettle and the wherewithal to make some tea, they could have fetched some stuff in from outside, been free of the terrors of the dining-room, and never needed to stir out of the room at all.

During the war when we stayed in boarding-houses we didn't actually board but took our own food: screws of tea, packets of sugar and tins of corned beef, cushioned by shirts and socks and bathing-costumes, all packed in a bulging cardboard box, cat's-cradled in string and fetched on the train from Leeds. So when we were on holiday there was no romance to the food: we ate exactly what we did at home. Come six o'clock, while the rest of the clientele at The Waverley or The Clarendon or The Claremont would be wiring into 'a little bit of plaice' or the 'spot of something tasty' which the landlady had provided, the Bennett family would be having their usual slice of cold brisket and a tomato. It was home from home.

ALAN BENNETT

The Duchess of Portland

The Duchess of Portland was another remarkable lady. Beautiful, unpredictable and slightly eccentric. She lived with the duke in almost royal splendour at Welbeck Abbey in Nottinghamshire, surrounded by thousands of acres. Welbeck was vast and ugly but filled with wonderful pictures and furniture, including the famous Portland vase. At the beginning of the Second World War the Eagle Squadron, consisting of American flying officers who had volunteered to come over and help us before the United States entered the war, were stationed near Welbeck. Michael Duff was their liaison officer and told me that Winnie Portland asked him to bring them over for a tour of the abbey. They trooped through room after room, the duchess explaining each treasure. At last the tour came to an end in a smaller room, where she said: 'That's a Rembrandt, that's a Titian, that's a Rubens and, pointing to an armchair, that's Portland (where dozed the comatose duke), that's a Raphael, that's a Van Dyck', and so on. The Americans were quite hysterical with laughter. Another story concerns a guest who was met at the station by a hired car. On the visitor's arrival at the abbey, Winnie said: 'So sorry, my dear, but the first eleven footmen are playing cricket against the first eleven chauffeurs.' When in Paris she liked walking everywhere looking at the shops but, since she didn't have a very good bump of locality, she had a piece of cardboard pinned to the back of her coat which read: *Si je suis perdue rendez-moi au Ritz*.

DAVID HERBERT

An Unusual Hotel

We had acquired the address through my mother. Mother was a joiner. She would join any organization of which her friends were presidents or committee members, provided, of course, the dues weren't excessive. Once having joined, she seldom did much about her affiliations, and dear knows never dreamt of going to any meetings, but she kept on joining others because, she'd explain, she thought they might prove useful sometime and besides such nice women belonged to them. One of her enthusiasms was an instructive little endeavor known as 'The Ladies' Rest Tour Association'. Its purpose was to provide lists of comfortable but inexpensive and, of course, highly respectable lodgings for ladies traveling alone and unprotected through Europe. It published a monthly pamphlet which contained sprightly articles penned by certain of the itinerant members, telling about the cosy inn one of them had found in Avignon, recommending a highly intellectual pension in Perugia, or putting fellow travelers on the trail of a Swiss tea-room where the coffee was 'just like home'. There was also issued a general European lodging list for the use of members only, they being supposedly on their honor not to pass the information along to any outsider (one of the aims of the society was to 'keep Europe unspoiled'). Mother had culled the address of a Rouen boarding house out of this invaluable pamphlet and had sent it to us. She may have written it down wrong, or the Ladies' Rest Tour publication may have been guilty of a misprint, but it was clear someone had blundered, for the hostelry proved to be one which had very little to do with 'rest' and Lord knows nothing remotely to do with 'ladies'. As surely as we were what our mothers would have called 'nincompoops', that house was one which our mothers also would have called 'of ill repute'.

We rang the bell and after a time the door was opened a crack by a frowsy maid who didn't seem to want to let us in. But we smiled and said, *Bon soir* and blandly asked to see *La Madame* (meaning 'landlady'). The maid looked slightly astonished and walked off, returning in a second with the landlady, who looked

even more astonished. She was awfully dressy and luridly made up, hardly the type one would associate with the Ladies' Rest Tour and the elderly New England gentlewomen who supported it. We told her we'd like a room for the night, a seemingly simple demand but one which obviously increased her astonishment, for she stepped back in a blank manner and gave no reply. I was afraid she thought that two girls arriving alone and on foot might detract from the gentility of her pension, so, to establish our respectability, I told her that her house had been recommended to us as just the place for *deux jeunes filles*. She murmured a faint *Ah?* and beckoning us to follow, led us down a hall. It was lined on either side with smallish rooms, rather elaborately decorated. Some of the doors were open, and we caught glimpses of the other guests who seemed quite surprised to see us and we were indeed surprised to see them. They all appeared to be young women in very striking evening dresses. This was certainly unusual, but we concluded they must all be waiting to go out to a dinner-party. It never once occurred to us that we weren't exactly in keeping with the *ton* of the place, I, in my Buster Brown panama and Emily in her pepper and salt tweeds.

Madame led us up several flights of stairs and allotted us a modest room quite removed from the more elaborate ones below. She explained we'd be more *tranquille* there. Then, in a faint, far-away voice, she asked how we'd happened to come to her place. We told her we'd read all about it in a book published by an American society. She hadn't said much up to now, but this item of information caused her to lose all power of articulation, for she opened and closed her mouth several times but nothing came forth. Finally, with a wan, Camille-like wave of the hand, she backed out of the room and closed the door. Her behavior had been very odd, but with our faith in the Ladies' Rest Tour ever bright, we dismissed her as being a 'character'.

We washed, went out and found a quiet nearby restaurant where we dined. We were less shy about going into restaurants than we'd been in London, possibly because there were no other places in which to eat. Then we returned to our snug abode. The frowsy maid, still looking astonished, admitted us, and we went down the long hall, tiptoeing because the doors were all closed now, and we didn't want to disturb anybody. We could hear the sound of laughter and music coming from a back room but we felt too tired to join in the fun, so we climbed the flights of stairs and went to bed. We were very comfortable but I couldn't help thinking that this was an eccentric sort of pension, and Emily remarked that it lacked that 'homey' quality of the one in Saint-Valery.

Once in the night we woke with a start. People were walking in the corridor outside, we could hear a man's voice and someone tried the handle of our door. Then we heard Madame speaking sharply to whoever it was and evidently she pulled him away. We thought it very nice and motherly of her to be up watching out for her boarders, but just in case we might be disturbed again we did take the precaution of pushing the bureau against the door. After which we slept the sleep of babes.

The following morning, bright and eager as daisies, we rose, packed and asked for the bill. Madame told us it was not her custom to make out a formal account but she named a sum which was most reasonable, and as we paid it we told her what a pleasant sojourn we had had there and how we'd most assuredly recommend her establishment to all our friends. Her eyes glazed over a bit at that, and faintly she asked us if we'd have the *bonté* to give her the name of the American *Société* which had informed us about her. She would like, she said, to write to them. We gave her the name and address of the Ladies' Rest Tour Association, and left her to start what, we trust, proved to be an interesting and illuminating correspondence.

CORNELIA OTIS SKINNER AND EMILY KIMBROUGH

Bar-sur-Seine

Sometime in the early 1950s, late April or early May, I am with my friend Maurice, in his three-wheel car that runs on a two-stroke motorcycle engine, and which he had acquired, by some devious means, from the *Wehrmacht*—it still had *Wehrmacht* camouflage on it. Maurice had used it, rather unwisely I would have thought, in 1943 and 44, to transport rustic wardrobes and massive Franc-Comtois dressers from his native Vellexon, in the Haute-Saône, to Paris, where he sold them on the flea market of Saint-Ouen. The dressers were the origin of the prosperity of my friend in the last two years of Occupation, when furniture would fetch enormous prices. The Resistance people had had a go at 'requisitioning' my friend's van and had threatened to shoot him, but he had got by somehow. I liked the van, its little engine made an agreeable sound, '*tuff-tuff*', and one sat rather high up in the nose of the thing; the single wheel was in the front, it did not need very much petrol and chugged along at a steady, soothing 40 or 50 km an hour. We had gone out of Paris for the day, with no particular purpose in view, there was nothing in the back, we had not brought anything with us, we both had a free day and had thought it would be nice to get out of the city in the spring sunshine. I remember we were chug-chugging along—'*teuf teuf*' —a very straight avenue cutting through a double bank of trees in the Forest of Fontainebleau, the road heading more or less south-east. We seem to have had the same thought at much the same time, and the silvery road, the shadows of the trees heavily marked at both sides and moving gently to a light breeze, stretched out ahead of us, dead straight, as if to invite us to go on and on, just to keep going, with no particular destination in view. Why not? Maurice said he could do with a visit to his parents, he might pick up one or two bits of furniture in Vellexon, let's make a leisurely trip, stop off for lunch, then dinner, and sleep in or under the van at whatever point we had reached by 10 p.m. or so. It really did seem quite a little adventure, all the better for having been totally unrehearsed. I had a bit of cash and my French PO book, no problem there; Maurice always travelled with quite a bit of cash, he never used cheques or banks. The silver road was almost empty, it was a Tuesday, outside any holiday period, and the traffic in these early 1950s was still very light. We had a very good lunch, I think at a Routier—it was before these had become fashionable and self-conscious—at Maison-Rouge. By evening we had reached Romilly, rather a seedy, semi-industrial town, very dusty, and with long grey walls of factories spelling out DÉFENSE D'AFFICHER. We had supper in Romilly, then found a quiet spot by the river; Maurice settled down to sleep in the van on some sacking, I decided to sleep underneath it, had a bad night and got bitten by masses of mosquitoes.

The van seemed to speed along as the road started climbing in rolling country, the green, gentle hills, heavily treed, separating the valleys of the Seine and the Aube. We stopped off for lunch at Bar-sur-Seine. It was another good lunch, the people in the restaurant were friendly, and I decided that I would leave Maurice at this point, and spend a night in Bar, to explore the place, and walk in the hills the other side of the river. The Seine at this point is quite a small stream, only about five feet deep in the middle, between banks covered in willows. It was very clear and one could see the big silver or greyish fish. First, I went to look for a hotel, and found one actually *on* the river, by a weir, at a place called Bourguignons—maybe that was where we had lunch, I cannot remember—anyhow I booked in for the night, the room was very cheap. As I had no luggage, I went into Bar, bought a sailor's sausage-shaped bag, pyjamas, a razor, soap, at a Prisunic. I had nothing to read, so went to a *tabac* and bought a cheap edition of Maupassant's *Une Vie*, his longest novel, and a very sad, hopeless one at that (I still have the copy, which is my reminder of Bar). I also bought the local paper, *Le Bien Public*, published in Dijon, but with a special Bar edition. I like local papers, they seem to help one to belong: news of sporting events, schools, weddings, *faits-divers* (nothing very alarming, poaching offences, illegal fishing, etc.). I spent the rest of the day by the river bank or walking up through the woods. I had dinner at the hotel in Bourguignons, with a bottle of red *vin du patron*, a light

burgundy, then a marc with my coffee, and went happily to bed about ten; I was very tired after the night under the van. The bedroom was white, walls and curtains, and I had a huge double bed, very high up and with a massive white bolster, an inviting *polochon*. I left the windows open and could hear the steady sound of the weir. I thought that I had been very lucky to have ended up in this spot. Furthermore no one knew where I was, and I had absolutely no reason to *be* where I was. I woke up to the crowing of the cocks. I had breakfast downstairs, brought to me by the son of the owners, a boy of about eleven, who was very polite. After breakfast I told the people I would be staying that night as well, it seemed a special luxury to have one whole day ahead of me, to explore further, and I had checked that there was a station and that I could get back to Paris by train. I wandered about all the morning, bought a towel, and had a swim, wearing my pants; it was very hot for May, and they were soon dry. Then I had an aperitif in the *tabac*, walked back to Bourguignons for lunch. I was the only person staying at the hotel, but there were several farm workers having lunch. In the afternoon I dozed by the tiny river. In the evening I had more than one marc and went to bed quite late. I had *Une Vie* out on the bedside table, but was too sleepy to read any of it. In fact it remained unread, though I had anchored it firmly in its place of purchase: 'R.C.C. ★★★*mai*, 1951—Bar-sur-Seine'.

I stayed there three more nights: the Thursday, the Friday, and the Saturday, having all my meals at the hotel. I felt as if I were playing truant, though in fact I wasn't missing anything, save my working days in the Archives Nationales. The unplanned holiday gave me a wonderful sense of freedom. No one knew where I was; I think I sent my mother a postcard of the parish church of Bar, that is all. I was completely on my own, in an unfamiliar place that I had all the time in the world to explore. I had established a regular daily and evening routine and begun to recognize the people who had aperitifs in the *tabac*, and those who had lunch in the dining-room of the hotel; they even greeted me and I did not have to be asked what drinks I would want, just '*Comme d'habitude, Monsieur?*'—the question mark a pure formality. There were rather more people at lunch on Saturday, a couple of families who had come by car, giving the place a weekend feeling, and this was not *quite* so nice as the quiet and the semi-isolation of the week. I could not afford to stay on into another week; I would take the train back on the Sunday afternoon. I could feel the Sunday difference: church bells in the morning, the *tabac* was closed, the men were in suits. I had been living outside time—no, that was not quite it, I had been *inside* time all right, each day: Wednesday, the first delight of exploration and discovery, Thursday, going over the same ground, Friday, striking out eastwards through the horse drives cutting through the thick woods as the yellow track climbed up to the top of the valley, with a view on to that *other* river, the Aube, and, if I could have seen it, the twin of Bar-sur-Seine: Bar-sur-Aube. Saturday a slight change of itinerary, to take in the station and look up train times. Every afternoon I had a swim, at much the same spot, beyond a bridge, where there was a deep hole in the river and the long green plants swirled around. On the Thursday I bought a pair of blue-and-red swimming trunks from Prisunic: another bid, too, to store up a claim to the location of my unplanned out-of-season holiday. Out of season, and all the better for that, the two local schools were noisy with children, giving Bar a feeling of everything as usual. Out of season, but the weather remained very warm, with a slight breeze; I had come without an overcoat or a mac, and their absence even added to my sense of freedom and truancy. I have done the same sort of thing in winter, but that curtails the time for exploration and out-of-doors habituation. When I paid my bill at the hotel on the Sunday morning, the family seemed really sorry to see me leave. They told me that, in the summer, quite a lot of English people came through on their way to Dijon and the Midi or the Alps. They knew I was English, because I had to fill in the thing for the Préfecture (no one knew where I was, but the police in Troyes, or may be Dijon, would, in due course, and on the Thursday, at the *tabac*, the *capitaine de gendarmerie* had given me a wave when I went past his table, on the Friday he had shaken my hand).

I returned to Paris refreshed. It had been a bit like an Italian film I had seen that year: *Quatre pas dans les nuages* was the French title; it was about a rather harassed commercial traveller from Rome who had taken a bus out into the remote countryside. On the bus he had met a girl, there had followed a week of semi-fantasy. I suppose I was a bit romantic myself; I had seen the film several times. But Bar-sur-Seine had produced no girl. I had just wanted to be completely on my own, unattached, in an unexpected place in which I had no business to be present. I met

Maurice on the Wednesday of the following week. I had called round in the evening at his ground-floor single room in the rue d'Obligado; he had cooked a meal on his tiny stove, which we ate at a small round table, while he put on the Can-Can Bal Tabarin record in his gramophone—also a product of *les puces*. His trip had been profitable, he had brought back two more heavy wooden wardrobes and had sold them at Saint-Ouen. He too was looking very well, refreshed, and even redder than usual. He asked me how I had spent my time in Bar; quite a nice little place, he had always thought, but had I not been a bit lonely? I did not really try to explain that I had not. Perhaps too I was being a bit coy, or a bit selfish: those few days in Bar had been my private treasure, another sort of pink cloud (as Mauricette had described our weekend encounters in 1947—she *would* have used the expression 'petits nuages roses'), my exclusive possession. Still, as always, it was nice seeing Maurice again, things were looking up for him and he had discovered a source of unrationed petrol for the *Wehrmacht* (or ex-*Wehrmacht*) van.

RICHARD COBB

The Singular Character of Ninon, called de l'Enclos

Ninon, the famous courtesan, who called herself Mlle de l'Enclos when age had forced her out of business, is a shining example of the triumph of vice, when directed with intelligence and redeemed by a little virtue. The disturbances that she made, and worse, the dissipations into which she led the noblest and most brilliant young men of her day, taxed even the patience of the Queen Mother, who was usually very lenient (not without good reason) to persons of easy and more than easy virtue. Finally she commanded her to retire into a convent. An officer of the Paris police brought the *lettre de cachet*, which Ninon read, noticing that no particular Order was mentioned. 'Monsieur,' she said, quite undismayed, 'the queen has had the immense goodness to allow me to choose my cloister. Pray tell her that I should prefer to live with the Franciscan monks in their Paris monastery,' and she handed him back the letter with a sweeping curtsey. The policeman was struck dumb by the brazen impudence of the reply, but the queen was so much amused that she left her in peace.

Ninon always had crowds of adorers but never more than one lover at a time, and when she tired of the present occupier, she said so frankly and took another. Yet such was the authority of this wanton, that no man dared to fall out with his successful rival; he was only too happy to be allowed to visit as a familiar friend. She sometimes remained faithful to one lover, if he pleased her greatly, for the entire duration of a campaign.

La Chastre boasted that he was one of those favoured few, when he set off for the wars. But apparently Ninon had made no definite promise, for he was foolish enough (indeed he was very foolish, and presumptuous into the bargain) to ask her to give it him in writing, which she did and he crowed over the paper. But the promise that it contained was ill-kept, and every time that she slipped, 'Oh! the note!' she cried. 'Oh! La Chastre's dear little note!' In the end, her new lover asked what she meant. She explained; he repeated; and La Chastre was overwhelmed with ridicule, which pursued him even to his post in the army.

Ninon made friends among the great in every walk of life, had wit and intelligence enough to keep them and, what is more, to keep them friendly with one another, or at least not openly at loggerheads. Everything about her was done with seemliness and that outward show of modesty, which is often lacking, even with high-born princesses in their frailties. For this reason, she numbered among her acquaintances the noblest and most fastidious men at court, so that it became the fashion to be received at her house. Indeed it was much to be desired, because useful connections were formed there. There was never any gaming, nor vulgar laughter, nor quarrelling, nor mocking at religion and politics; but much witty, polished talk of matters old and new and of the latest love-affairs, and all without scandal-mongering, for the tone was always light, well-mannered, and restrained. She knew how to begin a conversation and was well able to maintain one, because she was intelligent and well-versed in the affairs of every period.

The respect (strange to relate) and the number and quality

of her friends and acquaintances did not diminish when she no longer attracted society by her beauty, and when good taste and changing fashion forbade her to unite physical with spiritual charms. She knew all the intrigues of the old court and the new, both serious and otherwise. Her conversation was a delight, not self-centred but loyal, secret, safe to the last degree. Indeed it may truly be said that, frailty excepted, she was full of goodness and integrity. She often placed her purse and credit at the service of her friends and entered into important negotiations on their behalf, very honestly keeping the considerable monies and secrets which they entrusted to her. All of which caused her to be held in an esteem and respect, altogether remarkable.

She had been an intimate friend of Mme de Maintenon when the latter was living in Paris. This lady did not like her to be mentioned in her presence, but dared not disown her, and wrote cordial letters to her from time to time, until the day of her death. L'Enclos, as Ninon called herself after she abandoned the profession of her youth which was protracted, was not so distant with her old friends, and when she was strongly interested in anyone or anything (which she was judicious enough to make a rare event) she wrote to Mme de Maintenon, who obliged her promptly and efficiently. After the latter grew so great, they met but seldom, and then in secret.

L'Enclos was wonderfully quick at repartee. Two remarks, especially, which she made to the Maréchal de Choiseul, will never be forgotten. The first was an admirable rebuke; the second is a sketch from life. Choiseul, one of her oldest friends, had in his youth been gallant and handsome. He had fallen out of favour with M. de Louvois and was complaining of his ill-fortune when, in spite of the minister, the king gave him the Order in the general promotion of 1688. Choiseul did not in the least expect it, although he was nobly born and one of the best of the lieutenant-generals. He was therefore highly delighted and could be seen gazing at himself in the mirrors, decked in his blue ribbon. L'Enclos found him doing so on one or two occasions and at last lost patience. 'Monsieur le Comte,' she said loudly before the whole company, 'if I catch you doing that again, I shall tell you the names of your fellow-members.' And indeed some members of the Order were enough to make one weep, yet even they were better by birth and character than some of those made in 1724, and later.

226

This Maréchal was the very pattern of virtue, but he was dull company and not over-intelligent. After one very long visitation, l'Enclos yawned, looked at him, and then exclaimed: 'Oh, God! How you do make me hate virtue!' which is a line from some comedy or other, I forget the name.* You may imagine the laughter and the tittle-tattle. None the less, even this sally did not provoke a quarrel between them

L'Enclos lived to be well over eighty, sound in mind and body to the end and much sought after and respected. Her last years she gave to God, and her death made news. I have spread myself upon her portrait because she was a very remarkable woman.

DUC DE SAINT-SIMON

Edward de Vere, seventeenth Earl of Oxford,
1550–1604

Mr Thomas Henshawe, FRS, tells me that Nicholas Hill was secretary to Edward de Vere, the great Earl of Oxford, who spent forty thousand pounds per annum in seven years' travel. He lived at Florence in more grandeur than the Duke of Tuscany.

This Earl of Oxford, making of his low obeisance to Queen Elizabeth, happened to fart, at which he was so abashed that he went to travel [for] seven years. On his return the queen welcomed him home and said, 'My lord, I had forgotten the fart.'

JOHN AUBREY

* See Corneille: *La Mort de Pompée*, III, iv, 1072.

The Great Jane Eyre

One of the most notable persons who ever came into our old bow-windowed drawing-room in Young Street is a guest never to be forgotten by me, a tiny, delicate, little person, whose small hand nevertheless grasped a mighty lever which set all the literary world of that day vibrating. I can still see the scene quite plainly!—the hot summer evening, the open windows, the carriage driving to the door as we all sat silent and expectant; my father, who rarely waited, waiting with us; our governess and my sister and I all in a row, and prepared for the great event. We saw the carriage stop, and out of it sprang the active, well-knit figure of young Mr George Smith, who was bringing Miss Brontë to see our father. My father, who had been walking up and down the room, goes out into the hall to meet his guests, and then after a moment's delay the doors open wide, and the two gentlemen come in, leading a tiny, delicate, serious, little lady, with fair straight hair, and steady eyes. She may be a little over thirty; she is dressed in a little *barège* dress with a pattern of faint green moss. She enters in mittens, in silence, in seriousness; our hearts are beating with wild excitement. This then is the authoress, the unknown power whose books have set all London talking, reading, speculating; some people even say our father wrote the books—the wonderful books. To say that we little girls had been given *Jane Eyre* to read scarcely represents the facts of the case; to say that we had taken it without leave, read bits here and bits there, been carried away by an undreamed-of and hitherto unimagined whirlwind into things, times, places, all utterly absorbing and at the same time absolutely unintelligible to us, would more accurately describe our states of mind on that summer's evening as we look at Jane Eyre—the great Jane Eyre—the tiny little lady. The moment is so breathless that dinner comes as a relief to the solemnity of the occasion, and we all smile as my father stoops to offer his arm; for, genius though she may be, Miss Brontë can barely reach his elbow. My own personal impressions are that she is somewhat grave and stern, specially to forward little girls who wish to chatter; Mr George Smith has since told me how she afterwards remarked upon my father's wonderful forbearance and gentleness with our uncalled-for incursions into the conversation. She sat gazing at him with kindling eyes of interest; lighting up with a sort of illumination every now and then as she answered him. I can see her bending forward over the table, not eating, but listening to what he said as he carved the dish before him.

I think it must have been on this very occasion that my father invited some of his friends in the evening to meet Miss Brontë—for everybody was interested and anxious to see her. Mrs Crowe, the reciter of ghost-stories, was there. Mrs Brookfield, Mrs Carlyle, Mr Carlyle himself was present, so I am told, railing at the appearance of cockneys upon Scotch mountain sides; there were also too many Americans for his taste, 'but the Americans were as gods compared to the cockneys', says the philosopher. Besides the Carlyles, there were Mrs Elliott and Miss Perry, Mrs Procter and her daughter, most of my father's habitual friends and companions. In the recent life of Lord Houghton I was amused to see a note quoted in which Lord Houghton also was convened. Would that he had been present!—perhaps the party would have gone off better. It was a gloomy and a silent evening. Every one waited for the brilliant conversation which never began at all. Miss Brontë retired to the sofa in the study, and murmured a low word now and then to our kind governess, Miss Truelock. The room looked very dark, the lamp began to smoke a little, the conversation grew dimmer and more dim, the ladies sat round still expectant, my father was too much perturbed by the gloom and the silence to be able to cope with it at all. Mrs Brookfield, who was in the doorway by the study, near the corner in which Miss Brontë was sitting, leant forward with a little commonplace, since brilliance was not to be the order of the evening. 'Do you like London, Miss Brontë,' she said; another silence, a pause, then Miss Brontë answers, 'Yes and No,' very gravely; Mrs Brookfield has herself reported the conversation. My sister and I were much too young to be bored in those days; alarmed, oppressed we might be, but not yet bored. A party was a party, a lioness was a lioness; and—shall I confess it?—at that time an extra dish of biscuits was enough to mark the evening. We felt all the importance of the occasion; tea spread in the dining-room, ladies in the drawing-room; we roamed about inconveniently, no doubt, and excitedly, and in one of my excursions crossing the hall, after Miss Brontë had left, I was surprised to see my father opening the front door with his hat on. He put his fingers to his lips, walked out into the darkness, and shut the door quietly behind him. When I went back to the drawing-room again, the ladies asked me where he was. I vaguely answered that I thought he was coming back. I was puzzled at the time, nor was it all made clear to me till long afterwards, when one day Mrs Procter asked me if I knew what had happened once when my father had invited a party to meet Jane Eyre at his house. It was one of the dullest evenings she had ever spent in her life, she said. And then with a good deal of humour she described the situation—the ladies who had all come expecting so much delightful conversation, and the gloom and the constraint, and how finally, overwhelmed by the situation, my father had quietly left the room, left the house, and gone off to his club.

LADY RITCHIE (NÉE ANNE THACKERAY)

Rosa Lewis and the Cavendish Hotel

Much has been written, and even more spoken, about Rosa Lewis who owned the Cavendish Hotel. She was unknown to me, and if I had read Evelyn Waugh's *Vile Bodies*, I did not for a moment think that the character of Lottie Crump had a real-life counterpart.

Jermyn Street, running parallel to Piccadilly, is narrow and discreet, and was then almost unchanged in outlook since Edwardian days. That is, it catered entirely for men: Mrs White still made the best men's hats (my father frequently sent from Tipperary for them); Paxton and Whitfield were the finest grocers for delicacies that men enjoyed, and had the largest stock of cheeses in London; there were various shops for boots, ties, cravats, socks, and silk scarves; expensive jewellers, and antique shops with *objets d'art* to please the most discriminating or exacting mistress; apartments, called chambers, for men only, and if all else failed, Fortnum and Mason's side entrance on the corner, where you could get kitted out for game-hunting in darkest Africa.

Strolling up from St James's, the Cavendish was on the right-hand side, a pleasant brick building with a front entrance like a private house, a discreet brass plate with the name at the side. Inside, the Edwardian atmosphere continued. The hotel was run entirely for men: women generally, unless they were titled, were only tolerated because men liked to have them around. I don't think Rosa thought much of modern girls: she said they only came in to have a pee and pick someone up. At this time she would have been in her seventies: tall, erect, with silver-white hair, a ruddy complexion devoid of any make-up, and penetrating large blue eyes with as much warmth in them as a seagull's. She was always dressed in a long-skirted suit, cut like a riding habit, in various colours, with a white cambric man's handkerchief knotted around her neck.

Stories about her were copious and conflicting. She had been Edward VII's mistress—or was it her mother?—Lord Ribblesdale's, or Sir William Eden's; or a French duke's. Her mother had been cook to a French nobleman, and Rosa as a pretty girl, in this aristocratic household, had . . . The most likely was that as a young girl she had married a dull Welshman called Lewis, and they had separated. She then trained a troupe, if that is the right word, of pretty girls to serve at the tables of the rich, she being responsible for the food. The truth does not matter. Whatever Rosa's early life had been it had given her an undying love for the aristocracy and their way of living. Champagne was drunk all day long, and most of the night too, for Rosa never went to bed if there was a party on. When she slept is a mystery, for she was about first thing in the morning. There were always at least six or eight 'regulars', one usually being a rich American of impeccable family, whom she had met, or his father, at one of the grand houses before the 1914–18 war, or on her visit to the United States in the 1920s.

Ex-kings were especially welcome, as were dashing young blades of good, preferably noble, family. In fact 'blades' were expected to be dashing and were cold-shouldered if they were not. After Evelyn Waugh had immortalized her in *Vile Bodies*, a portrait which did not amuse her, writers were allowed only under scrutiny, and anyone she disliked was referred to as a writer and usually asked to leave. Painters, on the other hand, were both liked and encouraged, and if they were knighted or honoured, like her special friends the Irishman William Orpen, Alfred Munnings or Augustus John, so much the better.

It was not an hotel in the ordinary sense of the word, although there were many innocents who haphazardly chose it to stay in. I often wondered what they made of it. For Rosa was a Robin Hood of hoteliers. The rich got very large bills, and the poor none at all. Rosa decided who could pay and who couldn't, and there was no use arguing with her for you would be told, in the fruitiest cockney, to get out. Like a true Edwardian, her conversation was pungent and spiced with references to tarts, backsides and chamber pots. The servants, if such they can be called, were varied, and led by Moon, an extremely old, bent headwaiter, porter, odd-job man, who was reputed to have been the Duke of Blank's butler in former days. He was so slow and so deaf that it was pointless to ask for anything. You got what he thought you should have. I once asked for some brown bread and butter and after half an hour was given a large brandy. There were several elderly, bearded housemaids, dressed in nineteenth-century clothes, and a young boy, his face shining like lard, wrapped in an enormous green baize apron. He had no name, but answered to 'Cheeky'. The one who did most of the work was called Charles Ingram, and he was unmercifully teased by Rosa. There was also Edith, or Edie. I didn't know quite what her function was: small, shy, brown-haired, with eyes like a partridge, she was usually to be seen carrying round, and consulting, a large heavy ledger—no doubt trying, with Sisyphean labour, to balance the books. Rosa for many years had a succession of West Highland white terriers, all called Kippy. There was a small marble slab low down on the wall near the floor, in the main room, known as the Elinor Glyn, commemorating the death of the last one. It had been the dog's favourite place for lifting his leg. There was another one of these slabs outside the front door. The main dish served went under the name of Game Pie, but the nearest it got to that in wartime was rook. This was always on the go, and served for breakfast, lunch and dinner. I only once had a change of breakfast diet: it was a chunk of smoked haddock, which tasted like fish flannel, and I was glad to go back to the unspecified game pie.

Having two very strong-minded grandmothers, I had had a

little experience in handling self-willed old ladies. For several days we both watched each other, and although I was technically staying in the hotel, I was not yet wholly accepted by Rosa. One morning, grudgingly, she said:

'You're quite a nice girl, not like that saucy tart Francesca: go and put your name down in the hall.'

For there had been no signing of the hotel register on arrival. At the Cavendish you signed when you left, like a visitors' book in a private house. I was very glad, for if Rosa took one of her unpredictable dislikes to you there was no way of getting round her. To put it mildly, 'you had had it'.

It was impossible at any hour of the day or night to creep in without Rosa spotting you, for her sanctuary was a medium-sized room just inside the front door on the right as you came in. This resembled the comfortable study of a man of varied interests but little intellectual ability: leather armchairs, Rosa's winged armchair, a desk, heavy pieces of furniture of mixed antiquity, the walls plastered with signed portrait photographs, sporting prints, caricatures by 'Spy', yachting pictures, vintage motorcars, old and young men riding or leading in the winners of well-known races. The regulars spent most of the time in this room, only moving to the Elinor Glyn at the back of the hotel at night, if there was a party. This weird collection of an old lady's life interested me, and I spent some hours looking at it. I was, therefore, both surprised and delighted to see a photograph of my father leading in his horse, Victor Noir.

'That's Adam . . .'

Rosa was behind me, champagne bottle in hand.

'What's that to you, Miss Christabel?' Rosa always called me that, for she never bothered to remember anyone's name, preferring to christen them herself.

'He's my father!'

Rosa was delighted to be able to give me a label. Most of her introductions were in the nature of Lord Whats-his-name, Lady Thingummy, Pullman (Pulham) who-takes-all-the-photographs; Lulu Waugh (Evelyn Waugh) who-writes-all-the-books. Now it was Miss Christabel, whose-father-owns-all-the-horses. Elderly mahogany-faced gentlemen would sidle up and ask me for racing tips, for most of the regulars were great gamblers. Rosa too liked her daily flutter. I hated to think that their fortunes were made or lost by my haphazard predictions, but they were so insistent.

233

Once Rosa had been able to place me I was guarded like an Infanta. For Miss Christabel, although I did not know it at the time, was not a very friendly appellation. There had been a lawsuit regarding paternity in the 1920s, and one of the protagonists was Mrs Christabel Russell. A jingle of the time was:

> *I'm Mrs Russell's baby,*
> *Blue eyes and curly hair,*
> *I'm looking for my Daddy,*
> *All over Leicester Square.*

This rhyme I learned subsequently from my father, who was enchanted to hear of my brief connection with Rosa Lewis. For all the high jinks at the Cavendish, Rosa had quite a strict moral code. It was all right to 'carry on' if you were unmarried, but any sign of rumpling the 'sanctity of the home' was treated very roughly. A newly-married young Guards officer on leave, with his young wife pregnant in the country, was pursued by Francesca, or someone like her. She was told loudly and firmly in front of us all:

'Get your fat tart's arse out of my house.'

On another occasion, hearing one man say to another, 'May I speak to your wife?', Rosa misheard it as, 'May I sleep with your wife?', and the trio were out sharply, without realizing why.

At this stage of the war, after Dunkirk and the fall of France, anyone whom Rosa liked was given the kindest of welcomes. With vivid memories of the earlier, bloody war, she became hostess to endless children of the fathers and mothers she had known in the past. Frequently she mixed them up, and addressed them by their parents' names, but there was a jeroboam of champagne, called a cherrybum by Rosa, to speed them on their way. Edie usually retired to bed about midnight, taking the ledger with her. One morning at about three o'clock, Rosa went off to the dispensary to get another cherrybum. Her old handsome face was flushed, and she looked tired, so I followed, thinking I could at least carry back the wine. In the dim, torch-lit dispensary she was bending over with her back to me, pouring one bottle through a funnel into another. A harmless enough deception in the early hours of the morning, especially as the source of champagne from France had been cut off. She turned, saw me and spat out:

'Get out of here, you bloody little spy.'

'Rosa dear, I only came to help you carry back the bottle. I promise you . . .'

'All right, all right, don't make a song and dance about it. Hold this bloody torch.'

From then on we were in league, and many times thereafter I heard the crisp voice saying:

'Come on, Miss Christabel, get off your backside and fetch another bottle.'

For Peter and me it was like being on leave, after the gruelling journey through France with fear and apprehension as travelling companions. Although we were outwardly gay, there were times of deep depression. Peter had only the rag-bag jumble of clothes he stood up in. All his possessions and paintings he had had to leave behind, and the sole prospect was conscription into one of the forces, to which he was violently opposed. The only sure work for an actress was with ENSA, entertaining the troops. I would willingly have done this, but my talents did not lie in singing or dancing, which were what was wanted. Peter worried about his friends in France, especially those who had already been pronounced 'decadent' by the Germans, such as Max Ernst and Giacometti. For this reason he was always delighted when English people he knew turned up, which they often did in the evenings at the Cavendish, for entertainment was limited at this stage of the war—all cinemas being closed by nine o'clock at night (there was just time to see *Gone with the Wind* if one went in after lunch), likewise the few theatres like the Windmill which ran a non-stop girlie show. They were a marvellously assorted mixture of people: amongst them the handsome Hamish Erskine, soon to be reported missing; outrageous, delicious, homosexual sauce-box Brian Howard, on whom Evelyn Waugh modelled his characters Ambrose Silk in *Put Out More Flags* and Anthony Blanche in *Brideshead Revisited*. Brian joined the air force in his forties, as an aircraftsman, and when asked by a pompous air force officer in the Ritz Bar for his name and number, replied:

'My name is Mrs Smith!'

I was always very fond of Brian, also his young Irish friend Sam Langford, who came from Tralee, and I delighted Rosa by calling him 'The Rose of Tralee'.

Dashing Lord Shimi Lovat—who, kilted, and with bagpipes

235

playing, led the commando raid on Dieppe in 1942—was another of the regulars.

Witty Daphne Bath, gentle and tender as only big women, in every sense of the word, can be, seemed goddess-like to me. She was one of Rosa's 'specials', for Rosa had cooked for her grandmother, Mrs Harry McCalmont, when she entertained the Prince of Wales, later Edward VII, at her country house. Now Daphne Fielding, she has written an enchanting book, *The Duchess of Jermyn Street*, about the life and times of Rosa Lewis.

And there was Crabbe: his first name was Lionel, but he was always called Crabbe. He looked like a younger, more genial version of the sailor on the Player's cigarette package. He was at this time an AB in the navy, dressed in bell-bottomed trousers, and was most engaging; quite small, but so perfectly in proportion that he didn't look a short man. He seemed delighted that Peter had a girl who was looking after him, as he put it, and kept telling me that he had bought an early Pulham painting of which he was very proud. A little before this he had come into a small inheritance which he had decided to blow on a celebration at the Cavendish. Of course, he well overspent it, and Rosa in one of her unpredictable moods had made him seriously work off the debt. This he did for several weeks with good humour. Many times later he came to Chelsea to visit us, and it was always a special treat to see him, for he was bold, brave and amusing. He survived the war, but disappeared in April 1956, when he was last seen diving as a frogman under the *Ordzhonikidze*, the Russian cruiser, during the visit of Bulganin and Khruschev to England. The Cavendish was a very romantic house. There were endless passages all leading to the same place, and many suites (I never saw a single room), which were very charming. Besides the old-fashioned huge bathtubs, where the supply of hot water was capricious, the rooms were crammed with furniture of all descriptions, for Rosa was a great collector. She had a large Daimler motorcar, and for many years had resolutely attended auctions of the houses of the nobility. She was an emotional buyer and bought indiscriminately. With the war on, and many rich families abandoning their London houses, which were often used as offices, Rosa felt it her duty to buy up as much as she could. She was always delighted with her purchases.

As my main object in moving into central London had been to find a job and a flat, I was out most of the day, on those days when there hadn't been too many cherrybums the night before. As often happens, on this particular day I had found both, was utterly exhausted, and crept past Rosa's parlour to my room. At first I thought I must have mistaken the number, for as I opened the door it only went halfway. I groped for the light switch, and was confronted with a staircase. For a moment I thought I had lost my reason and went out to check the room number. I sat down in the corridor, wearily wondering whether I had the energy for the Elinor Glyn that night. Dammit, no, I said to myself, walk up the stairs and see what happens. So I walked up the staircase, round the corner, down the other side and eventually found my bed. The next morning when I awakened, there was Rosa sitting on the top half of the staircase with my breakfast tray (game pie again) on her lap.

'What d'you think of it? Beautiful carving isn't it? Got it cheap from Lord Whats-his-name's town house.'

Dear Rosa, how many hundreds of people she must have cheered in her life. Given them a welcome taste of lotus-eating and gaiety, even the grandchildren of her original friends. She stayed at the Cavendish all through the war, leaving only for a few days to stay at a nearby hotel when the Cavendish was twice badly bombed during the Blitz. On each occasion a hamper of champagne accompanied her. A few times she went to the air-raid shelter at the Ritz Hotel, but generally, as did many elderly people, she preferred to stay in her battle-scarred home, until the last year of the war, when severe illness made her go to a nursing home. But this was not to Rosa's liking, and she was back in a few weeks, with a new 'Kippy', the fourth terrier in succession. She died peacefully in 1952, aged eighty-five, at her beloved Cavendish.

When I unpacked my small amount of luggage in the new flat, there was, snuggled in a spotless white napkin, a cherrybum.

Requiescat in pace.

THEODORA FITZGIBBON

Meeting W. S. Gilbert

'Some people I knew took me over to lunch one Sunday at his house at Harrow Weald. This would have been in 1903, when I was a shy, timid lad of twenty-two. Or, rather, not quite twenty-two, because my birthday is in October, and this was June.'

'Get on, grandpa.'

'Dash it, let me establish atmosphere and build character and all that. The story's no good unless you realize how shy I was. I was just a shrinking floweret, and when I found fourteen other guests there, I felt relieved, because I saw that I could simply sit and be inconspicuous. It was about halfway through lunch when Gilbert started to tell a story.'

'What about?'

'I can't remember, but it was one of those very long stories which you make as dull as possible all through in order to stun the audience with the surprise smash at the finish. It went on and on, and then he paused, preparatory to delivering the snapperoo.'

'And was it worth the wait?'

'That we shall never know, because, as he paused, I, thinking the story was over, let out a yell of mirth. I had rather a distinctive laugh in those days, a little like an explosion of tri-nitro-toluol, and it lasted for about five minutes, by which time the company had begun to talk of other things and Gilbert never got the point of it in at all. I can still remember his face as he glared at me. His eyes were like fire, and his whiskers quivered. It was a horrible experience.'

'Still, you have the consolation of knowing that you are the only man who ever stopped W. S. Gilbert telling a funny story.'

'Yes, there's that,' said Plum.

P. G. WODEHOUSE
RECORDED BY GUY BOLTON

On Not Winning the Prize Again

When June came round I once more entered the academic lists. This time I had hopes of being finally done with it. My success was generally predicted. Even the members of the music section were saying that I was sure to get first prize. I had a great advantage over my fellow-competitors. None of them had done anything of note. I, on the other hand, had obtained a second prize. I was like a crowned head among so many bourgeois. I told myself that I was bound to win, and I reasoned—disastrously, as experience soon showed—that since they had already decided to give me the prize, there was no point in cramping my style as I had done the year before and writing their kind of music. Why not let myself go and write my own kind—something from the heart? I would take my task seriously and compose a really good cantata.

The subject was 'Cleopatra after the Battle of Actium'. The Queen of Egypt clasps the asp to her bosom and dies in convulsions; but before dying, she invokes the spirits of the Pharaohs and in holy fear demands to know if she, a queen of crimes and dissipations, may hope to enter those mighty vaults erected to the shades of monarchs distinguished for their fame and virtue.

Here was an idea worth expressing in music. I had often in my imagination conceived a musical equivalent of Juliet's wonderful monologue, 'How if, when I am laid into the tomb', a passage that had something in common, at least in its sense of dread, with the feelings contained in the invocation which our French rhymester had put into the mouth of Cleopatra. I was mad enough to write the line, in English, at the head of my score. This for a start was an unpardonable crime to Voltairean academicians like my examiners.

The music for this scene came easily to me. I wrote what I believe was an imposing piece, the rhythm strikingly original, the enharmonic progressions creating a rich and sombre effect, and the melody unfolding slowly and dramatically in a long sustained crescendo. I afterwards used it unchanged for the unison Chorus of Shades in my monodrama *Lélio*.

I have performed it at my concerts in Germany and know how it sounds. I cannot now remember what the rest of the cantata was like, but on the strength of this piece alone I think it deserved first prize. That was precisely why it did not get it. None of the other cantatas got it either.

The jury decided to award no first prize at all that year rather than give official encouragement to a young composer who 'betrayed such dangerous tendencies'. The day following this verdict, I met Boïeldieu on the boulevard.* I give the conversation word for word; it was too remarkable for me to have forgotten it.

When he saw me, he cried out, 'My dear boy, what have you done? The prize was in your hands and you simply threw it away.'

'I assure you, sir, I did my best.'

'That is exactly what we have against you. You should not have done your best. Your best is the enemy of the good. How can I be expected to approve of such things when you know that what I like most is soothing music?'

'Sir, it's a little difficult to write soothing music for an Egyptian queen who has been bitten by a poisonous snake and is dying a painful death in an agony of remorse.'

'Oh, I know you have an answer—you always do. But that proves nothing. It is always possible to be graceful.'

'Gladiators could die gracefully, but not Cleopatra. She hadn't the knack—it was not her way. Besides, she wasn't dying in public.'

'You exaggerate. We were not asking you to make her sing a quadrille. Then, what need was there to go and use such extraordinary harmonies in your invocation to the Pharaohs? I'm not much of a harmonist, you know, and I must own that those unearthly chords of yours were beyond me.'

I bowed silently; I could hardly make the obvious rejoinder: 'Is it my fault that you are not much of a harmonist?'

'And then,' he went on, 'why do you bring that absolutely unheard-of rhythm into your accompaniment?'

'I was not aware, sir, that one should avoid using new procedures when one had the good luck to hit on one, and it suited the character of the piece.'

* 2 August 1829.

240

'But my dear fellow, Madame Dabadie is a very fine musician, and yet one could see it took all her intelligence and powers of concentration to get through your cantata safely.'

'I see. This is also new to me. Music is meant to be performed without intelligence or concentration?'

'Ah, well, you've always got an answer, haven't you? Goodbye, take this lesson to heart and be more sensible next year, and meanwhile come and see me and we'll talk it over. I shall take you on again—like a good "French gentleman".' And he went off, very pleased with his exit line, as the comedy writers say. (To appreciate its subtlety, which was worthy of Elleviou himself,* it should be realized that he was, as it were, quoting from one of his own works, *Jean de Paris*, in which this courtly phrase is set to music.)

The artless Boïeldieu had merely been expressing current French ideas about the art of music. Yes, that was it, soothing music was what the general public in Paris wanted, even in the most violent situations; music that was not too dramatic, but lucid, rather colourless, safely predictable, innocent of unheard-of rhythms or harmonies or new procedures of any sort, modest in its demands on the intelligence and concentration of performer and listener alike: a 'French gentleman's' art, dressed in tights and top boots, never carried away, always correct, lively, urbane, chivalrous, pleasure-loving, Parisian.

HECTOR BERLIOZ

A Brief Encounter with Sibelius

During my stay in Helsinki someone suggested that I should pay a call on Sibelius, who, although he lived a life of the utmost quiet and seclusion, would, I was assured, be more than delighted to

* A famous actor at the Opéra-Comique who played the typical French gentleman of the Empire.

receive me. This, later, proved to be an overstatement. However, encouraged by the mental picture of the great Master being practically unable to contain himself at the thought of meeting face to face the man who had composed 'A Room with a View' and 'Mad Dogs and Englishmen', I drove out graciously to call upon him. His house was a few miles away in the country and my guide-interpreter and I arrived there about noon. We were received by a startled, bald-headed gentleman whom I took to be an aged family retainer. He led us, without any marked signs of enthusiasm, on to a small, trellis-enclosed veranda, and left us alone. We conversed in low, reverent voices and offered each other cigarettes and waited with rising nervous tension for the Master to appear. I remember regretting bitterly my casual approach to classical music and trying frantically in my mind to disentangle the works of Sibelius from those of Delius. After about a quarter of an hour the bald-headed man reappeared carrying a tray upon which was a decanter of wine and a plate of biscuits. He put this on the table and then, to my surprise, sat down and looked at us. The silence became almost unbearable, and my friend muttered something in Finnish to which the bald-beaded gentleman replied with an exasperated nod. It then dawned upon me that this was the great man himself, and furthermore that he hadn't the faintest idea who I was, who my escort was, or what we were doing there at all. Feeling embarrassed and extremely silly I smiled vacuously and offered him a cigarette, which he refused. My friend then rose, I thought a trifle officiously, and poured out three glasses of wine. We then proceeded to toast each

other politely but in the same oppressive silence. I asked my friend if Mr Sibelius could speak English or French and he said 'No'. I then asked him to explain to him how very much I admired his music and what an honour it was for me to meet him personally. This was translated, upon which Sibelius rose abruptly to his feet and offered me a biscuit. I accepted it with rather over-done gratitude, and then down came the silence again, and I looked forlornly past Sibelius's head through a gap in the trellis at the road. Finally, realizing that unless I did something decisive we should probably stay there until sundown, I got up and asked my friend—whom I could willingly have garrotted—to thank Mr Sibelius for receiving me and to explain once again how hon-oured I was to meet him, and that I hoped he would forgive us for leaving so soon but we had an appointment at the hotel for lunch. Upon this being communicated to him, Sibelius smiled for the first time and we shook hands with enthusiasm. He escorted us to the gate and waved happily as we drove away.

NOËL COWARD

Palmy Days at the Opera

When old-fashioned people deplore the decadence of the mod-ern theatre, and regret the palmy days of the drama, superstitious ones are apt to take the desirability of palminess for granted, with-out troubling themselves to ascertain the exact conditions which constituted it. On enquiry, we are led to infer that long runs, elaborate scenery and dresses, efficient performance of minor parts, and prose dialogue, are degenerate; but that prompters, changes of programme every night, poster playbills printed in blue colour that adheres to everything except the flimsy paper, and 'historical' costumes—i.e. costumes belonging to no known historic epoch—are palmy. Between the merits of these things, the young London playgoer can hardly judge; for he has no ex-perience of palminess. There are many persons of culture still under thirty who are familiar with the palmy flat, vanishing from the scene with the scene-shifters' heels twinkling at its tail; who have touched the orchestra palisade from the front row of a palmily stall-less pit; who have seen the creations of Shakespeare enter and quit the scene to the strains of Handel; and whose fingers have been a sorry sight after smudging the playbill for three hours. But these experienced critics are from the country, and began their playgoing careers whilst palminess and stock companies still lingered there, as they do, perhaps, to this day. But the West Londoner, who only visits first-class theatres, has only one way of studying palminess. He must go to the opera, where he will soon get quite enough of it to convince him that the theatre in John Kemble's time, when it was carried on much as Italian opera is now, had quite enough drawbacks to reconcile a reasonable man to the changes which have since taken place.

There are no long runs at the opera. Faust is played one night, and Lucia the next; Lohengrin follows, and so on. Here is a splendidly palmy training for the singers. No stagnation in one play for three hundred nights, until the characteristics of his part fasten themselves upon the actor as mannerisms, never afterwards to be got rid of. No rusting of one's powers of study by disuse, nor dawdling in drawing-rooms when one should be busy with the divine art at rehearsal. No season passing away without a single performance of one of Mozart's operas, as seasons so often pass without a representation of Shakespeare's plays. Development of powers in their fullest variety, by constant alternation of tragedy and comedy, classicism and romanticism, Italianism and Germanism; leading, of course, to enormous superiority of the lyric to the ordinary actor.

At this point it becomes somewhat obvious that the palmy theory lacks experimental verification. On the ordinary stage, crippled as it is supposed to be by long runs, everyone is expected to act; and the more important characters are expected to act very well. At the opera, the tenor is not expected to act at all; and the baritone, though admittedly an eminently dramatic figure, would not, if he condescended to spoken dialogue, stand the smallest chance of being allowed to play Rosencrantz at a revival of *Hamlet* at the Lyceum or Princess. And if, by bringing strong private influence to bear, he succeeded in getting cast for Bernardo, and attempted, at rehearsal, to apply to that part the treatment which gained general admiration for his Conte di Luna, he would undoubtedly be at once conveyed, under restraint, from the stage to bedlam. Fancy a Don Felix or a Benedick at any West-End theatre exhibiting the manners of an average Don Juan or Count Almaviva! Conceive any respectable dramatic company daring to act that great and neglected work of Molière's, *Le Festin de Pierre*, as our opera singers usually act the masterpiece which Mozart founded on it. Yet musical critics frequently speak of the dramatic power and tragic intensity of the latest and absurdest Lucia or Traviata in terms which no sober critic of the kindred profession ever applies to the most skilful achievements of Mrs Kendal.

But, then, the variety of resource, the freedom from mannerism—from Middlewickism! Unhappily that has not come off yet. Operatic actors, so far from being free from mannerisms, wholly substitute mannerisms of the feeblest sort for acting; and as for variety of resource, there is not a penny to choose between an average prima donna's treatment of any two of her parts, however dissimilar in conception. Her Lady Henrietta is exactly the same as her Marguerite; her Marguerite is not distinguishable by a deaf man from her Juliet, except by her dress and wig; and her Semiramis is only a swaggering Juliet. Even the few singers, male or female, who are specially celebrated for their acting, would be celebrated for their deficiency if they were placed in an equally prominent position in drama, and judged by the standard set by Ristori and Salvini.

As to the development of 'study', or the power of learning new parts by constant change of programme, it is to be noted that whereas the power of prompting and of taking a prompt during actual performance is becoming a lost art at our theatres, opera singers never venture before an audience without a prompter in the middle of the stage to pilot them through their business. As there is no possibility of sufficient rehearsal, it is part of their qualification, as it still is of the actor in the remote places where the palmy system is still rampant, to get through a part in which they are not even letter-perfect, much less note and letter-perfect. Who has ever heard an opera go absolutely without a hitch, except it was a very new opera which had been recently the subject of special effort in preparation, or a very old one played by a company of veterans? How many singers, when they have once picked up enough of their part to get through it without disgrace by dint of watching the prompter, ever give any further study to its details? At the ordinary theatres a hitch is as exceptional an occurrence as the forgetting of the Lord's Prayer or the benediction by a Dean. Our actors gain both study and practice from long runs. It is true that they are condemned too often to play for months shallow and characterless parts which they get to the bottom of in a week; but that is the fault of the abject condition of the drama in England, and not of the system of long runs, which gives artists time to get thoroughly inside their parts, and frees them during considerable periods from daily rehearsals, to dawdle in the drawing-room if they like, but also to study in the library, the picture gallery, the museum, the gymnasium, or the concert room, as their bodily or mental wants may suggest. The old system of a changed programme every night and a hurried rehearsal every day meant insufficient time to prepare one's part, and no time at all to prepare oneself for playing it. To the actor as to other men, leisure means light. He may not always make a good use of his leisure; but in that case he will eventually succumb to competition of the men who do.

As to the advantage of having performances of the greatest operas each season, it may be admitted that a few great works are included in the narrow and hackneyed repertory of our opera houses; but it must at the same time be asked whether such performance as they get is in any sense worthy of them. Don Giovanni is certainly kept before the public; but in what plight? With fine movements omitted in the second act; with the recitatives gabbled through in a manner which could not be adequately described without the employment of abusive epithets; and with most of the parts played so as to inspire a faint wonder as to whether ten or twenty more earnest rehearsals, followed by a run of a hundred nights, would suffice to reveal them to the players. When this is all we can do for Don Giovanni we had better keep it on the shelf, as we now keep Shakespeare when we have not time to take due trouble with him. The actor who knows one part, and consequently one play thoroughly, is superior to the actor who can scramble with assistance through a dozen. The one gets into the skin of one character: the other only puts on the clothes of twelve. One impersonation is worth more than many impostures. Long runs mean impersonations: palminess means imposture. Let us rejoice over the departure of the palmy days of the theatre.

GEORGE BERNARD SHAW

An Evening with Bach

The recital last evening in the Chamber Music Room of the Erawan Hotel by US pianist Myron Kropp can only be described by this reviewer as one of the most interesting experiences in a very long time. Mr Kropp had chosen the title 'An Evening with Bach'; the evening opened with the Toccata and Fugue in D minor. As I have mentioned on several other occasions, the Baldwin concert grand needs constant attention: in this humidity the felts tend to swell, causing the occasional key to stick, which apparently was the case last evening with the D in the second octave.

Some who attended the performance later questioned whether the awkward key justified some of the language which was heard coming from the stage during softer passages of the fugue. However, one member of the audience, who had sent his children out of the room by the midway point, commented that the workman who greased the stool might have done better to use some of the grease on the second octave D key. Indeed, Mr Kropp's stool had more than enough grease, and during one passage in which the music was particularly violent he was turned completely around. Whereas before his remarks had been largely aimed at the piano and were therefore somewhat muted, to his surprise and that of those in the Chamber Music Room he found himself addressing himself directly to the audience.

By the time the audience had regained its composure Mr Kropp appeared to be somewhat shaken. Nevertheless he swivelled himself back into position and, leaving the D major fugue unfinished, commenced on the Fantasia and Fugue in G minor. Why the G key in the third octave chose that particular time to begin sticking I hesitate to guess. However Mr Kropp himself did nothing to help matters when he began using his feet to kick the lower portion of the piano instead of operate the pedals. Possibly it was this jarring, or the un-Bach-like hammering to which the sticking keyboard was being subjected: something caused the right front leg of the piano to buckle slightly forward, leaving the entire instrument listing at approximately a 35-degree angle. A gasp went up from the audience, for if the piano had actually fallen, several of Mr Kropp's toes, if not both his feet, would surely have been broken.

It was with a sigh of relief, therefore, that the audience saw Mr Kropp slowly rise from his stool and leave the stage. A few men in the back of the room began clapping, and when Mr Kropp reappeared a moment later it seemed he was responding to the ovation. Apparently, however, he had left to get the red-handled fire axe which was hung backstage in case of fire, for when he returned that was what he had in his hand.

My first reaction at seeing Mr Kropp begin to chop at the left leg of the grand piano was that he was attempting to make it tilt at the same angle as the right leg. However, when the weakened legs finally collapsed altogether with a great crash and Mr Kropp continued to chop, it became obvious to all that he had no intention of going on with the concert.

The ushers, who had heard the snapping of piano wires and splintering of sounding board from the dining-room, came rushing in and, with the help of the hotel manager, two Indian watchmen and a passing police corporal, finally succeeded in disarming Mr Kropp and dragging him off the stage.

KENNETH LANGBELL

A Thomas Beecham Tale

Sammons was the first leader to enjoy Beecham's characteristic asides and confidences from the rostrum in mid-performance. Some of these were revealing. During a Diaghilev ballet season, Beecham was called to the rostrum unexpectedly because all other available conductors were sick. The programme included

among other pieces the Polovtsian Dances from *Prince Igor*. Did
he wish for a rehearsal with the dancers? enquired the management. Not at all, drawled Beecham benevolently. On the night,
at a point usually taken two-in-a-bar, he suddenly let fly to the
general consternation with a one-in-the-bar beat which had the
dancers winded after a couple of pages. 'Too fest, too fest!' they
gasped every time they came within earshot of the rostrum.
Beecham's face remained ironic and inflexible. At the end he
leaned down to Sammons and said, 'We made the b——s hop,
what?'*

CHARLES REID

Lost Empires

It might be the worst house of the week—and indeed most of
the people sitting near me looked stupid—but even so it was
wonderful in a way to leave the darkening and chilly streets of
Newcastle and then find oneself sitting in the fourth row at the
Empire. I think the secret of all these music-halls is that while
they seemed big—and most of them were—at the same time
they seemed warm, cosy, intimate. A lot has been written about
the magic of the playhouse, but it has always seemed to me very
pale and thin compared with the warmer and deeper magic of
the music-hall, which attracted more men than women to itself
because there was something richly feminine about it, belonging
half to some vast tolerant mother and half to some bewitching
mistress. I don't say I was putting all this into words as I stared
about me that night, saw the orchestral players switch on their
lights and try their instruments, noticed fat Mr Broadbent,
no longer out of temper, bobbing up, first to smile at two people

* I have heard the same incident ascribed to another occasion by another
orchestral leader. It seems to have happened more than once.

sitting just in front of me and then to tap with his baton, and heard his orchestra, with its desperate strings as usual fighting a losing battle with the woodwind and brass, scurrying through Grieg's *Norwegian Dances*; but I will swear some such thoughts were going through my head. And for the first time since I had promised to join Uncle Nick, instead of feeling confused, dubious, vaguely apprehensive, I felt quite happy about it. I was still going to be a watercolour painter—nothing could shake me about that—but until I could keep myself by painting, the variety stage, at five pounds a week instead of twenty-two-and-six, would be better than any office.

The first turn was a 'fill-in', a pair of trick cyclists, and of course I wasn't interested in them, only in the people I would be travelling with for the next few months. The first of these, the second act on the programme, were the Colmars, three male acrobats and a girl, Hislop's 'stunner', called Nonie. It was one of those acts, which had always rather bored me, in which the men stood on each other's shoulders and chucked the girl around a lot. (I saw one recently, on a TV circus programme, and it seemed just the same, unchanged in a world of bewildering transformations.) Nonie was rather small and seemed quite young, probably still in her teens, but there was nothing undeveloped about her figure. Her legs were magnificent in their tights, and her full breasts made her glittering bodice rise and fall. And the way she held herself and moved, among the three sweating males, suggested she was tremendously conscious of herself as a female. Her sex came over the footlights like a sharp challenge. In those days of long skirts, stays and demure blouses, we had to guess what girls really looked like; but Nonie Colmar (who plays an important part in this story, so I'm not wasting time on her) triumphantly displayed what a well-shaped girl had to offer. I don't think I was any more lustful than most of us were then, but my mouth almost watered at the sight of her.

Next was Harry G. Burrard, Eccentric Comedian, who came rushing on, with the band playing its loudest, waving his arms and hoarsely breaking at once into one of his hell-for-leather idiotic songs. His make-up and costume—a grotesque ginger wig, a white face and red nose, an enormous collar, a bottle-green tunic and peg-top patched pants—left the audience in no doubt that he was a funny man. But this Monday first house offered him only a few distant giggles. Perhaps like me they didn't think him funny.

'Diddy-diddy—oodah—oodah—oodah', he croaked away, still waving his arms; and nobody cared. I don't think I am being influenced by the knowledge of what happened afterwards if I say that, at first, he made me feel embarrassed, and then, as he went on and on without any encouragement, I began to feel sorry for him. I was near enough to see his eyes, and they seemed to me—though of course I might have been deceiving myself—fixed in a kind of despair. I know I felt relieved when he took himself off, with the band at its loudest again, pretending desperately that a little weary clapping was an ovation.

Uncle Nick was next, the last act before the interval. This was the time he preferred, because it meant that the wings were clear of people waiting to go on. The orchestra opened as usual with part of the *Ballet Égyptien*, and then there was the familiar *Ganga Dun* big set, some kind of glittering Indian temple, which Uncle Nick had designed himself. It looked important and showy, but also its structure and glitter helped his act. I watched it now of course with new and keener eyes, reminding myself that I would soon be taking part in it. Sam and Ben Hayes and Norman Hislop, hardly recognizable in Indian make-up and costume, came backing on, and then Barney, the dwarf, also an Indian now,

251

scuttled across the stage with squeals and backward looks of terror; and finally Cissie Mapes, a gauzily clothed Hindoo maiden, arrived to prostrate herself before some advancing figure off-stage. A gong sounded. And there—a tall, commanding, sinister figure—was the Indian magician himself, who announced his arrival by letting loose a vivid green thunderflash. There was no doubt that Uncle Nick was a superb showman. Even the stolid fat deadheads sitting all round me, waiting for death rather than for any entertainment, were not entirely unimpressed. But Ganga Dun, intent upon magical feats as if they were part of some religious rite, gave no sign that he was aware of the existence of any audience. Unsmiling, grave, he behaved as if they were not there.

At first, from seemingly empty bowls and vases, handed to him by the Hindoo maiden, he produced bunches of flowers, fruit, coloured silks, gold and silver coins; and then he performed the feat, a genuinely Oriental one, of covering a heap of sand with a cloth once, twice, three times, while a magical plant appeared to grow there. The Hindoo maiden was then carried by the magician's slaves and her rigid body placed across two trestles. Ganga Dun regarded her sombrely, made some mysterious passes, then beckoned the slaves to remove the trestles. The Hindoo maiden remained there, now apparently unsupported. A few more passes and she slowly rose about two feet higher. The magician passed—or appeared to pass—hoops round her body, to prove that no wires were holding it up. Another gong, another green flash, and the magician was holding her by the hand as she bowed and smiled. But then an angry rival magician, as tall as Ganga Dun and nearly as imposing, wearing a turban, a majestic beard, and stiff long robes that hid his feet, arrived rather slowly and shakily, to challenge the magic power of Ganga. This he did not in words—nothing was said throughout the act—but by means of various insulting gestures. Ganga soon lost his patience, went nearer, summoned the gong and the green flash again—and then there was no rival magician, only the robes in a heap on the floor. It was a very effective trick, and it would have left me puzzled if I hadn't noticed that it was Barney the dwarf who was wearing the beard and turban, so that I guessed he had been raised two feet or so by stilts or something, and that at the end of the trick he was hiding in the heap of robes. But now a pedestal, about four feet high and very fancy, was brought on to the stage, and a white box was placed on top of it. Cissie as Hindoo maiden climbed into the box, and even while its lid, which faced away from the audience, was still slowly closing, the box was lifted off the pedestal, securely roped, then fastened to a hook let down from the flies. The box remained in mid-air for a few moments. The magician scowled at it; there was a roll on the side-drum; as if in despair he plucked a pistol out of his robes and fired three times at the box, which was then lowered and opened, all its sides falling down, and was plainly seen to be empty. There was a chord from the orchestra; Ganga Dun, aware at last of the audience, bowed to it almost negligently: the act was over. I led the rather scattered applause, but did not succeed in bringing back the magician before the curtain to take a final bow. When the lights went up for the interval, I looked around me. The Monday first-house people looked just as stolid as they had done before. Their sense of wonder had not been touched and aroused, because they had none. If my uncle had brought on three elephants and made them disappear, those people would have hardly raised an eyebrow.

The house manager stood me a Bass in the Circle Bar, which was almost empty. 'Wonderful act—one of the best,' he said again. 'I must have seen that girl-in-the-box trick twenty or thirty times and I still don't know how it's done. You do, I suppose—um?'

'Yes, I do.' I tried not to sound too grand and condescending. He waited, obviously wanting me to tell him how it was done, but I wasn't having any. So now he frowned.

'You can tell him from me, I noticed he cut three minutes out of the act. Naughty—very naughty! I'm supposed to report him to head office for that, but of course I know he wouldn't do it to a full house. Always gets a wonderful reception with the right house. Great Showman—Nick Ollanton—though he can be naughty—very naughty. Staying in front for the next half, I hope? Good! Three very good turns coming on—Ricarlo the juggler—those girls, Susie and Nancy—then Tommy Beamish. You've seen Tommy before, I expect. Wonderful comedian, Tommy—and they worship him up here. He'll have 'em rolling before the week's out. But he may walk through it this first house. He can be a naughty boy too, Tommy. Lovely talent though—lovely. Well, off you go and enjoy yourself. Give 'em a hand if nobody else does.'

Ricarlo was an elegant and graceful though not handsome

Italian, probably about forty, who worked in full evening dress, and did most of his juggling, which was superb, with a top hat, a cane, and a cigar, to which he added, after a few minutes, a pair of yellow gloves. Throughout the band played, very softly, the same little tune, one I had never heard before, half gay and half melancholy. And indeed there was something half gay and half melancholy about Ricarlo himself and his act. His movements, so graceful and quick, so beautifully timed, had about them a kind of infectious joy; but his dark and big-boned face, with its ebony stare, seemed carved and dyed in melancholy, the sort of blank sadness that I have since noticed many Latin people seem to be sunk into, behind their noisiness and flash of teeth and eyeballs. As I watched him dreamily—there is something almost hypnotic about this sort of juggling—I felt that here was a man I might come to like. And once again I led such scattered applause as he received.

The front cloth of unbelievable shop windows, before which Ricarlo had appeared so elegantly and incongruously, gave place to a garden scene, first in a greenish moonlight, where two girls and three men began singing softly. This of course was the song-and-dance act of *Susie, Nancy and Three Gentlemen*. When the lights went up I saw that the three men were wearing grey

morning dress and grey toppers; and I also saw, with an interest that soon rose to excitement, that Susie and Nancy were quite bewitching creatures. Susie, the taller and older and the one I knew was married, was a ripe brunette. Nancy, who looked about eighteen, was a blonde with short curly hair, unusual in those days, a saucy look and manner, and legs that were both ravishing and witty. The whole act was out of the usual music-hall run, more like a visitation from musical comedy, and perhaps a trifle too deliberately 'refained'; the dancing, apart from Nancy's, was careful rather than brilliant; the songs were melodious nothings about Orange Girls and Kitty on the Telephone and so on; and no commanding talent was audible or visible; but—and I'll admit my instant infatuation with the adorable Nancy may have swayed my judgement—the act conveyed something that seemed to vanish from the world not long afterwards, something I never found again in any place of entertainment—a kind of young and innocent gaiety, a bit silly as youth itself can be silly, without any sort of depth in it, any weight of experience, but somehow enchanting and lingering in the memory as an enchantment, so that later, when everything was different, and fragments of the songs returned to my mind, I was at once haunted by a bright lost world that had taken my own youth with it. As for that little Nancy, so pert and saucy and yet somehow so innocent, I began to fall in love with her there and then. And as I clapped until my hands ached, and glared at the fat deadheads who turned their idiot faces my way, I thought how wonderful it was that Uncle Nick had asked me to join him, so that I would see this girl again, and again and again, and would soon go backstage where she existed. But I did not really think of her existing in the corridors, passages and spaces there that I had seen and smelt that morning, but in some unchanging sunlit garden, some perpetual Maytime: I was already touched, barmy.

Luckily for me, Tommy Beamish, topping the bill, came on next. I had seen him before, but not in this particular sketch, in which he was 'supported by Miss Julie Blane and Mr Hubert Courtenay, both well known in the West End Theatre'. He was one of those rare comedians who began to make me laugh as soon as they appeared. He was a born comic, a plumpish man with a round cherubic face, usually decorated with an improbably ginger moustache, and with rather bulging eyes that stared in bewilderment or suddenly blazed in droll indignation. He never bothered with the ordinary comedian's patter, told no funny stories, sang no comic songs. He would lose himself in a labyrinth of misunderstandings and cross-purposes, and would go on repeating some commonplace phrase or even one word, with deepening bewilderment or growing indignation, like a creature from some other world baffled by this one, until he had only to make the smallest gesture or mutter half a word to produce another roar of laughter from the nearest stalls to the high distant gallery, lost in the smoke. Like all the great variety artistes, he was able through the projection of his stage personality and his marvellous sense of timing to dominate every kind of audience, keeping them hushed and still when it suited him and then releasing their laughter as if he were pressing a trigger. He was the best comedian I ever saw on the stage—I am not forgetting Chaplin, but he belongs to the screen—and I have not seen his equal these past forty years or so; yet now there must be only a few of us, our memories already hazy, who remember him at all.

The sketch they played that night was simple enough in outline. Mr Hubert Courtenay, an old Shakespearean type of actor who suggested he was really the Doge of Venice or the banished Duke of Arden, was an immensely dignified country gentleman. Miss Julie Blane, though she could not keep the mischief out of her splendid eyes, played with some skill his anxious and delicate-minded daughter. They had sent for a vet for poor little Fido, and in his world of dubious communications and infinite cross-purposes, Tommy Beamish had found himself summoned to the house, though he was in fact a plumber. The resulting confusion created the atmosphere in which Tommy was at his best. The indignant Courtenay rolled out words like 'prevaricate' and 'dilatory' and 'callousness', which Tommy repeated in amazement, brought back to taste again, chopped in half and flung the pieces about when he felt himself at bay. His slightest reference to plumbing operations, to his astonishment and then despair, were regarded as outrages by the quivering Miss Blane, whom he followed round the stage, sometimes climbing over the furniture, hoping to make it clear to her that he was not some kind of monster. A decent well-meaning man, only anxious to be helpful and impressed by the gentility of his patrons, he floundered into deeper and deeper misunderstandings, sometimes almost ready to cry and at others leaping to a height of blazing indignation. Even the fat deadheads all round me had to laugh, though they hated doing it. And as for me, I laughed so much and so long that often I lost the sight of Tommy in that curious and disturbing red haze which comes with violent laughter just as it does—so we are told, though I have never experienced it— with sudden and terrible anger.

What with the delectable and tantalizing Nancy and then the sublime idiocies of Tommy Beamish, I had had as much as I could take and wanted to cool off, so I went out during the final turn, a 'fill-in' trampoline act, caring nothing, like most people then, about the inevitable flickering bioscope that would end the programme. (We never imagined that soon it would help to put an end to Variety itself.) I wandered around for a few minutes, passing the queues now waiting for the second house, my excitement cooling in the Newcastle night air, chilly and sooty like that of most industrial towns then, as if they were really one vast railway station. Then I found the stage door and asked for Uncle Nick's dressing-room.

He was sitting alone, smoking a cigar, still with his make-up on but without his turban. 'Well, Richard, how do you think the act's looking?'

'Better than ever,' I told him. 'Even with that rotten audience.'

'I cut the Magic Ball trick. I can't astonish those blockheads, so why waste one of my cleverest effects? You can watch it tonight from the side—no point in you sitting out front again. I want you to note very carefully from now on everything that young Hislop has to do, and if you can't do it better by the end of the week, then you'll have made a fool of me.' He sounded heavy and grumpy, as if he needed some champagne—there was none in sight—or the applause the second house would give him. 'You stayed on after the interval? No, no, quite right. Get the feel of the whole show. How was Tommy Beamish?'

'Funnier than ever, I thought,' I began enthusiastically, and then checked myself.

Uncle Nick took out his cigar and grunted at it. 'He doesn't like me, and I don't like him. I suppose he's a very successful comedian, but then I don't like comedians. They have to pretend to be even sillier than the people who are watching 'em—and that's saying a lot—and after a time it does something to 'em. Their brains soften, then their characters. Before the week's out, Tommy Beamish often has to be more than half-pissed before he can go on. That Blane woman, who lives with him, has a hell of a time. Here I'm lucky, lad. I haven't to pretend to be sillier than they are but cleverer, and that's all right because I *am* cleverer— though that's not saying much because, as you'll soon find out, most people who come to variety shows are half-witted. I could fool *them* in my sleep. I do my work for about one person out of every two hundred.' There was a rather timid knock, then Cissie Mapes looked in, still a Hindoo maiden.

J. B. PRIESTLEY

Quite the Comedienne

I also took my assistant stage-management duties extremely seriously, and in those few minutes before curtain up, although my heart was full of my village wench role, my head was methodically checking the prop table. Six drinking-cups, wooden platters, shotgun, stuffed partridge . . . It was a litany I knew by heart; nevertheless I went through the motions of checking each object off on a list. The partridge was my particular concern, because it was the hub of the director's favourite joke. Tom Jones fired his twelve-bore stage right, and the partridge plopped out of the wings stage left. 'Don't argue, boyo—it's a classic,' said the director, and I was so bewildered by his sense of humour that I failed to get neurotic about his apparent sexual confusion.

My cue came, and I fled the sanctuary of the prop table for the wide unknown of the stage. I had evolved a sort of Loamshire sound for my comic village maiden, uneasily aware that regional accents were not my forte. My false hairpiece tumbled over my shoulders; my eyelashes were still tangentially attached; I had heaved and padded my unabundant bosom into a respectable cleavage, and every visible extremity was painted rustic nut-brown. They laughed. I only had eight lines and they laughed at five of them. I had the incredible disadvantages of an Oxford degree, a posh voice and the physique of an overbred setter, but the audience had believed in my common sexy wench enough to laugh at her.

'Quite the comedienne, boyo,' said the director in the interval. Rashly confident, I essayed some crack about his gender mix-ups, and was rewarded with the laugh accorded to my status as comic.

Act Two began, and I cavorted at the back of the stage with two other ASMs, busily representing a mob of three thousand.

Tom Jones raised his gun. He fired. Nothing happened. Where was the partridge? Being a resourceful chap, the Star raised his gun again. 'Bang,' he said loudly. Suddenly I realized that I had hallucinated that bird on the prop table, that I had never set it there in the first place, absorbed in my own petty role, and that it was now up to me to Save the Play. Quick as a flash, I fell writhing to the ground, reasoning that as long as *something* died that Tom Jones wasn't aiming at, the director's favourite joke would remain intact. Unfortunately, a more practically minded member of our cavorting mob had simultaneously nipped off stage and thrown the partridge on. I never thought much of the original joke, but I can tell you with authority that when *two* things die that Tom Jones isn't aiming at, there is no joke at all. The entire episode was greeted with a bewildered silence.

I wept off my eyelashes as I swept the stage after curtain down, waiting for retribution. It arrived. 'Theatre is discipline, boyo. You can act your socks off, but it's no good if you're not reliable. Go back to your undergraduate amateurs where you can't spoil any more of my gags. You're fired.'

'But I bought three pairs of eyelashes for the run,' I sobbed, unable to believe that my career had ended the night it began. I trailed upstairs to pack up the barely used sticks of greasepaint, and wandered snuffling out of the stage-door. The Star was outside, engulfed in provincial pubescents waving autograph books. He took one look at my swollen face and led me to the nearest pub, heedless of the weeny-boppers' protestations. He extracted the story through my hiccups and gasps and towed me through a maze of carparks and alleys to another pub. I shied like a nervous horse when I saw the director propping up the bar, but the Star propelled me inexorably forward.

'Hallo,' he said pleasantly. 'I thought we'd find you here. I've brought Miss Initiative along for a drink.'

'She's fired,' said the director.

'No, I don't think so,' said the Star politely. 'I wouldn't feel the same about appearing here without her.'

I was dumbstruck. I'd never even spoken to him until that evening. By the time I refocused on what was happening, the Star and the director had their arms round each other's necks.

Later, much later, as they say in the women's magazines, I attempted to thank the Star.

'You've said thank you in the nicest possible way,' he said, putting on his clothes. 'Now I have to go home to my wife.'

My heart was broken, but I got my job back. I've never been able to look at a partridge since.

MARIA AITKEN

William the Conqueror

Upon a time when Burbage played Richard III, there was a citizen grew so far in liking with him that before she went from the play she appointed him to come that night unto her by the name of Richard the Third. Shakespeare overhearing their conclusion went before, was entertained, and at his game ere Burbage came. Then message being brought that Richard the Third was at the door, Shakespeare caused return to be made that William the Conqueror was before Richard the Third.

JOHN MANNINGHAM

Ralph Richardson Remembered

Over the years Ralph Richardson, always generous to a fault, gave me a number of presents which I greatly treasure, including a finely-bound set of Sheridan, an exquisite malacca cane with a rhinoceros-horn handle and a beautifully-carved walking stick, late seventeenth-century, made from a narwhal's tooth. All I ever gave him, I think, was a classic work on parrots when he bought

José, a highly-coloured bird, in Spain, and a white azalea on his seventieth birthday.

Some time ago, three days after an operation for a hernia and sitting up in a hospital bed, the door to my room was pushed slowly open. It was a Sunday afternoon and all was very quiet and dreary. I looked at the door expecting to see someone at eye level but the figure that entered was on the ground. Pushing a pile of books before him Ralph crawled in on all fours.

'Who', he asked immediately, 'is Miss Mackenzie?'

'Never heard of her,' I replied.

'She is your next-door neighbour. Shall we have her in?'

'Don't be ridiculous,' I said, 'she's probably just had an operation. Like I have.'

Ralph deposited the books on my bed and went to the adjoining wall and thumped on it.

'Miss Mackenzie? This is Ralph Richardson. I am in Alec Guinness's room. We would like you to visit us. Do you hear me, Miss Mackenzie?'

There was an ominous silence, but Ralph continued in spite of my protests.

'Are you lonely, Miss Mackenzie? Guinness is lonely too. He would appreciate your company.'

He sat on my bed, chatting for ten minutes, explaining how eyes were first formed by sea-worms rubbing against rocks, and then left the room, again on all fours. He must have had a very good lunch. I forgot about his visit until the floor sister woke me the following morning.

'Wasn't it awful about Miss Mackenzie!' she said cheerfully.

'What's happened?' I asked with some apprehension.

'Apparently she thought she heard strange voices and in the night she got up—she is very ill—and ran out of the hospital in her nightgown and went screaming round Bryanston Square before she was caught. Now she is heavily sedated.'

'Poor thing,' I said, and opened one of Ralph's books.

Such times as I visited him in his dressing-room he always poured me half a pint of champagne into a silver tankard; he appeared to knock back half a pint of gin himself with just a splash of water. On one occasion he rose to his feet, stood at attention and raised his beaker in a military-style toast. 'To Jesus Christ. What a splendid chap!'—and gulped it all down. He often made references to his Catholic and Quaker upbringing

261

but I never heard him discuss religious matters or politics. He seemed happiest, socially, when talking about books, his ferret, his rat, his parrot, painting, or his boyhood in East Sussex or his love of Northern England. He rarely talked of theatre or films and I never heard him mention one of his own performances.

We only appeared together in three plays, two films and one television. The television (*Twelfth Night*) was unfortunate; very uncharacteristically Ralph took a great dislike, and expressed it, to a young actor playing a small part whom he referred to, *sotto voce*, as 'Bright Eyes'.

'What about Bright Eyes?' he asked me one day early on in rehearsals.

'What about him?'

'I don't go much on Bright Eyes,' he said.

'Well, he's not very experienced.'

A day or two later Ralph enlarged on his displeasure.

'Bright Eyes,' he said. 'Have you noticed? He wears a bracelet.'

'It's only a plain gold bangle. Probably some sort of identification. A lot of young persons wear them nowadays.'

Ralph looked suspicious and a few days later cornered me again.

'Bright Eyes,' he said.

'Well?'

After a long pause he said, 'Not right for the part.'

He never mentioned Bright Eyes again or, as far as I know, ever spoke to him. He remained dejected throughout the remainder of the production but managed to be comforting to me. Joan Plowright was the Viola and Larry Olivier was invited to watch the final run-through of the play. Having quite a long gap with nothing to do I went up to the viewing box to see some of it. Larry caught me by the arm, saying, 'Fascinating, old dear. I never realized before that Malvolio could be played as a bore.' It was my fault for taking a peek and I was a little put out; I would hear the word 'bore' running through the rest of my performance. When I told Ralph he shrugged it off with, 'He's wrong, old cock. He *can* be wrong, you know. I think your performance is fine.' I was grateful to him for not adding, 'I can be wrong too.' It was generous of him, particularly as he was going through agonies with his own performance.

One night in Madrid, where we were filming *Dr Zhivago*, I

took him and his delightful wife, Mu, to a rather precious little restaurant I had been told about in the old quarter of the city. The food turned out to be not particularly good but the clientele was amusingly odd, largely consisting of aged Spanish grandees sitting at little rickety tables communicating with each other through enamelled ear-trumpets. Ralph, well-wined, got on to the subject of his beloved ferret, describing how it had chased a white-coated house-painter through his house. The ferret, Ralph insisted, had thought the painter was a rival rodent and was determined to get him by the throat. To tell his story Ralph acted it out, rising from his chair, hiding behind it, making a dash for another table and squatting on the floor beside some astonished old *marquesa*, rising on tip-toe with a hiss and finally dashing round the room pretending to be the painter on the run. Ear-trumpets followed him like Triffids, napkins were flicked in his direction and old voices croaked in horror. Out in the street, no taxis being available, Mu and I marched him for what seemed miles through the damp and cold. He was extremely cheerful and insisted we go to some very impoverished-looking bar which was just about to close. There were no other customers and the sweet, tired-looking woman who ran the bar poured us hefty brandies. Language was a difficulty but Ralph expressed great admiration for a highly-coloured oleograph of the Blessed Virgin, framed in seashells, which stood among the bottles on a shelf. 'You like?' asked the woman. 'I show you better. Please come.' So we followed her up steep, creaking stairs to her bedroom. There, among a muddle of knick-knacks, powder puffs, mantillas, fans, dolls and Spanish flags, stood a large statue of the Sacred Heart exposing his viscera, wearing a blue ribbon and surrounded by red and yellow feathers.

'You like?' she asked proudly.

'She's lovely,' said Ralph.

'Not she! He!' Mu said sharply.

'Ah!' Ralph sounded surprised. 'I hadn't noticed the beard.'

As we left the premises Ralph pushed a handful of high-denomination banknotes towards the woman—probably about £20-worth. Her mouth fell open with astonishment, tears filled her eyes, and as we went out of the door I saw her turn with gratitude towards the seashelled Madonna.

A few days later Ralph and Mu left for a fortnight in England and I felt excessively lonely. On the day they were due back in

Madrid I telephoned and asked them to dinner again but they declined, although Mu said I would be welcome to an omelette if I came round to their hotel fairly early; an invitation I jumped at.

A waiter with a menu opened the door for me to the luxurious Richardson suite.

'Who can one hit', said Ralph, 'if not one's friends?'

As he advanced across the hall I assumed it was to shake my hand; but there I was wrong. A fist landed unexpectedly on my jaw and I slumped to the carpet. The waiter, who had come to take an order for dinner, fled in panic. Mu, who had seen it all from the sitting-room, called out, by way of explanation, 'He's very tired.'

'What was all that about?' I asked rather peevishly as I picked myself up. But Ralph had already sunk into a deep armchair and was apparently fast asleep; and he remained that way for an hour or so.

It wasn't typical of him to welcome guests in that way, but it is a fair example of how unpredictable such a steady, kindly and courteous man could be if the mood seized him. You were always on the alert for some possible eccentricity and yet you were always taken by surprise. His timing was impeccable, though individual. He was decisive, practical and very aware even when he seemed to be dreaming. His motives were always honourable and I never heard him make a derogatory remark about anyone —except, by implication, about 'Bright Eyes' and an excessively camp understudy who had to go on at short notice at the Old Vic. Ralph watched the understudy for a while from the wings, wincing, and then turned to me, whispering under his breath, 'Oh dear! Oh no!' Then he strode on stage and pulled everything together.

The first time I met him must have been in about 1936, at a small party given by Peggy Ashcroft at her house on Campden Hill. We all were glancing anxiously towards a stout, middle-aged gentleman who looked as if he might be sick on the carpet; but Ralph frustrated him, picking him up like a child, running downstairs and depositing him in the gutter outside. Ralph made no comment when he rejoined the party except to apologize, with old-world gallantry, to John Gielgud's mother for having trodden on her feet.

As an actor he was compelling and could be wonderful to the point of greatness. His early Toby Belch (though not the per-

formance in the television *Twelfth Night* in which we found both ourselves floundering), his Cyrano, Peer Gynt and Bottom were superb; as were many of his modern parts (particularly in *For Services Rendered, Sheppey* and *Home*), but it was his Falstaff which was definitive and truly great—witty, cunning, bombastic and rather sad—a man regretfully saying goodbye to the pleasures of the flesh and cocking a quizzical eye at the foolishness of all men, including his own. Whatever Ralph touched he imbued with nobility; even his famous motorbike seemed like some splendid, black, medieval steed champing for its knightly rider to charge, though the targets were sometimes only windmills in the head. Of all the actors of repute in our time he was, I think, the most interesting as a man; original, shrewd,
knowledgeable, commonsensical and yet visionary, with a great love of animals, a respect for inanimate objects and a passion for books. He was pained that I couldn't share his enthusiasm for Conrad and could only meet him halfway over Henry James (preferring, as I do in that area, Edith Wharton). But he introduced me to many contemporary books which I could read with confidence and pleasure.

Dozens of actors imitate him well and amusingly (the best, in my experience, being Anthony Quayle and Michael Jayston) and in the past twenty years or so Ralph 'stories' have multiplied prodigiously and become theatrical legend. Most of them I believe to be true, which is rare in theatrical gossip.

When I was with him in Priestley's *An Inspector Calls* he came to my dressing-room one evening and said, 'Your patent leather shoes squeak horribly. Do something about it.' I explained that I had tried oil and vaseline but nothing seemed to help. 'Try water,' he said. The following evening when I went to put them on, during a fairly quick change of clothes, I found the shoes standing in a bucket of water. I squelched noisily through the last act and then missed two performances through near pneumonia. When I returned to the theatre I called on him to apologize for my absence. 'Oh, have you been off, cocky? I didn't notice.' The shoes were never mentioned.

A story I have always liked, told me many years ago by Beatrix Lehmann, concerned a fast car and a tiny aeroplane. Ralph invited her one Sunday to go for 'a little spin in the air' as he had hired a plane for the day. He drove her through London, with small regard to traffic lights or other cars, at eighty miles an hour with Bea screaming, 'Slow down!' and punching him hard on the arm. When they arrived at the airfield she got out, shakily, and shouted, '*Never* do that to me again! *Much* too fast!' They climbed into the plane and took off. The plane lolloped through the air desperately slowly with Bea now screaming, 'For God's sake *go faster!*' But no, they remained just airborne until they slumped in a field.

Beautiful cars were a joy to him but he objected to the ostentatious. He told me once, with a lot of chuckling laughter, of an outing he had with Jack Priestley who was at the wheel of his brand-new and flashy car. Priestley, appreciating Ralph's knowledge and love of cars, was seeking his approval and suggested a 'jaunt to Brighton'. After several miles of driving in silence Priestley turned to him and said in his broadest Yorkshire accent, 'Well, what do you think of the bus, eh?' Ralph hesitated before taking the bull by the horns. 'I'm sorry, Jack. I'm *really* sorry. I don't like it.'

'Why not?' snapped Jack.

'It's all very fine—but this dashboard! It's hellish! All these little bits of glass that look like fake diamonds and emeralds! And all this gilt work. I'm sorry, but it's *vulgar!*'

There was a horrible pause before Priestley said, 'I asked you out to enjoy yourself, not to criticize.'

They turned round and drove home. Ralph said it was months before Jack would forgive him.

A few years ago, after Ralph and Mu had given me dinner at a smart London hotel, we walked slowly across the road to his car while he fumbled in a pocket for a pound note. An obsequious commissionaire, with a sharp eye for a good tip, followed us, raising his top-hat and saying, 'Goodnight, Sir Alec. Nice to see you, sir. And goodnight to you, too, Sir John.' 'Bastard!' Ralph muttered, putting away the money. However, as we reached the car I noticed him surreptitiously take out the note again and slip it to the man. Ralph was lost in a dream and drove at a steady four miles an hour down Oxford Street leading a long line of exasperated buses.

The last time I was with him was on a summer day when he, Larry Olivier and I were to be photographed for a Christmas issue of *Vogue*. (Gielgud and John Mills were unavailable.) In the morning I telephoned to ask if he and Mu would dine with me at the Connaught that night, and when they accepted I called Larry to invite him and Joan Plowright as well but Larry said he wasn't feeling well enough and Joan had a prior engagement. It was arranged that a car should pick up Larry in mid-afternoon from his Chelsea address, collect me from my hotel and that we would then go to Chester Terrace to gather up Ralph. When Larry arrived I thought he looked dreadfully frail, and when he said, 'It's one of my bad days,' I tried to persuade him to go home but he wouldn't hear of it. His sense of duty, which seemed unnecessary on this occasion, has always been of paramount consideration with him, and his courage ever undaunted. We found Ralph, in a brown suit, with bowler hat and yellow gloves, leaning on a silver-knobbed cane on the steps to his house. I got out and whispered to him that Larry was feeling far from well. 'Oh, poor Laurence,' he said, obviously deeply concerned. Ralph got in the car and, sitting next to Larry, took his hand and held it. There was something very touching in the sight of those two elderly great actors sitting side by side; Ralph comforting Larry and Larry dismissing his illness lightly and with wit.

Arriving at the *Vogue* studio, somewhere in the area of Theobald's Road, Ralph bounded up the stairs with alacrity but it was a slower and more painful climb for Larry. At the top of the stairs stood a lovely *Vogue* lady who made, in my opinion, a tactical error; she was holding a tray of bottles of gin, vodka and whisky. 'Welcome!' she said. 'Welcome indeed,' said Ralph, following the tray into the studio.

The bottles were opened and large drinks were poured into outsize tumblers. I declined, rather prissily, saying I couldn't drink in the middle of a hot afternoon without falling asleep. Ralph, in antic disposition, struck a vast number of poses for the photographer while keeping up a soaring, fantastic and wildly

funny monologue which was designed, I am sure, to cheer up his old friend; rather like an uncle pulling mad faces to enchant a sad child. Larry began to blossom again and by the end of our session had shed ten years. Going down the stairs again it was Larry who led, almost jauntily, and Ralph who had to be more cautious. Outside the building Ralph refused a lift in the car, saying he intended to walk the two miles home. Bowler-hatted, elegantly accoutred, he waved his cane in a wild valediction and strode off in the wrong direction. 'I'll see you and Mu at eight,' I called after him. Secretly I thought that at about seven Mu would telephone to say they couldn't make it.

Sharp on eight o'clock the swivel doors of the Connaught swung round at speed, propelling Mu and a stately Ralph into the lobby. 'A drink before we go in to dinner?' I queried. 'Perhaps a dry martini,' Ralph said very gravely. Mu rolled her eyes. We sat rather silently before our drinks while ordering our meal. Ralph only wanted a Spanish omelette. 'He *always* has a Spanish omelette,' Mu explained when I protested that it was a dull idea. We eased our way into the crowded dining-room, which appeared to be full of Americans, including a bevy of elderly Southern Belles who sat at a round table near ours. Ralph complained that he couldn't hear anything because of the loud chatter all about us but he heard when Mu said, 'José bit Ralph's finger this evening,' because he held up a sore forefinger. 'You remember José?' asked Mu. José was the parrot, which had been bought in the flea-market in Madrid during the making of *Dr Zhivago* and had been brought back to England, not exactly in a diplomatic bag but with all sorts of government certificates obtained from the British Embassy. I think Ralph had fallen for my South African Grey which I had for nearly thirty years and talked about endlessly. (Percy, for that was his name, had on one occasion flown off across a cornfield and was missing for three days. Breakfasting out of doors on a bright morning Merula and I suddenly heard, coming from a distance, Percy sweetly whistling, 'Speed bonny boat from over the sea to Skye'. Following the sound we found him perched on a small branch over a fox's lair. When I picked him up he fainted with relief on my chest. Ralph was entranced by the story and immediately wanted to add a parrot to his entourage of rodents.) José, spotted on an afternoon walk, was the answer. He was brought to the Palace Hotel in Madrid by two small boys who had been his owners. No cage, no perch; so the parrot sat on the back of a gilded chair in the Richardson suite, swiftly demolishing most things around him. According to Ralph the two boys produced a camera and said they wanted a photograph, so Ralph obligingly posed. 'No, no!' they chorused, outraged. 'Fotografia of José!'

Mu, always beautiful, elegant and equal to any social occasion, did her best to pull the three of us together towards some animation but nothing could displace Ralph's gloom as he stared at his Spanish omelette. Finally, he said, 'Would you forgive me, old fellow, if I went home now?'

'Of course,' I said. 'Are you unwell?'

'No. Bored. I'd rather go home.'

He rose from the table and I followed him. As he passed the Southern Belles he caught his foot in a chair and fell flat on his face. The Belles all turned round and squealed with excitement, 'Why, if it isn't Sir Rafe Richardson!' I went to help him but he managed to pull me down on top of him. '*And* Sir Alex Gwines,' a blue-rinsed matron added. As waiters got us to our feet Ralph gave me a wicked look. 'Sneck up!' he said, quoting a line of Toby Belch's to Malvolio.

I offered to get him a taxi but he said he would prefer to walk. I watched him amble away across Carlos Place, day-dreaming and looking forlorn. He must have day-dreamed a lot as a boy, and continued to do so through a long life, for I often thought that the things he said were not always invented on the spur of the moment but were dredged up from years of contemplation. A day or two after our non-dinner at the Connaught he telephoned me.

'Did you walk all the way home?' I asked.

'Yes,' he replied. 'But I sat for a while on a bench in Oxford Street. It was very nice until a chap on a bicycle stopped by me. "I know you," he said. "Oh, yes?" I said. "Yes," he said. "You're Sir John Gielgud," he said. "Fuck off!" I said. Then I walked home. It was a lovely night for walking. So many stars.'

ALEC GUINNESS

269

Orson Welles in 'Moby Dick'

Moby Dick was an open-stage production with no scenery, consequently the actors were seen as soon as they entered the pass door.
Orson achieved his effects by lighting and stage grouping. In the
chapel sequence, where he played Father Mapple, he stood holding a chair-back for the pulpit with a multi-coloured spotlight
casting the glow of a stained-glass window over the scene. It was
economical and practical. When Orson spoke the lines, 'O Lord,
I have striven to be thine', he was both vulnerable and moving.
He used the stage area for the deck of the whaling ship *Pequod* and
the auditorium was the sea. We lowered a rostrum as a symbolic
boat into the front stalls when it came to the encounter with the
whale. Orson was playing Captain Ahab and told me, 'You will
be Fool to my Lear; kneel in the prow and I can tell my playing
positions by standing above you for the harpoon throwing.' This
was where he cried out, 'That whale—I'll have his blood!' It was
all right rehearsing such a scene in an empty theatre, but on the
night, with a packed house, it was a different matter. Sailors were
clambering into the stalls trying to lower the boat into the central
gangway while well-dressed spectators shrank in their seats from
the proximity of burly perspiration. One lady's box of chocolates
got squashed on her lap, and she protested loudly; and the spectators in the circle completely lost sight of the cast. They rose in
their seats to extend their view, provoking cries of 'Sit down'
from those seated behind. Orson, with his hand raised for the harpoon, was roaring 'Shut up' to the audience between his vengeful
curses to the whale, and we eventually returned to the stage
amidst considerable confusion.

In the interval I used to lie full-length on the dressing-room floor. The unaccustomed exercise had exhausted me and the continuity of the play was baffling because Orson frequently changed the scenes. One night I was playing the carpenter and during a long speech about carving Ahab a false leg made from ivory, Orson suddenly leant over my kneeling figure and muttered 'Get off.' I rose muttering a lame ad lib, 'God bless you, Captain,' and backed away into the wings with the scene unfinished. As there was no set, we had been instructed that when we exited, we were to stand still at the side of the stage, and I was frozen in this position next to Joan Plowright who was playing Pip the cabin boy. 'What happened?' she whispered and out of the side of my mouth I replied, 'He told me to get off.' She looked heavenward: 'What about your speech?' 'It's cut,' I whispered. At this point she realized it was her scene which followed the now absent carpenter episode. She rushed on saying her line, 'O Captain put thy hand in mine, the black and white together . . .' with such incoherent haste that Orson was quite taken aback, but Joan rattled on with the speed of a gatling gun about white being black and black becoming white, till it sounded like a high-speed detergent commercial.

Afterwards I went to Orson's dressing-room and asked why he had cut the dialogue so drastically. 'You bored me,' he said shortly, and if there's a snappy answer to that I haven't found it.

KENNETH WILLIAMS

A Solemn Masque*

One day a great feast was held, and after dinner the representation of Solomon his Temple and the coming of the Queen of Sheba was made, or, as I may better say, was meant to have been

* Performed before the King of Denmark at the court of James I in 1606.

made, before their Majesties, by device of the Earl of Salisbury and others. But alas! As all earthly thinges do fail to poor mortals in enjoyment, so did prove our presentment hereof. The Lady who did play the Queens part did carry most precious gifts to both their Majesties; but forgetting the steppes arising to the canopy, overset her caskets into his Danish Majesties lap, and fell at his feet, tho I rather think it was in his face. Much was the hurry and confusion; cloths and napkins were at hand to make all clean. His Majesty then got up and would dance with the Queen of Sheba; but he fell down and humbled himself before her, and was carried to an inner chamber and laid on a bed of state; which was not a little defiled with the presents of the Queen which had been bestowed on his garments; such as wine, cream, jelly, beverage, cakes, spices, and other good matters. The entertainment and shew went forward and most of the presenters went backward, or fell down, wine did so occupy their upper chambers. Now did appear in rich dress, Hope, Faith, and Charity: Hope did assay to speak, but wine rendered her endeavours so feeble that she withdrew, and hoped the King would excuse her brevity. Faith was then all alone, for I am certain she was not joyned with good works; and left the Court in a staggering condition. Charity came to the Kings feet, and seemed to cover the multitude of sins her sisters had committed: in some sorte she made obeysance and brought giftes, but said she would return home again, as there was no gift which Heaven had not already given his Majesty; she then returned to Hope and Faith, who were both sick and spewing in the lower hall.

Next came *Victory*, in bright armour, and presented a rich sword to the King, who did not accept it, but put it by with his hand; and, by a strange medley of versification, did endeavour to make suit to the King; but Victory did not tryumph for long, for, after much lamentable utterance, she was led away like a silly captive, and laid to sleep in the outer steps of the antechamber. Now did Peace make entry, and strive to get foremoste to the King; but I grieve to tell how great wrath she did discover unto those of her attendants, and, much contrary to her own semblance, most rudely made war with her olive brance, and laid on the pates of those who did oppose her coming. I have much marvelled at these strange pageantries, and they do bring to my remembrance what passed of this sort in our Queens days; of which I was sometime an humble presenter and assistant; but I neer did see such lack of good order, discretion, and sobriety, as I have now done . . .

JOHN HARRINGTON

Show Some Respect

I went along to help with the laying-out and make-up. At first I was very clumsy. I used too much rouge, and smeared it down the cheekbones.

'Show some respect,' said the woman, 'the dead have their pride.' We always had a checklist with the burial instructions, and soon this became my particular task. I went round making sure that the dead had everything they wanted. Some just asked for a prayer book or their Bible, or their wedding ring, but some were positively Egyptian. We did photograph albums, best dresses, favourite novels, and once someone's own novel. It was about a week in a telephone box with a pair of pyjamas called Adolf Hitler. The heroine was a piece of string with a knot in it.

JEANETTE WINTERSON

Remembering Needleman

It has been four weeks and it is still hard for me to believe Sandor Needleman is dead. I was present at the cremation and at his son's request, brought the marshmallows, but few of us could think of anything but our pain.

Needleman was constantly obsessing over his funeral plans and once told me, 'I much prefer cremation to burial in the earth, and both to a weekend with Mrs Needleman.' In the end, he chose to have himself cremated and donated his ashes to the University of Heidelberg, which scattered them to the four winds and got a deposit on the urn.

I can still see him with his crumpled suit and grey sweater. Preoccupied with weighty matters, he frequently would forget to remove the coat hanger from his jacket while he wore it. I reminded him of it one time at a Princeton Commencement and he smiled calmly and said, 'Good, let those who have taken issue with my theories think at least that I have broad shoulders.' Two days later he was committed to Bellevue for doing a sudden back somersault in the midst of a conversation with Stravinsky.

Needleman was not an easily understood man. His reticence was mistaken for coldness, but he was capable of great compassion, and after witnessing a particularly horrible mine disaster once, he could not finish a second helping of waffles. His silence, too, put people off, but he felt speech was a flawed method of communication and he preferred to hold even his most intimate conversations with signal flags.

When he was dismissed from the faculty of Columbia University for his controversy with the then head of the school, Dwight Eisenhower, he waited for the renowned ex-general with a carpet beater and pelted him until Eisenhower ran for cover into a toy store. (The two men had a bitter public disagreement over whether the class bell signaled the end of a period or the beginning of another.)

Needleman had always hoped to die a quiet death. 'Amidst my books and papers like my brother Johann.' (Needleman's brother had suffocated under a rolltop desk while searching for his rhyming dictionary.)

Who would have thought that while Needleman would be watching the demolition of a building in his lunch hour, he would be tapped on the head by a wrecking ball? The blow caused a massive shock and Needleman expired with a broad smile. His last, enigmatic words were, 'No thanks, I already own a penguin.'

As always, at the time of Needleman's death he was at work on several things. He was creating an Ethics, based on his theory that 'good and just behavior is not only more moral but could be done by phone.' Also, he was halfway through a new study of semantics, proving (as he so violently insisted) that sentence structure is innate but that whining is acquired. Finally, yet another book on the Holocaust. This one with cutouts. Needleman had always been obsessed by the problem of evil and argued quite eloquently that true evil was only possible if its perpetrator was named Blackie or Pete. His own flirtation with National Socialism caused a scandal in academic circles, though despite everything from gymnastics to dance lessons, he could not master the goose step.

Nazism was for him merely a reaction against academic philosophy, a position he always attempted to impress on friends and then would grab at their faces with feigned excitement and say, 'Aha! Got your nose.' It is easy to criticize his position on Hitler at first, but one must take into account his own philosophical writings. He had rejected contemporary ontology and insisted that man existed prior to infinity though not with too many options. He differentiated between existence and Existence, and knew one was preferable, but could never remember which. Human freedom for Needleman consisted of being aware of the absurdity of life. 'God is silent,' he was fond of saying, 'now if we can only get Man to shut up.'

Authentic Being, reasoned Needleman, could only be achieved on weekends and even then it required the borrowing of a car. Man, according to Needleman, was not a 'thing' apart from nature, but was involved 'in nature', and could not observe his own existence without first pretending to be indifferent and then running around to the opposite end of the room quickly in the hopes of glimpsing himself.

His term for the life process was *Angst Zeit*, loosely meaning Anxiety-Time, and suggested man was a creature doomed to exist in 'time' even though that was not where the action was. After much reflection, Needleman's intellectual integrity convinced him that he didn't exist, his friends didn't exist, and the only thing that was real was his IOU to the bank for six million marks. Hence, he was charmed by the National Socialists' philosophy of power, or as Needleman put it, 'I have the kind of eyes that are set off by a brown shirt.' After it became apparent that National Socialism was just the type of menace that Needleman stood against, he fled Berlin. Disguised as a bush and moving sideways only, three quick paces at a time, he crossed the border without being noticed.

Everywhere in Europe Needleman went, students and intellectuals were eager to help him, awed by his reputation. On the run, he found time to publish *Time, Essence, and Reality: A Systematic Reevaluation of Nothingness* and his delightful lighter treatise, *The Best Place to Eat While in Hiding*. Chaim Weizmann and Martin Buber took up a collection and obtained signed petitions to permit Needleman to emigrate to the United States, but at the time the hotel of his choice was full. With German soldiers minutes from his hideout in Prague, Needleman decided to come to America after all, but a scene occurred at the airport when he was overweight with his luggage. Albert Einstein, who was on that same flight, explained to him that if he would just remove the shoe trees from his shoes he could take everything. The two frequently corresponded after that. Einstein once wrote him, 'Your work and my work are very similar although I'm still not exactly sure what your work is.'

Once in America, Needleman was rarely out of public controversy. He published his famous *Non-Existence: What To Do If It Suddenly Strikes You*. Also the classic work on linguistic philosophy, *Semantic Modes of Non-Essential Functioning*, which was made into the hit movie, *They Flew By Night*.

Typically, he was asked to resign from Harvard because of his affiliation with the Communist party. He felt only in a system with no economic inequality could there be real freedom and cited as the model society an ant farm. He could observe ants for hours and used to muse wistfully, 'They're truly harmonious. If only their women were prettier they'd have it made.' Interestingly, when Needleman was called by the House Un-American Activities Committee, he named names and justified it to his friends by citing his philosophy: 'Political actions have no moral consequences but exist outside of the realm of true Being.' For once the academic community stood chastened and it was not until weeks later that the faculty at Princeton decided to tar and feather Needleman. Needleman, incidentally, used this same reasoning to justify his concept of free love, but neither of two young coeds would buy it and the sixteen-year-old blew the whistle on him.

Needleman was passionate about the halting of nuclear testing and flew to Los Alamos, where he and several students refused to remove themselves from the site of a scheduled atomic detonation. As minutes ticked off and it became apparent the test would proceed as planned, Needleman was heard to mutter, 'Uh-ho,' and made a run for it. What the newspapers did not print was that he had not eaten all day.

It is easy to remember the public Needleman. Brilliant, committed, the author of *Styles of Modes*. But it is the private Needleman I will always fondly recall, the Sandor Needleman who was never without some favorite hat. Indeed, he was cremated with a hat on. A first, I believe. Or the Needleman who loved Walt Disney movies so passionately and who, despite lucid explanations of animation by Max Planck, could not be dissuaded from putting in a person-to-person call to Minnie Mouse.

When Needleman was staying at my house as a guest, I knew he liked a particular brand of tuna fish. I stocked the guest kitchen with it. He was too shy to admit this fondness for it to me, but once, thinking he was alone, opened every can and mused, 'You are all my children.'

At the opera in Milan with my daughter and me, Needleman leaned out of his box and fell into the orchestra pit. Too proud to admit it was a mistake, he attended the opera every night for a month and repeated it each time. Soon he developed a mild brain concussion. I pointed out that he could stop falling as his point had been made. He said, 'No. A few more times. It's really not so bad.'

I remember Needleman's seventieth birthday. His wife bought him pajamas. Needleman was obviously disappointed as he had hinted for a new Mercedes. Still, it is the mark of the man that he retired to the study and had his tantrum privately. He re-entered the party smiling and wore the pajamas to the opening night of two short plays by Arabel.

WOODY ALLEN

A Last Request

Elsie de Wolfe, later Lady Mendl, decided that when she died she should be placed in a large cannon and shot out over her beloved Versailles, where she had lived for many years. But when the time came, as she was dying, she regained consciousness for a second or two. Her last words were: 'They can't do this to me!'

DAVID HERBERT

Index: There Is No Index

Readers of books, I mean worthwhile readers, like those who read this volume, will understand how many difficulties centre round the making of an Index. Whether to have an Index at all? Whether to make it a great big one, or just a cute little Index on one page? Whether to have only proper names, or let it take in ideas—and so so. In short the thing reaches dimensions that may raise it to the rank of being called the Index Problem, if nothing is done about it.

Of course one has to have an Index. Authors themselves would prefer not to have any. Having none would save trouble and compel reviewers to read the whole book instead of just the Index. But the reader needs it. Otherwise he finds himself looking all through the book, forwards and then backwards, and then plunging in at random, in order to read out to a friend what it was that was so darned good about Talleyrand. He doesn't find it, because it was in another book.

278

So let us agree, there must be an Index. Now comes the trouble. What is the real title or name of a thing or person that has three or four? Must you put everything three or four times over in the Index, under three or four names? No, just once, so it is commonly understood; and then for the other joint names, we put what is called a cross-reference, meaning, 'See this' or 'See that'. It sounds good in theory, but in practice it leads to such results as— *Talleyrand, see Périgord* . . . and when you hunt this up, you find— *Périgord, Bishop of, see Talleyrand.* The same effect can be done flat out, with just two words, as *Lincoln, see Abraham* . . . *Abraham, see Lincoln.* But even that is not so bad because at least it's a closed circle. It comes to a full stop. But compare the effect, familiar to all research students, when the circle is not closed. Thus, instead of just seeing Lincoln, the unclosed circle runs like this, each item being hunted up alphabetically, one after the other— *Abraham, see Lincoln* . . . *Lincoln, see Civil War* . . . *Civil War, see United States* . . . *United States, see America* . . . *America, see American History* . . . *American History, see also Christopher Columbus, New England, Pocahontas, George Washington* . . . the thing will finally come to rest somehow or other with the dial point at *see Abraham Lincoln.*

But there is worse even than that. A certain kind of conscientious author enters only proper names, but he indexes them every time they come into his book, no matter how they come in, and how unimportant is the context. Here is the result in the Index under the Letter N:

Napoleon—17, 26, 41, 73, 109, 110, 156, 213, 270, 380, 460. You begin to look them up. Here are the references:

> Page 17—'wore his hair like Napoleon'.
> Page 26—'in the days of Napoleon'.
> Page 41—'as fat as Napoleon'.
> Page 73—'not so fat as Napoleon'.
> Page 109—'was a regular Napoleon at Ping-pong'.
> Page 110—'was not a Napoleon at Ping-pong'.
> Page 156—'Napoleon's hat'.
> Page 213, 270, 380, 460, not investigated.

Equally well meant but perhaps even harder to bear is the peculiar kind of Index that appears in a biography. The name of the person under treatment naturally runs through almost every page, and the conscientious Index-maker tries to keep pace with him. This means that many events of his life get shifted out of their natural order. Here is the general effect:

John Smith: born, p. 1; born again, p. 1; father born, p. 2; grandfather born, p. 3; mother born, p. 4; mother's family leave
Ireland, p. 5; still leaving it, p. 6; school, p. 7; more school, p. 8;
dies of pneumonia and enters Harvard, p. 9; eldest son born,
p. 10; marries, p. 11; back at school, p. 12; dead, p. 13; takes his
degree, p. 14; . . .

Suppose, then, you decide to get away from all these difficulties and make a Perfect Index in which each item shall carry with
it an explanation, a sort of little epitome of what is to be found in
the book. The reader consulting the volume can open the Index,
look at a reference, and decide whether or not he needs to turn
the subject up in the full discussion in the book. A really good
Index will in most cases itself give the information wanted.
There you have, so to speak, the Perfect Index.

Why I know about this is because I am engaged at present in
making such an Index in connection with a book on gardening,
which I am writing just now. To illustrate what is meant, I may
be permitted to quote the opening of the book, and its conversion into Index Material:

As Abraham Lincoln used to say, when you want to do gardening, you've got to take your coat off, a sentiment shared by
his fellow enthusiast, the exiled Napoleon, who, after conquering all Europe, retaining only the sovereignty of the spade
in his garden plot at St Helena, longed only for more fertilizer.

As arranged for the Index, the gist, or essential part of this sentence, the nucleus, so to speak, appears thus:

Abraham Lincoln: habit of saying things, p. 1; wants to do gardening,
p. 1; takes his coat off, p. 1; his enthusiasm, p. 1; compared with
Napoleon, p. 1.
Coat: taken off by Abraham Lincoln, p. 1.
Gardening: Lincoln's views on, p. 1; need of taking coat off, for, p. 1;
Napoleon's enthusiasm over, p. 1; see also under spade, sover-
eignty, St Helena.

Napoleon: his exile, p. 1; conquers Europe, p. 1; enthusiastic over gardening, p. 1; compared with Lincoln, p. 1; retains sovereignty of spade, p. 1; plots at St Helena, p. 1; longs for fertilizer, p. 1; see also under Europe, St Helena, fertilizer, seed catalogue, etc., etc. . . .

That's as far as I've got with the sentence. I still have to write up *sovereignty, spade, sentiment, share, St Helena,* and everything after S. There's no doubt it's the right method, but it takes time somehow to get the essential nucleus of the gist, and express it. I see why it is easier to do the other thing. But then sin is always easier than righteousness. See also under Hell, road to, Pavement, and Intentions, good.

STEPHEN LEACOCK

281

Acknowledgements

Every effort has been made to contact copyright holders; in the event of an omission or error, the editorial department should be notified at The Folio Society Ltd, 44 Eagle Street, London, WC1R 4FS.

The Folio Society wishes to acknowledge with gratitude the following writers, publishers and literary representatives:

Maria Aitken: 'Quite the Comedienne', taken from *A Night at the Opera*, ed. Ronald Harwood (Methuen, 1982). Copyright © Maria Aitken 1982. Reprinted by kind permission of the author.

Woody Allen: 'Remembering Needleman', taken from *Side Effects* by Woody Allen. Copyright © 1976 by Woody Allen. Reprinted by permission of Random House, Inc.

Sybille Bedford: 'A Hotel in Guadalajara', taken from *A Visit to Don Otavio* by Sybille Bedford. Copyright © Sybille Bedford 1953, 1960. Reprinted by permission of Eland Books.

Robert Benchley: 'J'Accuse', taken from *From Bed to Worse* by Robert C. Benchley. Copyright © 1934 by Robert C. Benchley, renewed © 1961 by Gertrude Benchley. Reprinted by permission of HarperCollins Publishers, Inc.

Alan Bennett: 'Observations in a Harrogate Hotel', adapted by permission of the author, Faber and Faber Ltd and Random House, Inc., from *Writing Home* by Alan Bennett. Copyright © Forelake Ltd, 1994, 1995, 1997, 2000. Printed by permission of Faber and Faber Ltd and Random House, Inc.

Hector Berlioz: 'On Not Winning the Prize Again', taken from *The Memoirs of Hector Berlioz*, trans. and ed. David Cairns (Victor Gollancz, 1969). Translation copyright © 1969, 1975, 1977, 1987 by David Cairns. Reprinted by permission of Victor Gollancz Ltd.

Jeffrey Bernard: 'Life History', taken from *Low Life* by Jeffrey Bernard. Copyright © Jeffrey Bernard 1986. Reprinted by permission of Jane Conway-Gordon.

George Bernard Shaw: 'Palmy Days at the Opera', taken from *How to Become a Musical Critic* by George Bernard Shaw (Rupert Hart-Davis, 1960). Copyright by George Bernard Shaw. Reprinted by permission of The Society of Authors on behalf of the Bernard Shaw Estate.

John Betjeman: 'Indoor Games Near Newbury', taken from *John Betjeman's Collected Poems* (fourth edn, John Murray, 1980). Copyright © John Betjeman 1958, 1962, 1970, 1980. Reprinted by permission of John Murray (Publishers) Ltd.